# Business Intelligence and Analytics

# Business Intelligence and Analytics

Delilah Murdock

Willford Press
www.willfordpress.com

Published by Willford Press,
118-35 Queens Blvd., Suite 400,
Forest Hills, NY 11375, USA





ISBN: 978-1-68285-976-6

**Cataloging-in-Publication Data**

Business intelligence and analytics / Delilah Murdock.
p. cm.
Includes bibliographical references and index.
ISBN 978-1-68285-976-6
1. Business intelligence. 2. Management--Data processing. 3. Industrial management--Statistical methods.
4. Business planning. 5. Strategic planning. 6. Decision making--Mathematical models. I. Murdock, Delilah.
HD38.7 .B87 2021
658.472--dc23

For information on all Willford Press publications
visit our website at www.willfordpress.com

Willford Press

# Table of Contents

# Preface

This book is a culmination of my many years of practice in this field. I attribute the success of this book to my support group. I would like to thank my parents who have showered me with unconditional love and support and my peers and professors for their constant guidance.

The set of strategies and technologies used by various enterprises mainly for data analysis of business information is known as business intelligence. Diverse functions of business intelligence technologies involve reporting, business performance management, benchmarking, complex event processing, etc. Historical, current and predictive views of business operations are provided in business intelligence technologies. By enabling electronic data interchange and data sharing, it can facilitate collaboration both inside and outside the business. Business analytics refers to the skills, practices and technologies used for continuous iterative investigation and exploration of previous business performance. Its main purpose is business planning. Analytics involves online analytical processing, prescriptive and predictive analytics, data and process mining, etc. This book elucidates the concepts and innovative models around prospective developments with respect to business intelligence and analytics. Most of the topics introduced herein cover new techniques and the applications of this field. Those in search of information to further their knowledge will be greatly assisted by this book.

The details of chapters are provided below for a progressive learning:

Chapter - What is Business Intelligence?

Business intelligence refers to the methodologies and strategies used by various firms and organizations to analyze data and business information. Some of its concepts are collaborative business intelligence, real time business intelligence, data collection, big data, knowledge management, etc. This is an introductory chapter which will briefly introduce all these significant concepts of business intelligence.

Chapter - Applications of Business Intelligence

Business intelligence is a vast subject consisting of various applications that provide assistance to the business. These include performance metrics, benchmarking, analytics, business reporting, electronic data interchange, data sharing, etc. This chapter has been carefully written to provide an easy understanding of the varied applications of business intelligence.

Chapter - Business Analytics and its Types

Business analytics deals with exploration of past business information by the substantial use of analytical modeling and numerical analysis, including explanatory and predictive modeling. Some of its types are decision analytics, descriptive analytics, predictive analytics, etc. All these diverse types of business analytics have been carefully explained in this chapter.

Chapter - Basic Domain in Business Analytics

There are numerous domains in which applications of business analytics can be applied. Behavioral analytics, cohort analysis, collection analytics, financial analytics, market analytics, pricing analytics, retail analytics, supply chain analytics, etc. are some of the examples. This chapter closely examines these business analytics domains to provide an extensive understanding of the subject.

Chapter - Applications of Business Analytics

Business analytics has a wide range of applications in different fields. Such fields include finance, HR analytics, customer relationship management, manufacturing, marketing, sales forecasting, credit card companies, etc. The topics elaborated in this chapter will help in gaining a better perspective about these diverse applications of business applications.

Chapter - Business Intelligence Technologies

Technology plays a vital role in business analytics by providing the ability to extract valuable information from business data in the most feasible way. Data warehousing, dashboards, ad-hoc reporting, data discovery, cloud business intelligence, etc. are some of the technologies that fall under this domain. All these business intelligence technologies have been carefully analyzed in this chapter.

Chapter - Modeling in Business Intelligence

Data modeling refers to the process of constructing a data model to store data in the database. Such model which deals with business data is referred to as data modeling for business intelligence. This chapter delves into concepts such as business intelligence applications and tools, business intelligence model roadmap, etc. to provide in-depth knowledge for the subject.

Chapter - Business Intelligence Tools and Software

Business intelligence consists of various applications such as spreadsheets, online analytical processing, digital dashboards, business activity monitoring, etc. It makes use of several software to aid these applications such as BIRT project, JasperReports, TACTIC and Orange. These diverse applications and software of business intelligence have been thoroughly discussed in this chapter.

**Delilah Murdock**

# 1

# What is Business Intelligence?

Business intelligence refers to the methodologies and strategies used by various firms and organizations to analyze data and business information. Some of its concepts are collaborative business intelligence, real time business intelligence, data collection, big data, knowledge management, etc. This is an introductory chapter which will briefly introduce all these significant concepts of business intelligence.

Business intelligence is defined as a process of collecting and processing business information to derive insights and make profitable business decisions. It is also used as an umbrella term, which bundles business intelligence software along with other tools, applications and best practices used to collect intelligent business insights, analyze the information for optimizing overall business performance.

Business intelligence depends on the process of business research to gather data. Analysis of the collected data by using comprehensive technological tools helps in getting actionable insights. The business intelligence comprises of collection, analysis, and presentation of business-related information and is more often considered as an outcome of business research enabling smarter business actions.

For example, a restaurant owner wants to understand the preference of his customers, type of cuisine they like, and why they like that specific cuisine. The restaurant went on to conduct a survey using business intelligence software and feedback is collected from customers about different types of cuisines. The restaurant owner using prominent features in the software analyzes the customer mindset and derives valuable insights about cuisines served in the restaurant. Empowered with information about what cuisine is liked by what people and what cuisine is ordered most on what day, etc., he then creates business strategies that are appealing as well as satisfying for his customers and profitable for his business.

The goal of business intelligence is to collect information and analyze it; so that a forward-thinking organization like yours can make better business decisions. Some of the trends related to business intelligence shortly are as follows:

- Increased investment in AI technology.
- Big data.

- The increasing importance of data governance.
- Increase in self-service business intelligence software and tools.
- Data interpretation through storytelling.
- Collaborative business intelligence.
- Embedded business intelligence.
- Cloud analytics.

Undoubtedly, in today's competitive business world, the ability to use data and technology in real-time is one of the most important parameters to succeed. It doesn't matter what industry you represent, but what matters is the access to quick information. Such access to intelligent insights helps organizations to make productive, analytical and impactful decisions. Although, what needs to be clear is that data collection alone is not enough for insights; processing and analyzing that data is what leads to actionable insights that drive business decisions.

## Business Intelligence: Types and Methodologies with Examples

To make strategic business decisions and gain competitive advantage, an organization must have a clear idea of market trends, customer needs, and consumer opinions.

There are a variety of online business intelligence tools using which you can access numerous ways to collect business insights, here are some of the widely recommended methodologies widely used to gather business intelligence.

## Step 1 – Data Collection

The first step in acquiring business intelligence is data collection. There are various methods to collect data, which can provide reliable information for statistical analysis and help an organization to make data-driven decisions.

### Surveys

Web/Online surveys – Online Survey remains the most reliable, economical, and widely used method to reach a larger audience for data collection. As it is complicated to create, distribute, and analyze the survey results manually, most of the researchers depend on survey maker tools to get the job done. The major benefits of using an online business intelligence gathering platform are a real-time analysis of the results, cost-efficiency, ease of use, and flexibility.

For example – A company wants to understand the level of customer satisfaction with their customer service department and also want an opinion from customers on how to become more customer-centric. The company decides to conduct a customer service survey using a business intelligence platform for gathering valuable information about the staff, product and the overall quality of service provided to them. The results achieved through the survey can be used to gauge Net Promoter Score (NPS), Customer Satisfaction Score (CSAT) or even Customer Effort Score (CES).

All these results contribute to analyzing what customers feel about the current status of the service, areas that need improvement, what customers expect and what their necessities are. All these insights enabled the company to incur some changes, implement strategies, and initiate employee engagement ensuring a successful journey to become a more customer-centric organization.

In-person surveys – In-person surveys are face-to-face interviews. For years, it has been the most effective method of collecting the most accurate information. As this approach to gather business intelligence relies on direct communication, observing body traits, behavior, and reactions of the respondent also play a vital role. Suppose if certain questions make the interviewee uncomfortable, disinterested, agitated or frown it is better to skip those questions. In addition to that, interviewees body language, tone of speech, and mannerism also determine if the feedback he/she is giving is right or wrong.

In-person surveys is a costlier method compared to other methods used for collecting business intelligence. Additionally, the interviewer needs to be experienced having exceptional expertise in observing and analyzing people.

For example – Conducting face-to-face interviews of employees to evaluate their immediate supervisors is a common practice amongst many organizations. Although, the majority of these organizations have a detailed questionnaire ready, sometimes using a supervisor evaluation survey template questionnaire to gather accurate information and promote a better work culture is a good option.

Mail surveys – This is an age-old traditional method used to gather information from a larger set of audience. As technology has reached every nook and corner of the world this method to gather business intelligence has become distinct. Moreover, there are few other factors like time-consumption, expensive, error-prone, and low response rate contributed to lower adoption of this method. Online surveys have quickly emerged as a better substitute for this method. However, geographies where tablets, computers or laptops are still inaccessible, mail surveys are the best way of collecting actionable business intelligence from them.

For example – The Government wanted to survey for understanding public opinion about the use of plastic bags and was interested to evaluate their awareness regarding government initiative to abolish them. They mailed the use of plastic bags survey to the selected audience from different localities for gathering business intelligence for that area, and accordingly corrective measures were taken by the Government to eradicate the use of plastic bags.

Telephone surveys – Telephone surveys are a little costlier than online surveys but much inexpensive compared to face-to-face surveys. Such a method has a few drawbacks like the availability of the respondent or even establishing a friendly equation with the respondent.

For example – A church wanted to survey to understand why parishioners attend church and evaluate if their spiritual needs are being met by the church. A church survey template enabled them to conduct telephonic surveys with all the parishioners and get reliable information to help them understand their opinions.

## Questionnaires

A questionnaire is a set of questions used for research purpose which can be qualitative as well as quantitative in nature. A questionnaire may or may not be in the form of a survey, however, a survey always has a questionnaire.

For example – An HR of a company wanted to conduct an exit interview to find out the opinion of an employee for his time spent at the organization. The used the elaborative and highly engaging Exit interview questions to gauge the opinions and record the feedback of the employees who decided to leave. These insights were then used by the company to formulate their employee retention strategies for lowering the attrition rate.

### Polls

Polls are a little different than surveys and this approach usually consists of only one question. The response rate for polls is extremely high, as it is very easy to answer and it takes very less time.

For example – The best example for a poll would be election polls. Polls are conducted to find out which party is favored and preferred by voters that would govern the specified area in a particular term.

### Forms

Forms are a type of survey itself, however, forms are generally used to collect specific information from a respondent in each field such as age, income, gender, etc., unlike surveys which are used to gather generalized data such as opinions, attitudes, values, etc.

For example – A bank needs specific information from its customers to open a bank account. In such a scenario, a form is provided to the customer to collect specific information required by the bank to open an account.

## Step 2 – Analysis

This is the step where all the data comes under a single platform. A Business Intelligence software will enable you to collect as well as analyze data with advanced analytical tools embedded in the same software. Analyzing the data collected through various methods helps an organization to understand their customer's opinions and find out areas needing improvement. The software allows you to compare scores (such as NPS, CES, CSAT) for varied periods and also among departments. You can use the same BI Software to analyze the data under advanced pretexts such as Conjoint Analysis, Maxdiff Analysis, Trend Analysis, Text and Sentiment Analysis and many more. This way, you would get a solid snapshot of where your organization stands among your customers at any given time.

For example – The Hospitality industry must measure customer experience and satisfaction on an ongoing basis. By analyzing and monitoring customer satisfaction scores and NPS scores consistently, the organization can improve their customer's experience and become more customer-centric to achieve higher revenues and customer loyalty.

## Step 3 – Reporting and Presentation

After analysis, the next step is to understand what the metrics mean. This step is the most important, as the wrong interpretation of the data can send your organization down a cliff. Conversion into visual infographics can sometimes make it easier for a person to understand. Such understanding will enable the organization to find answers to most pressing business, operational and marketing questions.

These steps will help you to start using business intelligence software effectively, however, this is not the final step. An organization needs to continuously monitor and analyze real-time data to stay in the competition and keep meeting the ever-changing customer needs or even figure out the next best steps for the future. Following this path to utilize business intelligence effectively will provide an organization to spend money and time more wisely and tackle future goals, needs, and trends successfully.

## Advantages of Business Intelligence

Business Intelligence has a direct impact on an organization's strategic, tactical and operational business decisions. It supports fact-based decision making using historical data rather than assumptions and gut feelings. These tools perform data analysis and create reports, summaries, dashboards, maps, graphs, and charts to provide users with detailed intelligence about the nature of the business. Following are some advantages of Business Intelligence:

- A right Business Intelligence software helps to boost productivity in the organization by displaying the gathered data using reports, analytical dashboards, and infographics.
- It provides an organization with a holistic view of the company, segmented into various departments, products, services, etc., making it easier to identify areas that need attention or improvement.
- Complex processes in an organization can be streamlined using advanced automated analytics, enabling a company to reduce time and effort leading to faster and efficient business processes.
- Visual infographics and easy to understand reports can be generated using BI software allowing even non-technical individuals to understand the meaning of their metrics.

## Importance of Business Intelligence in an Organization

In today's ever-changing business environment, there is a need for business intelligence to enjoy a competitive advantage. Business intelligence helps an organization to evaluate customer opinions, the market and customer behavior, which gives them an upper hand in winning higher market shares and reaping higher revenues. Following are some reasons why business intelligence is an asset to any organization:

- Gather actionable insights – Business intelligence is transforming business-oriented raw data into usable information. Raw data will not give you actionable insights about your business parameters but BI will provide an organization with a comprehensive analysis of data to identify pain points or opportunities that can be used to devise more customer-centric strategies.
- In-depth understanding of the organization – It is difficult to understand the business as a whole if you don't know each component of the business, including those that are often overlooked. Business intelligence enables an organization to identify each component that requires attention and make improvements accordingly.
- Achieve sales and marketing targets – Achieving those sales and marketing goals are difficult if the company does not understand the target market, the trends or the ever-changing

customer needs. Business intelligence delivers in-depth analysis to kickstart an organization's sales, boost the performance of the marketing function and help in synchronizing both the teams to achieve those sales and marketing goals.

- Anticipate buyer behavior and trends – Customer engagement is a buzzword often discussed in today's business world. Hence, drawing prospective customers to you is essential, rather than relying on old outdated techniques based on a hard sell. A business intelligence software enables a company to create holistic customer profiles based on their every interaction or every feedback during the customer journey. This allows them to gather valuable intelligence, which provides them with detailed insights on buyer behavior and trends, thus allowing them to improve sales, marketing or growth strategies accordingly.
- Boost overall productivity – Many organizations have inefficient bottlenecks, old traditional processes and manual routine tasks that hinder the growth of an organization. Business intelligence software can release these bottlenecks, automate routine tasks and refine processes bringing new levels of organization and prioritization to everybody's work. This enables efficient and highly responsive customer service, better use of human resources, accurate measurement of marketing campaigns thereby boosting the overall productivity across the organization.
- Data governance and regulations – The new GDPR law has put many restrictions on the way personal data is being collected, used, stored, processed, and shared. The new laws include requirements to keep data accurate and up-to-date, to demonstrate grounds for processing data and formulate a clear privacy policy for improved transparency. A GDPR compliant business intelligence software e helps you to centralize all the data which in turn improves transparency and exposes inaccuracies and gaps. Furthermore, it enables a company to be in a position of meeting the global regulations and laws to avoid being blacklisted by the regulators and the customers as well.
- Accelerated ROI – Last but not the least, business intelligence helps an organization to accelerate ROI by managing day-to-day efficiency, sales conversion metrics and customer experience through analysis and modeling. It also enables a company to get valuable insights into consumer buying behavior, customer experience, and customer needs, putting the organization on a path of success.

Gone are the days when organizations relied on making the best guess or going with a gut feeling. Business intelligence empowers organizations with accurate data and updates in real-time. It also explored the upcoming market trends, and forecasting means and even at times allowing to predict "what-if" scenarios to eradicate the need to guess or estimate.

## Stages of Business Intelligence

Business Intelligence is the process of transforming related business data into information, information into knowledge and with repetitive identification turning knowledge into Intelligence.

- Data: It is a raw data i.e. it represents reality, facts and figures.

- Information: It is a data that is processed and interpreted.
- Knowledge: After the information is processed, it becomes more sensible containing some meaning and understanding.

Business Intelligence (BI) is a wide category of applications and technologies for collecting, storing, analysing, and providing access to data to help the enterprise users make better decision making. BI applications supports the activities decision support systems, querying and reporting, online analytical processing (OLAP), statistical data analysis, forecasting and data mining.

Some important definitions of Business Intelligence are:

- Business Intelligence is a set of methodologies, processes, architectures, and technologies that transform raw data into meaningful and useful information used to enable more effective strategic, tactical, and operational insights and decision-making.
- A set of methodologies, processes, architectures, and technologies that leverage the output of information management processes for analysis, reporting, performance management, and information delivery.
- Business Intelligence is neither a product nor a system. It is an architecture and a collection of integrated operational as well as decision-support applications and databases that provide the business community easy access to business data.
- BI is the delivery of accurate, useful information to the decision makers within the needed time frame to enhance decision making.
- BI is not just some facts and figures on a printed report or computer screen. BI provides foundational information on which to base a decision. BI also provides feedback information that can be used to evaluate a decision.
- BI systems enable organization to provide the users an insight about the company's information assets.

## The Five Stages of Business Intelligence

- Data sourcing: Business Intelligence is about extracting information from multiple sources of data. The data might be: text documents – e.g. memos or reports or email messages; photographs and images; sounds; formatted tables; web pages and URL lists. The key to data sourcing is to obtain the information in electronic form. So typical sources of data might include: scanners; digital cameras; database queries; web searches; computer file access etc.
- Data analysis: Business Intelligence is about synthesizing useful knowledge from collections of data. It is about estimating current trends, integrating and summarizing disparate information, validating models of understanding and predicting missing information or future trends. This process of data analysis is also called data mining or knowledge discovery.
- Situation awareness: Business Intelligence is about filtering out irrelevant information, and setting the remaining information in the context of the business and its environment. The user needs the key items of information relevant to his or her needs, and summaries

that are syntheses of all the relevant data (market forces, government policy etc.). Situation awareness is the grasp of the context in which to understand and make decisions. Algorithms for situation assessment provide such syntheses automatically.

- Risk assessment: Business Intelligence is about discovering what plausible actions might be taken, or decisions made, at different times. It is about helping you weigh up the current and future risk, cost or benefit of taking one action over another, or making one decision versus another. It is about inferring and summarizing your best options or choices.
- Decision support: Business Intelligence is about using information wisely. It aims to provide warning you of important events, such as takeovers, market changes, and poor staff performance, so that you can take preventative steps. It seeks to help you analyze and make better business decisions, to improve sales or customer satisfaction or staff morale. It presents the information you need, when you need it.

## Collaborative Business Intelligence

Collaborative BI (collaborative business intelligence) is a convergence of a Business Intelligence system with functionality for persisting knowledge and making better decisions using collective intelligence and social networking capabilities. In a top-down enterprise BI implementation, Collaborative BI allows end-users of the BI system to provide feedback into the traditionally read-only dashboarding solution. In advanced Collaborative BI solutions such as BITeamwork, the feedback created through comments and annotations, are especially point-of-view aware so that context of data perspectives when the feedback was authored will always be persisted with the comment or annotation. Collaborative BI has an emphasis on group problem solving, reducing knowledge silos, and increasing user adoption of the BI system.

Some Collaborative BI solutions such as BITeamwork provide a contextual framework for linking the BI system and an enterprise social network such as Salesforce.com's Chatter and Microsoft's Yammer. Collaborative BI tools do not seek to replace either a BI system or an enterprise social network.

Collaborative BI fulfills a need as a framework for teaching companies how to technically expand traditional BI functionality by allowing users to tell the whole story about an organization's data which is already surfaced through the BI tool, and it provides conversation-like functionality traditionally seen in a social network.

Often, Collaborative BI frameworks will include other ancillary functionality such as splash pages, notifications, and management utilities for the Collaborative BI aspects embedded within the BI system.

### Benefits of Collaborative BI

- Faster and more Informed Decision-making – Subject matter experts and decision makers can quickly share ideas and drive cohesive fact-based decisions.

- Knowledge Sharing – Encourages diverse groups to interact with a common focus and gather ideas that otherwise may not have been visible to the decision makers.
- Employee Satisfaction – Empowers employees by giving them a means of voicing thoughts and ideas in a targeted way, and enables them to better see an association between a decision and the conversations that led up to it.
- Stakeholder Involvement – With the right tools and/or processes, stakeholders can respond at a time that is convenient to them; this is especially important when stakeholders have busy schedules and are in multiple time zones.
- Audit Trail – Decisions and conversations can be saved and referred back to at a later date; having a documented decision trail can also reduce decision churn and prevent having the same discussion multiple times.
- Security – More cutting edge collaboration tools integrate security with their collaboration offering. This enforces report permissions for those being asked to review a report and ensure they authorized to view it.

Collaborative BI does have it's challenges – Too many conflicting voices can make it difficult to come to agreement on an issue and, as with physical meetings, strong personalities can overwhelm a discussion if not managed appropriately.

# Real Time Business Intelligence

Real-time business intelligence is an approach to data analytics that enables business users to get up-to-the-minute data by directly accessing operational systems or feeding business transactions into a real-time data warehouse and business intelligence (BI) system.

The technologies that can be used to enable real-time BI include data virtualization, data federation, enterprise information integration (EII), enterprise application integration (EAI) and service-oriented architectures (SOA). Complex event processing tools can be used to analyze data streams in real time and either trigger automated actions or alert workers to patterns and trends.

Real-time BI can help support instant decision-making, which is necessary, for example, if a company sells clothing online. The company's website and representatives at the company's call center need to have the same up-to-the-minute data regarding inventory levels so if a customer places an order and a particular size or color is sold out, the customer can be notified and redirected to another, similar item. A real-time approach isn't required for every part of a company's business, however. Most BI users can meet their business goals by looking at weekly or monthly business performance numbers and long-term trends such as year-over-year comparisons. Similarly, finance groups aren't likely to require real-time data to analyze financial metrics or compare actual budgets to forecasts.

Because real-time BI implementations can increase the overall cost of a BI system, the best practice for organizations is to deploy real-time BI technology only when it's absolutely required.

## Advantages of Business Intelligence

Here are some of the advantages of using Business Intelligence System:

### Boost Productivity

With a BI program, It is possible for businesses to create reports with a single click thus saves lots of time and resources. It also allows employees to be more productive on their tasks.

### To Improve Visibility

BI also helps to improve the visibility of these processes and make it possible to identify any areas which need attention.

### Fix Accountability

BI system assigns accountability in the organization as there must be someone who should own accountability and ownership for the organization's performance against its set goals.

### It gives a Bird's Eye View

BI system also helps organizations as decision makers get an overall bird's eye view through typical BI features like dashboards and scorecards.

### It Streamlines Business Processes

BI takes out all complexity associated with business processes. It also automates analytics by offering predictive analysis, computer modeling, benchmarking and other methodologies.

### It allows for easy Analytics

BI software has democratized its usage, allowing even nontechnical or non-analysts users to collect and process data quickly. This also allows putting the power of analytics from the hand's many people.

## Trends in Business Intelligence

The following are some business intelligence and analytics trends that you should be aware of:

Artificial Intelligence: Gartner' report indicates that AI and machine learning now take on complex tasks done by human intelligence. This capability is being leveraged to come up with real-time data analysis and dashboard reporting.

Collaborative BI: BI software combined with collaboration tools, including social media, and other latest technologies enhance the working and sharing by teams for collaborative decision making.

Embedded BI: Embedded BI allows the integration of BI software or some of its features into another business application for enhancing and extending it's reporting functionality.

Cloud Analytics: BI applications will be soon offered in the cloud, and more businesses will be shifting to this technology. As per their predictions within a couple of years, the spending on cloud-based analytics will grow 4.5 times faster.

## Financial Intelligence

Finance intelligence is skill set comprising of the following four competencies; understanding the foundation, understanding the art, understanding the analysis and understanding the big picture. All the four competencies need to be put into practice and implemented for whole hearted success of finance intelligence. Finance is the business language recognized and used across all organizations. It is common denominator on which all the organizations are measured.

### Understanding the Foundation

Organization needs to build on strong foundation for its non-finance manager to understand the concept of finance. The foundation requires basic understanding of income statement, cash flow and balance sheet. Non-finance managers should not be baffled when presented with an array of numbers. The purpose of finance intelligence is to ensure that when non-finance managers are presented numbers, they should be competent enough to make business sense out of them.

### Understanding the Art

Finance as well as accounting is considered science and art. Both the discipline tries to quantify what cannot always be represented as numbers. This quantification of concept is based upon rules, assumption and principles. Non-finance managers should be able to apply this art/science to scenarios and make financial sense out of them. By doing this, they are prepared for any challenging scenarios.

### Understanding the Analysis

Once the basic idea of finance and its utility is formulated, the application part comes from the picture. Numbers presented to non-finance managers can be better understood, right questions can be asked, and further analysis can be done around that. Finance intelligence equips managers to make sense of various ratio analyses, return on investment, etc. The new understanding helps them make informed and calculated decisions.

### Understanding the Big Picture

It has been observed that the financial numbers alone do not tell the complete story about what is happening within the organization. A financial result or analysis needs to be understood from top level or broader perspective. A financial result should be analyzed considering the macro environment under which the company is operating. The macro factors which influence financial results are competitive environment, government regulations, changing demographics, evolving technologies, etc.

### Finance Intelligence and Beyond

Understanding the finance concepts and finance intelligence competency are first steps in gaining broader financial knowledge. It should prepare managers to look beyond the finance numbers with an analytic eye and make informed decisions.

## Data Collection

Data becomes information after it has been processed to add context, relevance and purpose. Most companies collect a large amount of data from their business operations. The ability to analyze and act on data is increasingly important to businesses. The pace of change requires companies to be able to react quickly to changing demands from customers and environmental conditions. Although prompt action may be required, decisions are increasingly complex as companies compete in a global marketplace. Managers may need to understand high volumes of data before they can make the necessary decisions. Effective business intelligence (BI) tools assist managers with decision making.

## Knowledge Management

KM can be defined as a systematic approach that provides efficient disciplines and procedures to enable knowledge to grow and create value for organisations.

KM has become one of the most important trends in modern businesses across the globe. A general goal of KM is to improve the systematic handling of knowledge and potential knowledge within the organisation. Knowledge must be refreshed by the organisation, and therefore knowledge networks are needed to ensure employees have opportunities to share knowledge. In addition, Labedz et al. stated that KM processes that have been integrated into work processes can be used to correct dysfunctional organisational behaviour.

KM systems can be categorised as falling into the following groups: groupware, document management systems, expert systems, semantic networks, relational and object-oriented databases, simulation tools and artificial intelligence.

KM is crucial for maintaining and gaining competitive advantage, as it supports more effective knowledge acquisition and transfer.

Gummesson stated that the key task of the organisation is acquiring institutional knowledge and knowledge of the social interaction processes. KM system can improve a firm's operational processes. KM efforts focus on organisational objectives such as improved performance, competitive advantage innovation, the sharing of lessons learned, integration and continuous improvement of the organisation. KM effort needs to convert internalised tacit knowledge into explicit knowledge in order to share it, but the same effort must also permit individuals to internalise and make meaningful any codified knowledge retrieved from the KM effort.

## The Integration of BI and KM

KM is distinct from BI in many aspects. The majority of models used in the KM field, such as the tacit and explicit knowledge framework for a dynamic human process of justifying personal belief toward the truth are typically non-technology oriented. In addition, KM deals with unstructured information and tacit knowledge which BI fails to address.

According to Stevan Dedijer (the father of BI), KM emerged in part from the thinking of the 'intelligence approach' to business. Dedijer thinks that 'Intelligence' is more descriptive than knowledge. "Knowledge is static, intelligence is dynamic".

In addition, the visions of integration of BI and KM are diversified, and issues of whether KM should be viewed as a subset of BI or vice versa are still under debate in these two well-established fields. While both KM and BI are influenced by the approaches of the research and practitioners' communities, the way of integration of KM and BI seems not unique. There have been several models of integration of BI and KM reported in the literature. In addition, Malhotra has proposed general models of integration of KM and BI for routine structured information processing and non-routine unstructured sense making.

## Proposed BI Module Approach

The proposed approach consists of five main stages, namely storing data, pre-processing data, indices computation and calculation metrics, application of hierarchical clustering, and application of the PCA and e-business usage assessment. The first three stages are based on the framework described in detail in Kazanidis et al. and Valsamidis et al., and facilitate the extraction of useful information from the data logged by a web server running a web application.

The main advantages of the proposed approach are that:

- It uses the log file for web usage analysis.
- It proposes indices and metrics to be used for the first time in e-business system.
- It uses two algorithms for clustering and classification in a different way.
- It can be easily adapted to any e-business system.
- It visualises the results in a user friendly environment.

The five distinct stages of the approach are depicted in Figure. After the logging of data from e-business system which stands in a web server, the data are pre-processed in order to be ready for data analysis. It is worth mentioning that the recorded information by the module secures uses one-to-one mapping between URI and per product stored information in terms of pages.

Indices and metrics which were firstly introduced by the authors are used for the measurement of the usage of the e-business system.

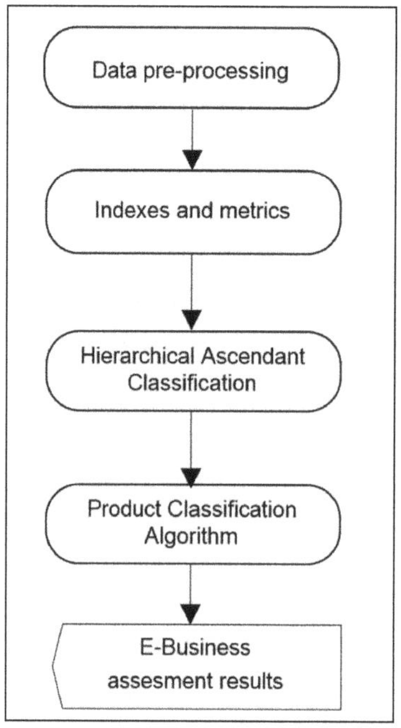


Stages of the e-business assessment approach.

## Logging the Data

This stage involves the logging of specific data from e-business systems. The data recording module is embedded in the web server of the e-learning platform and records specific web shop platform fields at the web shop database. More specifically, the following fields are being recorded:

1. Remote_host: The IP of the host that the user connected to the web shop as well as location info of the connected IP address taken from a who is request.
2. Session_id: Session id created at the web system upon user authentication. If a user does not identify itself with the web shop, a random session_id denoted to the user based on an md5 hash of its remote IP address.
3. User_name: The username of a logged in user. If user did not log in to the web store then anonymous username is used (user name can be used in order to extract gender or age attributes from the e-shops database by performing post-processing analysis).
4. Module_id: The e-shop component module_id. The web shop modules identified are product, new_product, offer_product, wish_productprice_reduction_product, news, links, payment modules, shipping modules and pricing modules.
5. Request_uri: The e-shop webpages that a session_id visits. Each page is identified by a module_id field. For product, new_product, offer_product, wish product modules, a product_id field and cat_id field, identifies each product page additionally. If it is an informatory page such as e-shop news or link page, then it is identified by an unique news_id or a link_id number. If it is a payment or shipping product module then it is identified by a payment type id or a ship type id accordingly.
6. Request_uri_duration: The time in seconds that a user visits a specific page.

7. Session_duration: The total session duration.
8. User_order_id: The order_id of a completed e-shop cart transaction, with transaction date included.
9. User_payment: The total amount of cart transaction cost.
10. User_wishlist_id: The id of a new product put into user's wish list from the wish list module.
11. User_payment_type: The cart enabled payment type selected by customer.
12. User_ship_type: The cart enabled shipping type selected by the customer.
13. User_red_id: The link of a product proposed by the user for a price reduction from the reduction_product_list_module.
14. User_red_value: The product reduction value.

These fields are being recorded with the use of an Apache module, developed in Perl programming language, as a first step.

The development of such a module has the following advantages:

- Rapid storage of user information, since it is executed straight from the server API and not by the e-business application, or database.
- The produced data are independent of specific formulations used by the web shop system.

## Data Pre-processing

The second stage is data pre-processing. The data of the log file contain noise such as missing values and outliers. These values have to be pre-processed in order to prepare them for data analysis. Specifically, in this stage the recorded data are filtered. Outlier detection is performed and extremes in values are removed. This step is not performed by the e-business system, but in the web server, thus can be embedded into a variety of e-business system.

The produced log file, from the previous step, is filtered, so it includes only the following fields:

- ProductID, which is the identification string of each product.
- SessionID, which is the identification string of each session.
- Page Uniform Resource Locator (URL), which contains the requests of each page of the platform that the user visited.

## Indices and Metrics

Although, the aforementioned fields contain information about the e-business process, more metrics and rates are proposed in order to adequately facilitate the assessment of product web usage.

Table: Attributes name and description.

| Index/metric name | Description of the index/metric |
|---|---|
| Session | The total number of sessions per product viewed by users |
| Pages | The number of pages per product viewed by users |
| Unique pages | The number of unique pages per product viewed by users |
| Unique pages per Product ID | The number of unique pages per product viewed by users per session |
| Homogeneity | The homogeneity of products |
| Enrichment | The enrichment of products |
| Disappointment | The disappointment of users when they view pages of the products |
| Interest | It is the one's complement to the disappointment |

Metrics are used for the facilitation of the product usage assessment. First, the indices Sessions, Pages, Unique pages, Unique Pages per ProductID per Session (UPPS) are computed with the use of a Perl program. Then, the metrics Enrichment, Disappointment, Interest and Homogeneity are calculated. Finally, the rates, mean rate and the Score are calculated based on the previous metrics.

The number of sessions and the number of pages viewed by all users are counted for the calculation of viewed by many users but there were also some other pages not so popular. To refine the situation, we define another index which is called unique pages and metrics the total number of unique pages visited per product viewed by all users. It counts each page of the product only once, independently of how many times they were viewed by the users. The Unique Pages per Product per Session (UPPS) index expresses the number of Unique Pages per Product visited in one Session; it is used for the calculation of the product activity in an objective manner. Because some novice users may navigate in a product and visit some pages of the product more than once, UPPS eliminates duplicate page visits, since it considers the visits of the same user in a session only once.

Enrichment is a metric which is proposed in order to express the 'enrichment' of each product in terms of educational material. Enrichment is defined as the complement of the ratio of the unique pages over total number of product webpages as proposed in Valsamidis et al.

Enrichment = 1 – (Unique Pages/Total Pages),

where Unique Pages ≤ Total Pages.

Enrichment values are in the range [0, 1). When users follow unique paths in a product this is 0 while in a product with minimal unique pages this is close to 1. Since it offers a metric of how many unique pages were viewed by the users, it shows how much information included in each product is handed over to the end user inferring that the product contains rich educational material.

Disappointment is a metric which combines sessions and pages viewed by users and it metrics the disappointment of the users in the product, in the sense that when a user views few pages of the product, he or she logs out of the product.

Disappointment = Sessions/Total Pages.

In other words, the disappointment metric reflects how quickly the users discontinue viewing pages of the products. Disappointment values are in the range (0, 1]. Owing to the negative nature of the Disappointment metric, it was replaced by another metric which has a positive sounding manner, Interest. Interest metric is defined as the complement to the disappointment.

Interest = 1 – Disappointment.

Both disappointment and interest metrics were proposed in Valsamidis et al.

Homogeneity metric is another metric, which is defined as the ratio of unique visited product pages to the number of sessions that visited the product.

Homogeneity = Unique pages/Total Sessions.

where Total Sessions per product ≫ Unique product pages.

Homogeneity metric value ranges from [0, 1), where 0 means that no user followed a unique path and 1 that every user followed unique paths. It is a product quality index and characterises the percentage of product information discovered by each user participating in a product. The aforementioned metrics contribute to the assessment of product usage.

# Data Integration

Data integration is the process of combining data from different sources into a single, unified view. Integration begins with the ingestion process, and includes steps such as cleansing, ETL mapping, and transformation. Data integration ultimately enables analytics tools to produce effective, actionable business intelligence.

There is no universal approach to data integration. However, data integration solutions typically involve a few common elements, including a network of data sources, a master server, and clients accessing data from the master server.

In a typical data integration process, the client sends a request to the master server for data. The master server then intakes the needed data from internal and external sources. The data is extracted from the sources, then consolidated into a single, cohesive data set. This is served back to the client for use.

## Integration Helps Businesses Succeed

Even if a company is receiving all the data it needs, that data often resides in a number of separate data sources. For example, for a typical customer 360 view use case, the data that must be combined may include data from their CRM systems, web traffic, marketing operations software, customer — facing applications, sales and customer success systems, and even partner data, just to name a few. Information from all of those different sources often needs to be pulled together for analytical needs or operational actions, and that can be no small task for data engineers or developers to bring them all together.

Let's take a look at a typical analytical use case. Without unified data, a single report typically involves logging into multiple accounts, on multiple sites, accessing data within native apps, copying over the data, reformatting, and cleansing, all before analysis can happen.

Conducting all these operations as efficiently as possible highlights the importance of data integration. It also showcases the major benefits of a well thought-out approach to data integration:

### Improves Collaboration and Unification of Systems

Employees in every department — and sometimes in disparate physical locations — increasingly need access to the company's data for shared and individual projects. IT needs a secure solution for delivering data via self-service access across all lines of business.

Additionally, employees in almost every department are generating and improving data that the rest of the business needs. Data integration needs to be collaborative and unified in order to improve collaboration and unification across the organization.

### Saves Time and Boosts Efficiency

When a company takes measures to integrate its data properly, it cuts down significantly on the time it takes to prepare and analyze that data. The automation of unified views cuts out the need for manually gathering data, and employees no longer need to build connections from scratch whenever they need to run a report or build an application.

Additionally, using the right tools, rather than hand-coding the integration, returns even more time (and resources overall) to the dev team.

All the time saved on these tasks can be put to other, better uses, with more hours earmarked for analysis and execution to make an organization more productive and competitive.

### Reduces Errors (and Rework)

There's a lot to keep up with when it comes to a company's data resources. To manually gather data, employees must know every location and account that they might need to explore — and have all necessary software installed before they begin — to ensure their data sets will be complete and accurate. If a data repository is added, and that employee is unaware, they will have an incomplete data set.

Additionally, without a data integration solution that synchronizes data, reporting must be periodically redone to account for any changes. With automated updates, however, reports can be run easily in real time, whenever they're needed.

### Delivers More Valuable Data

Data integration efforts actually improve the value of a business' data over time. As data is integrated into a centralized system, quality issues are identified and necessary improvements are implemented, which ultimately results in more accurate data — the foundation for quality analysis.

## Data Integration in Modern Business

Data integration isn't a one-size-fits-all solution; the right formula can vary based on numerous business needs. Here are some common use cases for data integration tools:

### Leveraging Big Data

Data lakes can be highly complex and massive in volume. Companies like Facebook and Google, for instance, process a non-stop influx of data from billions of users. This level of information consumption is commonly referred to as big data. As more big data enterprises crop up, more data becomes available for businesses to leverage. That means the need for sophisticated data integration efforts becomes central to operations for many organizations.

### Creating Data Warehouses and Data Lakes

Data integration initiatives — particularly among large businesses — are often used to create data warehouses, which combine multiple data sources into a relational database. Data warehouses allow users to run queries, compile reports, generate analysis, and retrieve data in a consistent format. For example, many companies rely on data warehouses such as Microsoft Azure and AWS Redshift to generate business intelligence from their data.

### Simplifying Business Intelligence (BI)

By delivering a unified view of data from numerous sources, data integration simplifies the business intelligence (BI) processes of analysis. Organizations can easily view, and quickly comprehend, the available data sets in order to derive actionable information on the current state of the business. With data integration, analysts can compile more information for more accurate evaluation without being overwhelmed by high volumes.

Unlike business analytics, BI doesn't use predictive analysis to make future projections; instead, it focuses on describing the present and past to aid in strategic decision-making. This use of data integration is well-suited to data warehousing, where high-level overview information in an easily consumable format aligns nicely.

### ETL and Data Integration

Extract, Transform, Load, commonly known as ETL, is a process within data integration wherein data is taken from the source system and delivered into the warehouse. This is the ongoing process that data warehousing undertakes to transform multiple data sources into useful, consistent information for business intelligence and analytical efforts.

### Challenges to Data Integration

Taking several data sources and turning them into a unified whole within a single structure is a technical challenge unto itself. As more business build out data integration solutions, they are tasked with creating pre-built processes for consistently moving data where it needs to go. While this provides time and cost savings in the short-term, implementation can be hindered by numerous obstacles.

Here are some common challenges that organizations face in building their integration systems:

- How to get to the finish line — Companies typically know what they want from data integration — the solution to a specific challenge. What they often don't think about is the route it will take to get there. Anyone implementing data integration must understand what types of data need to be collected and analyzed, where that data comes from, the systems that will use the data, what types of analysis will be conducted, and how frequently data and reports will need to be updated.
- Data from legacy systems — Integration efforts may need to include data stored in legacy systems. That data, however, is often missing markers such as times and dates for activities, which more modern systems commonly include.
- Data from newer business demands — New systems today are generating different types of data (such as unstructured or real-time) from all sorts of sources such as videos, IoT devices, sensors, and cloud. Figuring out how to quickly adapt your data integration infrastructure to meet the demands of integrating all these data becomes critical for your business to win, yet extremely difficult as the volume, the speed, the new format of data all pose new challenges.
- External data — Data taken in from external sources may not be provided at the same level of detail as internal sources, making it difficult to examine with the same rigor. Also, contracts in place with external vendors may make it difficult to share data across the organization.
- Keeping up — Once an integration system is up and running, the task isn't done. It becomes incumbent upon the data team to keep data integration efforts on par with best practices, as well as the latest demands from the organization and regulatory agencies.

## Integration Strategies for Business

There are several ways to integrate data that depend on the size of the business, the need being fulfilled, and the resources available:

- Manual data integration is simply the process by which an individual user manually collects necessary data from various sources by accessing interfaces directly, then cleans it up as needed, and combines it into one warehouse. This is highly inefficient and inconsistent, and makes little sense for all but the smallest of organizations with minimal data resources.
- Middleware data integration is an integration approach where a middleware application acts as a mediator, helping to normalize data and bring it into the master data pool. (Think about adapters for old electronic equipment with outdated connection points). Legacy applications often don't play well with others. Middleware comes into play when a data integration system is unable to access data from one of these applications on its own.
- Application-based integration is an approach to integration wherein software applications locate, retrieve, and integrate data. During integration, the software must make data from different systems compatible with one another so they can be transmitted from one source to another.

- Uniform access integration is a type of data integration that focuses on creating a front end that makes data appear consistent when accessed from different sources. The data, however, is left within the original source. Using this method, object-oriented database management systems can be used to create the appearance of uniformity between unlike databases.
- Common storage integration is the most frequently used approach to storage within data integration. A copy of data from the original source is kept in the integrated system and processed for a unified view. This is opposed to uniform access, which leaves data in the source. The common storage approach is the underlying principle behind the traditional data warehousing solution.

### Data Integration Tools

Data integration tools have the potential to simplify this process a great deal. The features you should look for in a data integration tool are:

- A lot of connectors: There are many systems and applications in the world; the more pre-built connectors your Data Integration tool has, the more time your team will save.
- Open source: Open source architectures typically provide more flexibility while helping to avoid vendor lock-in.
- Portability: It's important, as companies increasingly move to hybrid cloud models, to be able to build your data integrations once and run them anywhere.
- Ease of use: Data integration tools should be easy to learn and easy to use with a GUI interface to make visualizing your data pipelines simpler.
- A transparent price model: Your data integration tool provider should not ding you for increasing the number of connectors or data volumes.
- Cloud compatibility: Your data integration tool should work natively in a single cloud, multi-cloud, or hybrid cloud environment.

## Data Quality

Recent days the usage of BI solutions in the company such as data ware houses and data mining tools that allows the people in the business to analyze and understand the data which helps to make good decisions are increasing. Bad and inconsistent data will leads to bad decisions. For example department of health want to know how many drugs they need for the winter for outbreaks and to negotiate with the manufacturers. If they work with the bad quality data which in this case old data for the prediction then the prediction will be end up with uneven count of medicines and therefore negotiation too. Then health department has to buy additional medicines which will increase the cost of negotiation with the manufacturer and sometimes medicines will not deliver on time. This example highlights two problems – low quality data and the lack of awareness of analyst to identify the bad data and so the decisions will be inaccurate.

In business intelligence bad data quality paves path for bad business decisions. The economic experts in a company have to know everything about the data and what are the steps they have to take when the data falls short which means they have to take precautions about the bad data quality when they are doing analytics. "The abundant amount of data that is available at present making economists to ensure that their employees in different sections and units are using the same data units and inputs". The normal definition of data quality is about the bad data which is an incomplete data or the data which is incorrect whereas the broad definition of data quality is the consistent, relevant and timely data. A website named TDWI (The Data Warehousing Institute) declared the problems of data quality costs about $600 billion every year for USA companies. Generally to fix any problem we have to take responsibility for it. In the case of data quality taking that responsibility is a huge barrier. To achieve a high quality of data we have to view the data as an entire organization perspective. Sometimes the data in silo is correct but the information is inconsistent and untimely when it view across the organization but in general the data has to be consistent across the organization but not just within business function.

Bad data quality is always expensive, avoidable and sometimes it is an embarrassment for the company. for example if there is an error in your reservation of a hotel room, errors like wrong name or wrong room number then it is no big deal and there is no revenue to lost. But if the same thing happens in the other cases like banks then it will leads to a huge problem and nuisance. The banks and finance firms have so many problems related to the data quality are both optimistic and pessimistic. With the bad data they lose the customers and business due to their wrong information and in some situations it is even more embarrassing like when they couldn't retrieve the customer's name. In some cases financial firms loses their ability of selling the products because they are not familiar with the person they are talking to. In a company, the data of bad quality affects CFO more whenever he has to sign a financial report which is based on the bad data and whenever CFO releases the financial information of the company to the press with the bad quality data. This cases will lead to the suspending CFO from the company and in worse case it leads to legal actions against CFO. This scenarios will happen in any company which needs to operate efficiently regardless of its size and market. If the companies have to run with the bad data, how can they construct and process performance management system in the company, how teams can collaborate having different data for different team and management meeting will become hassle with various people with different data. Enterprise Data Management is the program which will improve the quality of the data across the enterprise.

Data quality can be measured using 6 types of elements:

## Definition

The degree of data quality numbers that are consistent with their original ones are depend upon definitions. Before the data consistency measure, first the definition has to be exist. The quality of the data is begins with the understanding of the whole data inventory and the information regarding the data is very crucial as the data itself.

## Accuracy

The degree to which the data value is correct and accurate and the values are usually compared with their original values for exactness but still it will be inaccurate. If the data values are equal to that of the original values then certain data has to be compared with the reference values.

## Completeness

The degree to which the user received the whole data that is expected. The completeness of the data can be measured by two ways:

Does the user received all the data that is sent by the provider? This can be measured by comparing the data count of provider with the received data count.

Does the provider sent all the information that is available with them or just some data? This is tough to find as some systems of the provider might have glitches and so records will be missed from the user's feed.

## Coverage

The degree to which all the fields are filled with the data. This can be measure by taking the missing data percentage from the columns and compare with the expected missing data percentage.

## Timeliness

The degree to which the files of the providers are received, processed and send them to data marts. The timeliness is measured by comparing the actual receipt files to the expected receipt times. The data files which are missed or received late are marked and reported. If the lag time increases then it will be reported to the provider in order to request the delivery soon.

## Validity

The degree to which the relationship between the different data are valid. For example data of the zip code is 06605 which is accurate and the data of the state is New Jersey is accurate. But the zip code 06605 is invalid for New Jersey.

## Findings

In any organization the impact of data quality is mostly effects on analysis and decision support department. The proliferation of the business intelligence which acquires data from various systems and application can decrease the quality of the data and this will leads to the degrading of confidence of the user in the BI reports. On the other hand the data with good quality leads the company to run more effectively and decisively. To deal with the problems that caused by low data quality companies invests in the technologies which will drives the competition and results of the company. Successful adoption of BI in the organization can help to determine it's health, identify the key indicators and supervise everyday operations of the company in growth standard.

Increased demand for the large data is driving the BI adoption across the organizations from executives to business users. Such a big adoption for BI to update to the advanced technologies like dashboards, visualization techniques. This means that as the data access increases then it need to be fast and accessible such that it has to be consumable for BI. Most of the traditional BI concentrates on analytics and queries but now a days the advanced BI is using as a aid for the organization's operational decisions. The user's action mostly depends upon the quality of data and the trust that user has on the data. But user is unable to decide the analyzing data is good quality or not. With these nauseous feeling, the business actions are subjected to delays and sometime it halts the action. So trust must be gained on data and the trust between the business users and BI teams has to be stimulated. If the data is incomplete and inaccurate then users will lost interest in the BI tools and trust will be derogated. Along with the data cleansing methods and match trust need to be built around the data warehouses, operational department and applications where huge amount of data is generated throughout the organization.

For any organization data quality is a base to allocate the assets of data against the business expectations with specific rules. Data quality problems can be analyzed by a data quality dimension framework which includes elements which can identify and categorizes the various data quality problems. If an organization comes up with data quality problems then using this framework we can analyze the level of data quality. Level of data quality means if certain data quality is said to be 80% which means duplicates and percentage of conformity included in it.

The data quality framework looks as the below figure. Both IT and business users have to contribute and agree with the elements that are included in this frame work. Organizations can change the framework depending on the level of maturity and priorities.

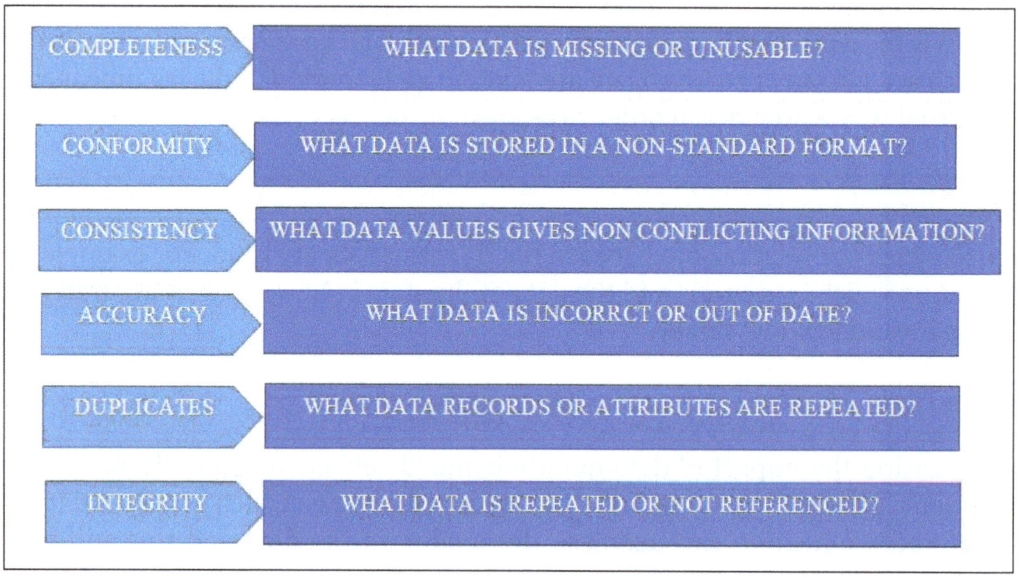


As the business intelligence deployment spreads to the different departments the managing the quality of master data beyond the other types of data is very crucial. Other types of data includes financial data, banking data and product data etc. which all are exists in different platforms like ERP, relational databases and semi structured data sources. Another crucial thing is that as the data volume increases, the intensity and performance of the data quality management processes has to be advanced. So for this reasons the processes for cleansing and delivering the data has to be delivered accurately regardless of the data size at any time and it is the fundamental to the BI success. With good data BI process will be fasten up and it stimulates the confidence. With the increased confidence in data, executives and other users can recognize the data quality of high accuracy. The data quality management process will increases the clarity and accuracy of the reports which are important for business risk management.

The consistent, real time and accurate data which is used for several BI applications is important to many organizations. If the data ware houses are unable to deliver the good quality of data consistently then the entire BI system will be problematic to determine the current situation of the organizations and it unable to take the right actions to run the business and compete effectively. By implementing the enterprise data quality method, the analysts can design the score cards, dashboards, OLAP analysis and on demand alerts with greater confidence.

The solutions of the data quality can synergizes with the present data integration methods that have the ability to access all the master data that is available in the organization. The final result will be perfect and far greater than the use of traditional data quality technology which mostly about the cleansing the customer's data. The successful processing of data quality at organizational level helps certain company to return their investment on BI.

## BI Software and its Benefits

### Get Valuable Insights into your Business

Business intelligence software benefits and functionality constantly collect and analyze data in order to deliver actionable insights for your business. Professionals can generate reports on a variety of data sets like expenses, operations processes, staffing and customer service.

There are numerous types of reports you can create using BI tools. All BI platforms will offer pre-formatted reporting capabilities that collect data for common KPIs. Businesses can also generate customized or self-service BI reports, applying BI's excellent visuals to unique, organization-specific data sets. If neither of these options give you what you need, users can run an ad-hoc report, which is put together entirely by users and usually focuses on a very specific KPI that can't be targeted by other types of reports.

Another unique benefit of business intelligence reports is the relevance of information. Because reports contain relevant data collected within your business operations, businesses are better able to act based on the information contained in BI reports. Plus, you don't have to be a data scientist to use BI tools — the data visualizations generated by these tools are easy to understand and explain. In SelectHub's recent survey of organizations in the market for BI software, 48 percent of buyers listed reporting as a desired feature.

### Visualize Important Information

Operational reports can be difficult to interpret, reducing an organization's ability to recognize and act on key metrics. One of the key benefits of BI software is that it provides excellent data visualization capabilities, allowing users to create intuitive data visuals that are easy to understand and simple to interpret.

Charts, graphs, videos, animations and infographics are more engaging ways to transmit information than blocks of numbers or spreadsheets. This is partly because the human brain is hardwired to process cognitive information — information that takes more than a glance to interpret and digest — much slower than visual information. Of those surveyed in SelectHub's recent survey, 81 percent of respondents expected visualization features from their BI platform.

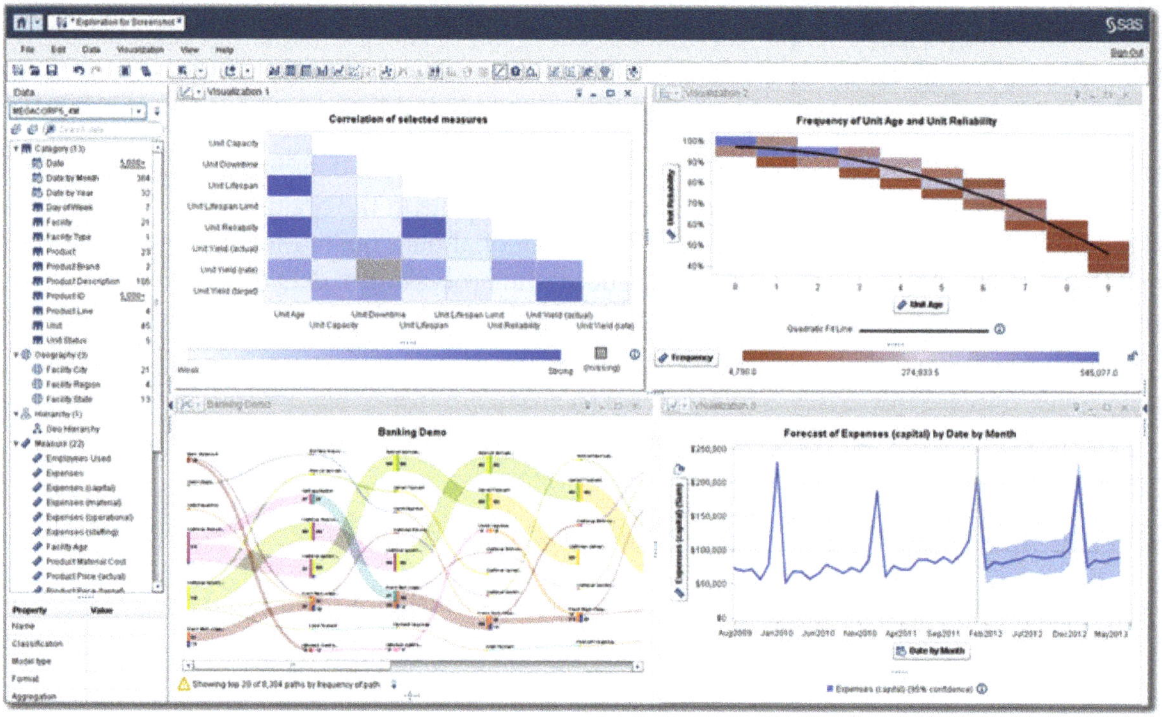


SAS BI offers powerful data visualization capabilities.

## Data Mining

BI analytics tools are exceptionally well-suited for powerful data mining. Data mining is the process of seeking patterns in data in order to identify trends and draw insights. It can be broken into five steps: collection, warehousing and storage, organization, analysis, and presentation. Some BI platforms can perform all of these steps for an organization, although others require support from business analytics tools, Big Data analytics systems or data warehousing platforms.

BI analyzes, processes and renders vast amounts of data that cannot be managed with weaker programs. It integrates with data warehousing solutions, in-house databases (e.g. SQL servers), as well as both structured and unstructured data. This allows easy access to valuable information and enhanced decision-making processes that businesses might otherwise miss.

Because BI software is able to instantaneously analyze incoming data, it helps companies catch fleeting opportunities that they might otherwise miss. With the customized reports produced by BI connected to a data warehouse, companies can more easily pick up on trends in company spending, staffing, operations, client development and more.

## Establish Benchmarking

Fast thinking and effective decision-making is important in achieving success in a business endeavor. Often, those in charge of running a business don't have the time to conduct a large-scale research project and a particular industry development or product release. Using business intelligence software is like constantly having an in-depth research project in progress that's compiling information for groundbreaking decision-making.

Benchmarking is a valuable data analysis tool businesses use to gauge their productivity, revenue and overall success relative to that of their competitors. Organizations often struggle with benchmarking, but BI simplifies the process, providing actionable information and reports that are easily understood. That's why benchmarking is one of the core BI requirements users look for in a BI platform.

Benchmarking reports offer accurate, timely data that allow businesses to evaluate their performance against individual KPIs or trends over time, providing valuable insight into the organization's current state. With predictive analytics capabilities, users can take these benchmarks and implement them proactively, getting ahead of their competitors instead of chasing behind them.

### Performance Management

BI also helps track, manage and implement performance goals. With BI tools, businesses can input data-based goals such as sales goals or target delivery time, then track progress on a daily basis. This tracking mechanism is known as performance management, and it provides some of the most effective and easily implemented goal management available.

BI applications make information readily accessible that would ordinarily take hours or weeks to track down and organize. Another business intelligence benefit is that by using dashboards and real-time data, users can easily organize important information and get moment-to-moment updates. This makes for a great deal of time savings and allows you to deal with problems immediately.

With BI's intuitive visual analytics capabilities, professionals can track goal fulfillment and use that information to gauge overall organizational productivity. When properly implemented, BI tools can boost your performance significantly.

### Sales Intelligence

One of the most important BI benefits is that it enhances awareness. Those who design business intelligence software know companies can't take advantage of opportunities they're not aware of. They therefore design software to make those fleeting opportunities noticeable and provide the details that allow companies to make the most of them.

The reports and data produced by business intelligence systems are great when you need to back up your claims with hard data when negotiating with potential clients. It can also be helpful to make quick sales decisions with real-time data and mobile BI reports. A business intelligence system might just turn out to be the most powerful tool you have when you're trying to convince clients, vendors or suppliers of the potentials and capabilities offered by your company's products and services.

When it comes to sales, this type of software is not only effective at supporting your arguments. It also helps you identify trends in customer preferences so you'll be the first in your industry to know what to offer customers in order to maximize sales. Plus, nothing tops off a pitch like a beautiful visualization of data — BI has your back.

A sales analytics dashboard from Domo BI.

## Streamline and Trim Operations

A lesser-praised advantage of business intelligence software is its ability to cut down waste. Anything that doesn't add value to your company can be considered waste: this includes operational and administrative work that can be automated with a BI system. BI does the work that data entry employees or data analysts would typically get saddled with like data organization, de-duplication and other repetitive tasks.

This benefits business intelligence: first, employees can devote their time to more intensive tasks, increasing productivity. It can also save time, money and reduce human error. It also allows users to identify how well the organization is doing with the current staff so you can grow or downsize accordingly.

BI systems can identify waste in your overall operations as well. It does this by pinpointing pain points, bottlenecks and inefficiencies in manufacturing, operations and sales. With predictive analysis features, BI will even offer suggestions to alleviate these problem areas.

## Eliminate Guesswork

Without business intelligence software, companies are basically forced to gamble when making many important decisions regarding management, finances, marketing efforts and more. With business intelligence software, the decisions made by company leaders are more data-driven and often result in a competitive advantage for your organization.

BI implements a data structure to encourage data-driven decision-making and helps you know the best plan — not just guess at it. This business resource will not only lead to greater profitability, but it will take a great deal of the stress and uncertainty out of running a business.

## Improve Inventory Management

The advantages of business intelligence systems can even extend into purchasing, procurement and inventory management. Users can generate reports detailing stockroom needs to determine when to purchase new inventory. BI also tracks inventory going out, so you can better prepare for future buying trends and reduce inventory waste.

## Get a Competitive Edge

The number of businesses utilizing BI is only increasing. According to Forbes, 53 percent of companies they interviewed use some form of BI — up from only 17 percent in 2015. It's not unreasonable to predict that in the next 10 to 20 years BI adoption will be the norm. This is especially true as the BI market gains increasing pervasiveness and traction. The future is bright for BI.

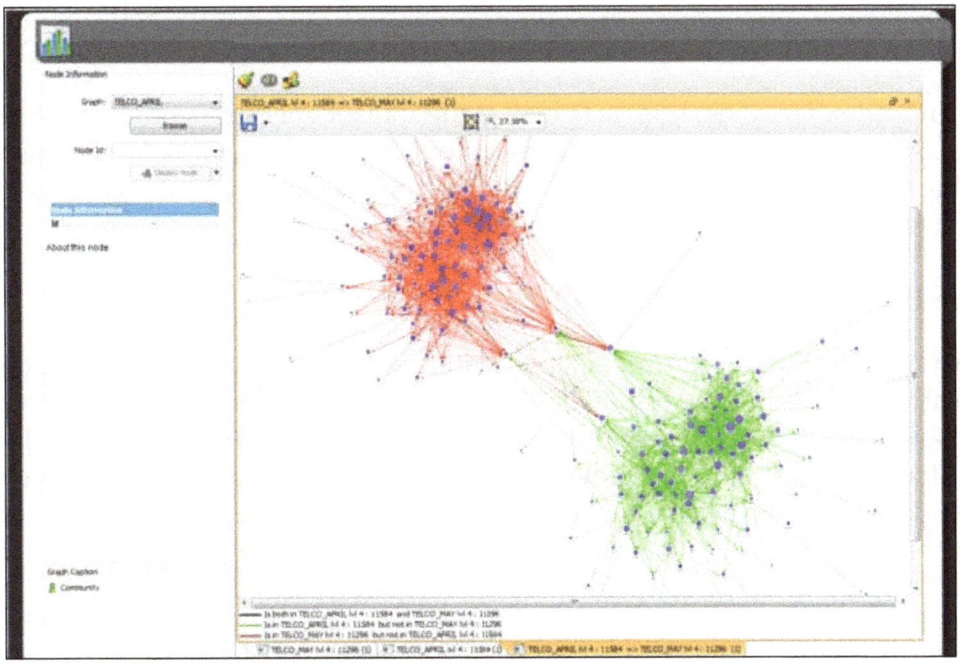

Predictive modeling from SAS.

Business intelligence gives organizations a tangible competitive edge in an ever-increasingly competitive market. Making quick decisions in the business world is part of the job, but knowing those decisions are based soundly in data-driven insights offers another level of security and confidence.

BI even offers fraud monitoring and risk management features! By tracking patterns and monitoring data behavior, BI can identify how likely it is that a transaction, person or network is fraudulent. The same data mining feature that can give sales teams insight into customer desires can be used to make risk assessments and predictions, protecting your organization.

There are a range of advantages of business intelligence software. It is a growing industry that has many proven advantages when properly implemented. It allows users to gain targeted insight into your organization's past, present and future to make informed business decisions. To accomplish this, BI software collects, organizes, mines and visualizes crucial KPIs. It eliminates waste and guesswork, promotes efficient inventory management, and improves sales intelligence. This powerful combination of features and benefits of BI software offers users a competitive edge that can make all the difference in the modern age.

# Elements of Business Intelligence

The five primary components of BI include:

### OLAP (Online Analytical Processing)

This component of BI allows executives to sort and select aggregates of data for strategic monitoring. With the help of specific software products, a certification in business intelligence helps business owners can use data to make adjustments to overall business processes.

### Advanced Analytics or Corporate Performance Management (CPM)

This set of tools allows business leaders to look at the statistics of certain products or services. For instance, a fast food chain may analyze the sale of certain items and make local, regional and national modifications on menu board offerings as a result. The data could also be used to predict in which markets a new product may have the best success.

### Real-time BI

In a mobile society, this particular component of BI is becoming increasingly popular. Using software applications, a business can respond to real-time trends in email, messaging systems or even digital displays. Because it's all in real-time, an entrepreneur can announce special offers that take advantage of what's going on in the immediate. Marketing professionals can use data to craft creative limited-time specials such as a coupon for hot soup on a cold day. CEO's may be interested in tracking the time of day and location of customers as they interact with a website so marketing can offer special promotions in real-time while the client is engaged on the website.

### Data Warehousing

Data warehousing lets business leaders sift through subsets of data and examine interrelated components that can help drive business. Looking at sales data over several years can help improve product development or tailor seasonal offerings. Data warehousing can also be used to look at the statistics of business processes including how they relate to one another. For instance, business owners can compare shipping times in different facilities to look at which processes and teams work most efficiently. Data warehousing also involves storing huge amounts of data in ways that are beneficial to different divisions within the company.

### Data Sources

This component of BI involves various forms of stored data. It's about taking the raw data and using software applications to create meaningful data sources that each division can use to positively impact business. BI analysts using this strategy may create data tools that allow data to be put into a large cache of spreadsheets, pie charts, tables or graphs that can be used for a variety of business purposes. For example, data can be used to create presentations that help to structure attainable team goals. Looking at the strategic aspect of data sources can also help organizations make fact-driven decisions that take into account a more holistic view of the needs of the company.

# Big Data

The term big data can be defined simply as large data sets that outgrow simple databases and data handling architectures. For example, data that cannot be easily handled in Excel spreadsheets may be referred to as big data.

Big data involves the process of storing, processing and visualizing data. It is essential to find the right tools for creating the best environment to successfully obtain valuable insights from your data.

Setting up an effective big data environment involves utilizing infrastructural technologies that process, store and facilitate data analysis. Data warehouses, modeling language programs and OLAP cubes are just some examples. Today, businesses often use more than one infrastructural deployment to manage various aspects of their data.

Big data often provides companies with answers to the questions they did not know they wanted to ask: How has the new HR software impacted employee performance? How do recent customer reviews relate to sales? Analyzing big data sources illuminates the relationships between all facets of your business.

Therefore, there is inherent usefulness to the information being collected in big data. Businesses must set relevant objectives and parameters in place to glean valuable insights from big data.

Big data isn't only about massive amounts of data or the way how we consume it, but also about the structure of that data with the purpose of delivering added value to the organization.

Increasingly present in our lives, big data is changing our everyday life. Both in our personal as in our business environment we create, whether we like it or not, a non-stop continuous stream of GPS data, phone records, text messages and other information that is captured and ready to analyze:

- Social media platforms, such as Twitter and Facebook, but also professional networking platforms, such as Linkedin, are processing millions of records per second.
- Intelligent devices, like smart energy meters, smartphones, GPS trackers, heart rate monitors in hospitals, etc., communicate with each other and store useful information.
- The presence of RFID tags and sensors on products present a clear picture of specific situations.

A couple of years ago, online retailers changed the way they looked at customers. Trying to understand a customer, it was not only important to know what they actually bought but also what products they looked at, how long they visited a specific webpage, how customers were influenced by promotion emails, how they navigated through the website, etc.

Because of the digital evolution it is now even possible to add peoples' opinions and other information in the process of understanding customers. Imagine, for example, receiving a text message while walking by a big sports equipment reseller stating the bike you last week liked on Facebook now will be sold half the price it was. This could become possible by embracing the power of big data.

There is a big pile of big data created every second awaiting to be processed and analyzed but for data to be more meaningful it must integrate sales, finance, marketing, product data with social data, sentiment data, demographic data, competitors data, etc.

## Business Intelligence vs. Big Data

Big data is often called the successor to Business Intelligence, but is this really the case?

The main thing both systems have in common is their existence to provide answers to business questions. But Big Data can and does go further than traditional BI systems. Big data analytics are similar to BI analytics for one of the so-called V's (Value) but slightly differ in the other 3:

- Variety: Data can be divided in 3 individual groups:
    - Structured (data from data structures generated out of data models),
    - Semi-structured (data that conforms to some kind of structure without having a data model) and
    - Unstructured (data with no pre-defined data model).

The scope of BI is limited to structured data while big data can handle all kinds of data (database tables, XML, audio- and video-files, etc.). Unlocking the possibilities of handling unstructured data is one difference between Big Data and BI.

- Volume: 90% of the worlds' data that exists today is created in the last 2 years. This load of new data is giving enterprises the opportunity to work with a lot of data (gigabytes, terabytes, petabytes, etc.) in just one single data set. BI specific technologies such as data warehouse appliances, column and in-memory databases can also handle big data and therefore it all comes down to whether the challenge is volume and performance, variety and complexity, or combinations thereof.
- Velocity or the frequency of data generation or frequency of data delivery. Data warehouse are mostly built using batch-oriented data flows or using data aggregated in virtual databases (data virtualization). Big data on the other hand makes it possible to process data streams in real-time or near real-time and therefore (re)act more agile than competitors.

## Business Intelligence and Big Data

When deploying big data technologies in the context of your existing data warehouse initiatives, you can take the advantage to speed up your data warehouse, making it more fault-tolerant, explore and discover new insight in your business, speed up time-sensitive processes and take quicker decisions.

Most of the data warehouses are using temporary locations where data from different sources are moved to for further loading it into the data warehouse. These are typically called staging areas. By replacing this data staging area by a big data file system, new data sources (semi-structured and unstructured) can be used to create metrics that can be loaded into the existing data warehouse. Unstructured data like tweets or consumer comments will provide the necessary information for discovering new insights and ideas, and providing explanations for long burning questions. You'll be able to dig deeper on the why, where, what and how questions provided by the BI system.

ETL processes are responsible for transforming and loading data from different source applications into the staging area and eventually into different data marts. The MapReduce paradigm can be seen as a way to transform data, in a scalable and parallel manner, and prepare it into a consumable format. One could therefore argue that writing MapReduce code is actually another way of designing ETL scripts. The thing that makes MapReduce special is the script execution is taking place near where the data resides while traditional ETL flows are mostly processed on a different server so data needs to be moved from one system to another which implies an unnecessary move and hence a slowdown.

As for the translation of transformed data into meaningful business information, there are different methods for querying on top of Hadoop. Batch-oriented MapReduce processing as well as direct querying on the big data file system delivers data on supported business intelligence systems (Qliktech, Microstrategy, etc.), for the immediate need of data there exists real-time query processing and in-stream processing.

The bigger picture Big data will be no replacement for your existing BI system but provides unique opportunities if you succeed in combining the richness of both technologies. It will widen your data view enabling much more detailed and complete data to be analyzed.

## Structured, Semi-structured and Unstructured Data

### Structured Data

Often thought of as "traditional data," structured data can be stored in Relational Databases (RDBMS). Common examples are fixed-length data points such as social security numbers, phone numbers, and zip codes. Most structured data consists of customer information in the form of variable length text strings, provided they are well organized and stored in an RDBMS format.

Before the advent of Big Data, structured data was what organizations used to drive business decisions. Data of this kind is typically stored in data warehouses and easy to digest, which make analytics possible through the use of traditional, legacy data mining solutions.

Common RDBMS applications include bank ATMs, inventory management solutions, airline reservation systems, and most CRM data.

### Unstructured Data

Essentially, unstructured data is all the data that – while it has an internal structure – does not conform to pre-defined data models. It can consist of textual or non-textual information and is typically the result of streaming data coming from platforms such as social media, location services, mobile apps and Internet of Things (IoT) enabled technologies.

Given the diversity among unstructured data sources, organizations struggle to store and analyze it using traditional data warehouse and data mining methods. But unstructured data is both too valuable and too prevalent to ignore, making up more than 80% of enterprise data. Companies need to find new solutions and creative methods for analyzing it alongside traditional structured data to gain the advantages promised by digital transformation.

### Semi-structured Data

The third type of data structure, semi-structured data uses internal tags and markings to let users identify different data elements, which in turn enables grouping and hierarchies.

While it makes up only 5-10% of the total data pie, semi-structured data still has several key business use cases. A typical example of the semi-structured data type is email: email's native metadata lets users classify and search information with the use of additional tools.

Most semi-structured data systems are used for data transport purposes. Sensor data, electronic data interchange (EDI), many social media platforms, and NoSQL databases are all examples of semi-structured data at work.

## Metadata

Modern data architectures promise the ability to enable access to more and different types of data to an increasing number of data consumers within an organization. Without proper governance, enabled by a strong foundation of metadata, these architectures often show initial promise, but ultimately fail to deliver.

Let's take logistics distribution as an analogy to explain metadata, and why it's critical in managing the data in today's business environment. When you are shipping one package to an international destination, you want to know where in the route the package is located in case something happens with the package delivery. Logistic companies keep manifests to track the movement of packages and the successful delivery of packages along the shipping process.

Metadata provides this same type of visibility into today's data rich environment. Data is moving in and out of companies, as well as within companies. Tracking data changes and detecting any process that causes problems when you are doing data analysis is hard if you don't have information about the data and the data movement process. Today, even the change of a single column in a source table can impact hundreds of reports that use that data—making it extremely important to know beforehand which columns will be affected.

Metadata provides information about each dataset, like size, the schema of a database, format, last modified time, access control lists, usage, etc. The use of metadata enables the management of a scalable data lake platform and architecture, as well as data governance. Metadata is commonly stored in a central catalog to provide users with information on the available datasets.

Metadata can be classified into three groups:

### Technical Metadata

Technical metadata captures the form and structure of each dataset, such as the size and structure of the schema or type of data (text, images, JSON, Avro, etc.). The structure of the schema includes the names of fields, their data types, their lengths, whether they can be empty, and so on. Structure is commonly provided by a relational database or the heading in a spreadsheet, but may also be added during ingestion and data preparation. There are some basic technical metadata that can be obtained directly from the datasets (i.e., size), but other metadata types are derived.

## Operational Metadata

Operational metadata captures the lineage, quality, profile, and provenance (i.e., when did the data elements arrive, where are they located, where did they arrive from, what is the quality of the data, etc.). It may also contain how many records were rejected during data preparation or a job run, and the success or failure of that run itself. Operational metadata also identifies how often the data may be updated or refreshed.

## Business Metadata

Business metadata captures what the data means to the end user to make data fields easier to find and understand, for example, business names, descriptions, tags, quality, and masking rules. These tie into the business attributes definition so that everyone is consistently interpreting the same data by a set of rules and concepts that is defined by the business users. A business glossary is a central location that provides a business description for each data element through the use of metadata information. Metadata information can be obtained in different ways. Sometimes it is encoded within the datasets, other times it can be inferred by reading the content of the datasets, or the information can be spread across log files that are written by the processes that access these datasets.

In all cases, metadata is a key element in the management of the data lake, and is the foundation that allows for the following data lake characteristics and capabilities to be achieved:

- Data visibility.
- Data reliability.
- Data profiling.
- Data lifecycle and age.
- Data security and privacy.
- Democratized access to useful data.
- Data lineage and change data capture.

Data lakes must be architected properly to leverage metadata and integrate with existing metadata tools; otherwise, it will create a hole in organizations' data governance process because how data is used, transformed, and related outside the data lake can be lost. An incorrect metadata architecture can often prevent data lakes making the transition from an analytical sandbox to an enterprise data platform.

Ultimately, most of the time spent in data analysis is in preparing and cleaning the data, and metadata helps to reduce the time to insight by providing easy access to discovering what data is available and maintaining a full data tracking map.

# Business Performance Management

BPM is the abbreviation for business performance management. It is a business management approach that entails aspects of reviewing the overall business performance and determining how the business can better reach its goals. These activities are aided by software tools, called BPM tools.

BPM is often thought of as a business strategy that enables businesses to efficiently collect, aggregate and analyze data from various sources in order to take the most appropriate business action. It enables businesses to:

- Improve productivity.
- Monitor and analyze business processes.
- Automate tasks.
- Increase efficiency.
- Identify cost savings opportunities.
- Generate new business.
- Measure key performance objectives.
- Analyze risks.
- Predict business outcomes.

Business performance management requires the alignment of strategic and operational objectives to the business activities in order to manage performance. By collecting and analyzing data, business managers are more informed about the company's position and can make better decisions as a result.

Successful BPM enables mangers to identify problems and produce more accurate and reliable forecasts. Business performance management is also used to analyze risks and predict business outcomes.

## References


- Business-intelligence: questionpro.com, Retrieved 31 March, 2019
- The-five-stages-of-business-intelligence, business-analysis: mbaknol.com, Retrieved 14 July, 2019
- What-is-collaborative-bi-collaborative-business-intelligence: biteamwork.com, Retrieved 17 May, 2019
- Collaborative-business-intelligence: plastergroup.com, Retrieved 19 April, 2019
- Real-time-business-intelligence-bi, definition: techtarget.com, Retrieved 5 February, 2019
- Business-intelligence-definition-example: guru99.com, Retrieved 26 July, 2019
- Finance-intelligence: managementstudyguide.com, Retrieved 21 May, 2019
- Knowledge-management-for-business-intelligence-measurement-in-an-e-business-system: researchgate.net, Retrieved 8 January, 2019
- What-is-data-integration, resources: talend.com, Retrieved 13 May, 2019

# 2

# Applications of Business Intelligence

Business intelligence is a vast subject consisting of various applications that provide assistance to the business. These include performance metrics, benchmarking, analytics, business reporting, electronic data interchange, data sharing, etc. This chapter has been carefully written to provide an easy understanding of the varied applications of business intelligence.

## Performance Metrics

Performance metrics are defined as figures and data representative of an organization's actions, abilities, and overall quality. There are many different forms of performance metrics, including sales, profit, return on investment, customer happiness, customer reviews, personal reviews, overall quality, and reputation in a marketplace. Performance metrics can vary considerably when viewed through different industries.

Performance metrics are integral to an organization's success. It's important that organizations select their chief performance metrics and focus on these areas because these metrics help guide and gauge an organization's success. Key success factors are only useful if they are acknowledged and tracked. Business measurements must also be carefully managed to make sure that they give right answers, and that the right questions are being asked.

Traditionally, businesses have viewed the following financial measurements as indicators of success:

- Return on capital employed or return on investment (ROI).
- Profit.
- Market share.
- Earnings growth.
- Stock price.

Non-financial measurements are also useful to help assess, report, and drive success. Most notably, the Malcolm Baldrige National Quality Award's Criteria for Performance Excellence non-financial success metrics include:

- Customer satisfaction.
- Process excellence.
- Employee satisfaction.

Organizations across most industries rely on these indicators as well as:

- Fast, responsive time to market.
- A loyal customer base.
- Outstanding processes for quality and timeliness.
- Mechanisms that ensure learning, growth, and continual improvement.

Organizations may define their own indicators of performance in key areas. Such metrics are often useful because they reduce complex measurements and results to a single value that can be tracked, managed, and improved. These "shortcuts" can be misleading, however, when used either for process improvement or for other feedback such as promotion, recognition, or compensation.

## Benchmarking

Benchmarking is the practice of comparing business processes and performance metrics to industry bests and best practices from other companies. Dimensions typically measured are quality, time and cost.

Benchmarking is used to measure performance using a specific indicator (cost per unit of measure, productivity per unit of measure, cycle time of x per unit of measure or defects per unit of measure) resulting in a metric of performance that is then compared to others.

Also referred to as "best practice benchmarking" or "process benchmarking", this process is used in management in which organizations evaluate various aspects of their processes in relation to best-practice companies' processes, usually within a peer group defined for the purposes of comparison. This then allows organizations to develop plans on how to make improvements or adapt specific best practices, usually with the aim of increasing some aspect of performance. Benchmarking may be a one-off event, but is often treated as a continuous process in which organizations continually seek to improve their practices.

In project management benchmarking can also support the selection, planning and delivery of projects.

In the process of best practice benchmarking, management identifies the best firms in their industry, or in another industry where similar processes exist, and compares the results and processes of those studied (the "targets") to one's own results and processes. In this way, they learn how well the targets perform and, more importantly, the business processes that explain why these firms are successful. According to National Council on Measurement in Education, benchmark assessments are short assessments used by teachers at various times throughout the school year to monitor student progress in some area of the school curriculum. These also are known as interim assessments.

The term benchmark, originates from the history of guns and ammunition, in regards to the same aim as for the business term; comparison and improved performance. The introduction of gunpowder arms replaced the bow and arrow from the archer, the soldier who used the bow. The archer now had to adapt to the new situation, and learn to handle the gun. The new weapon left only a mark on the target, where the arrow used to be visible, and with the bow gone, the soldiers title changed to marksman, the man who put the mark. The gun was improved already in the early beginning, with rifling of the barrel, and the rifle was born. With the industrialization of the weapon-industry in the mid-1800's, The mass production of ammunition as a cartridge replaced the manual loading of black-powder and bullet into the gun. Now, with standardized production of both the high-precision rifle, as well as the cartridge, the marksman was now the uncertain variable, and with different qualities and specifications on both rifle as well as ammunition, there was a need for a method of finding the best combination. The rifled weapon was fixed in a bench, making it possible to fire several identical shots at a target to measure the spread.

In 2008, a comprehensive survey on benchmarking was commissioned by The Global Benchmarking Network, a network of benchmarking centres representing 22 countries.

- Mission and Vision Statements and Customer (Client) Surveys are the most used (by 77% of organizations) of 20 improvement tools, followed by SWOT analysis (strengths, weaknesses, opportunities, and threats) (72%), and Informal Benchmarking (68%). Performance Benchmarking was used by 49% and Best Practice Benchmarking by 39%.
- The tools that are likely to increase in popularity the most over the next three years are Performance Benchmarking, Informal Benchmarking, SWOT, and Best Practice Benchmarking. Over 60% of organizations that are not currently using these tools indicated they are likely to use them in the next three years. benchmarking mainly depends on SWOT analysis and will also be using in future for almost 4-5 years.

## Procedure

There is no single benchmarking process that has been universally adopted. The wide appeal and acceptance of benchmarking has led to the emergence of benchmarking methodologies. One seminal book is Boxwell's *Benchmarking for Competitive Advantage*. The first book on benchmarking, written and published by Kaiser Associates, is a practical guide and offers a seven-step approach. Robert Camp developed a 12-stage approach to benchmarking.

The 12 stage methodology consists of:

- Select subject,
- Define the process,
- Identify potential partners,
- Identify data sources,

- Collect data and select all partners,
- Determine the gap,
- Establish process differences,
- Target future performance,
- Communicate,
- Adjust goal,
- Implement,
- Review and recalibrate.

The following is an example of a typical benchmarking methodology:

- Identify problem areas: Because benchmarking can be applied to any business process or function, a range of research techniques may be required. They include informal conversations with customers, employees, or suppliers; exploratory research techniques such as focus groups; or in-depth marketing research, quantitative research, surveys, questionnaires, re-engineering analysis, process mapping, quality control variance reports, financial ratio analysis, or simply reviewing cycle times or other performance indicators. Before embarking on comparison with other organizations it is essential to know the organization's function and processes; base lining performance provides a point against which improvement effort can be measured.
- Identify other industries that have similar processes: For instance, if one were interested in improving hand-offs in addiction treatment one would identify other fields that also have hand-off challenges. These could include air traffic control, cell phone switching between towers, transfer of patients from surgery to recovery rooms.
- Identify organizations that are leaders in these areas: Look for the very best in any industry and in any country. Consult customers, suppliers, financial analysts, trade associations, and magazines to determine which companies are worthy of study.
- Survey companies for measures and practices: Companies target specific business processes using detailed surveys of measures and practices used to identify business process alternatives and leading companies. Surveys are typically masked to protect confidential data by neutral associations and consultants.
- Visit the "best practice" companies to identify leading edge practices: Companies typically agree to mutually exchange information beneficial to all parties in a benchmarking group and share the results within the group.
- Implement new and improved business practices: Take the leading edge practices and develop implementation plans which include identification of specific opportunities, funding the project and selling the ideas to the organization for the purpose of gaining demonstrated value from the process.

## Costs

The three main types of costs in benchmarking are:

- Visit Costs - This includes hotel rooms, travel costs, meals, a token gift, and lost labor time.
- Time Costs - Members of the benchmarking team will be investing time in researching problems, finding exceptional companies to study, visits, and implementation. This will take them away from their regular tasks for part of each day so additional staff might be required.
- Benchmarking Database Costs - Organizations that institutionalize benchmarking into their daily procedures find it is useful to create and maintain a database of best practices and the companies associated with each best practice now.

The cost of benchmarking can substantially be reduced through utilizing the many internet resources that have sprung up over the last few years. These aim to capture benchmarks and best practices from organizations, business sectors and countries to make the benchmarking process much quicker and cheaper.

## Technical/Product Benchmarking

The technique initially used to compare existing corporate strategies with a view to achieving the best possible performance in new situations, has recently been extended to the comparison of technical products. This process is usually referred to as "technical benchmarking" or "product benchmarking". Its use is well-developed within the automotive industry ("automotive benchmarking"), where it is vital to design products that match precise user expectations, at minimal cost, by applying the best technologies available worldwide. Data is obtained by fully disassembling existing cars and their systems. Such analyses were initially carried out in-house by car makers and their suppliers. However, as these analyses are expensive, they are increasingly being outsourced to companies who specialize in this area. Outsourcing has enabled a drastic decrease in costs for each company (by cost sharing) and the development of efficient tools (standards, software).

## Types

Benchmarking can be internal (comparing performance between different groups or teams within an organization) or external (comparing performance with companies in a specific industry or across industries). Within these broader categories, there are three specific types of benchmarking: 1) Process benchmarking, 2) Performance benchmarking and 3) Strategic benchmarking. These can be further detailed as follows:

- Process benchmarking - The initiating firm focuses its observation and investigation of business processes with a goal of identifying and observing the best practices from one or more benchmark firms. Activity analysis will be required where the objective is to benchmark cost and efficiency; increasingly applied to back-office processes where outsourcing may be a consideration. Benchmarking is appropriate in nearly every case where process redesign or improvement is to be undertaking so long as the cost of the study does not exceed the expected benefit.

- Financial benchmarking - Performing a financial analysis and comparing the results in an effort to assess your overall competitiveness and productivity.
- Benchmarking from an investor perspective - Extending the benchmarking universe to also compare to peer companies that can be considered alternative investment opportunities from the perspective of an investor.
- Benchmarking in the public sector - Functions as a tool for improvement and innovation in public administration, where state organizations invest efforts and resources to achieve quality, efficiency and effectiveness of the services they provide.
- Performance benchmarking - Allows the initiator firm to assess their competitive position by comparing products and services with those of target firms.
- Product benchmarking - The process of designing new products or upgrades to current ones. This process can sometimes involve reverse engineering which is taking apart competitors products to find strengths and weaknesses.
- Strategic benchmarking - Involves observing how others compete. This type is usually not industry specific, meaning it is best to look at other industries.
- Functional benchmarking - A company will focus its benchmarking on a single function to improve the operation of that particular function. Complex functions such as Human Resources, Finance and Accounting and Information and Communication Technology are unlikely to be directly comparable in cost and efficiency terms and may need to be disaggregated into processes to make valid comparison.
- Best-in-class benchmarking - Involves studying the leading competitor or the company that best carries out a specific function.
- Operational benchmarking embraces everything from staffing and productivity to office flow and analysis of procedures performed.
- Energy benchmarking - Process of collecting, analysing and relating energy performance data of comparable activities with the purpose of evaluating and comparing performance between or within entities. Entities can include processes, buildings or companies. Benchmarking may be internal between entities within a single organization, or - subject to confidentiality restrictions - external between competing entities.

## Tools

Benchmarking software can be used to organize large and complex amounts of information. Software packages can extend the concept of benchmarking and competitive analysis by allowing individuals to handle such large and complex amounts or strategies. Such tools support different types of benchmarking and can reduce the above costs significantly.

The emerging technology of benchmarking engines automates the stage of going from data to noteworthy comparative insights, sometimes even expressing the insights in English sentences.

## Metric Benchmarking

Another approach to making comparisons involves using more aggregative cost or production information to identify strong and weak performing units. The two most common forms of quantitative analysis used in metric benchmarking are data envelope analysis (DEA) and regression analysis. DEA estimates the cost level an efficient firm should be able to achieve in a particular market. In infrastructure regulation, DEA can be used to reward companies/operators whose costs are near the efficient frontier with additional profits. Regression analysis estimates what the average firm should be able to achieve. With regression analysis, firms that performed better than average can be rewarded while firms that performed worse than average can be penalized. Such benchmarking studies are used to create yardstick comparisons, allowing outsiders to evaluate the performance of operators in an industry. Advanced statistical techniques, including stochastic frontier analysis, have been used to identify high and weak performers in industries, including applications to schools, hospitals, water utilities, and electric utilities.

One of the biggest challenges for metric benchmarking is the variety of metric definitions used among companies or divisions. Definitions may change over time within the same organization due to changes in leadership and priorities. The most useful comparisons can be made when metrics definitions are common between compared units and do not change so improvements can be changed.

## Social Media and Benchmarking

Social media is beginning to penetrate more and more into existing business processes. In this sense, benchmarking is no exception. Because of their inherent characteristics, it can even be argued that social media will have a significant impact on benchmarking. Here are some of the benefits associated with this.

- Joint benchmarking is, in fact, a social activity, and social media provide many new and effective ways for social interaction.
- Social media opens the way to new additional sources of information and data collection channels.
- Benchmarking is becoming increasingly business-oriented, and social media is supporting this type of continuous engagement, different from working on individual projects.

## Role of Benchmarking in Driving Business

Overall, the goal of benchmarking is to:

- Determine what improvements are needed.
- Analyze internal and external data on targeted areas of improvement.
- Use gathered information to make strategic business decisions.

A great example of benchmarking in action is in the sports arena. A team or athlete measures and analyzes statistics to see where they fall in the rankings and what they need to do to improve. The same principles apply in the business world, but it is much more complex than tracking batting averages or yards scored.

A company can benchmark everything from financial statements to the emotional intelligence of employees. Yet, many businesses only focus on benchmarking their bottom line. This omission can have disastrous consequences to the growth of the company.

## Benchmarking Digital Performance

If a company is not actively measuring its digital performance, then it becomes highly susceptible to disruption in today's digital world. Case in point: I doubt the music industry was benchmarking digital performance before Spotify, SoundCloud, or YouTube emerged and now it's scrambling to catch up.

So, how do you measure digital performance? And what is that you're measuring? While every company has different benchmarking needs, it's best to approach this process from both a macro and micro perspective.

## Macro Benchmarking

The macro approach to benchmarking digital performance provides an overview on where the company is in the market. When taking a macro approach, you'll want to look at your entire business model in order to:

## Monitor Trends Inside and Outside of your Industry

Keeping your finger on the pulse of tech trends could breathe new life into your business. Take the growth of Uber and the sharing economy. This was a trend the restaurant industry should have been keeping a keen eye on. While ridesharing has little to do with food, this trend bled over into the restaurant world with the emergence of Doordash, Postmates, UberEATS, and more. Had a savvy company in the restaurant world benchmarked this particular trend, they could have created a food delivery app and dominated the field before anyone else could.

## Track the Competition's Digital Innovation and Adoption

When FitBit started the fitness industry's wearable trend, apparel companies took notice. Nike saw the potential in wearables and released their fitness device, FuelBand, in fall of 2013. The problem, however, is that FuelBand wasn't radically different from FitBit and simply tracked users' physical activity, steps taken, and energy burned. Sales for FuelBand were disappointing and, in less than six months, Nike discontinued the tech.

Under Armour, on the other hand, watched the rise and fall of Nike's attempt and acted accordingly. Instead of developing another fitness wearable that functions the same as FitBit, Under Armour created HealthBox--a more robust system of wearable health trackers. HealthBox not only tracks steps and activity but also measures sleep, resting heart rate, workout intensity, body weight, and body fat percentage. It also sends alerts, works as an alarm clock and workout log, and allows users to control music volume and selection. Considering this product has been on the market for over a year now, it's safe to say it's already performing better than Nike's initial wearables attempt.

## Analyze the Digital Methods in which you Serve your Customer

Are you still sending paper statements to customers? Is your competition creating seamless omni-channel experiences? Can you afford to invest in VR tech to attract more prospects? Evaluate the current digital state of your offerings, research options for improving, and decide if (and how) you can use those options to better serve the customer.

### Micro Benchmarking

After measuring your company's digital performance at a macro level, you'll also need to monitor specific digital platforms or channels within your business. This type of benchmarking provides a company with granular data on performance.

The main micro digital performance areas to benchmark revolve around web, social, and mobile app analytics. Benchmarking Key Performance Indicators (KPIs)-such as usage, traffic, time spent on site, bounces, etc. will give your company valuable insight into the customer experience. This will also provide your company with concrete data regarding performance.

## Analytics

Analytics is the discovery, interpretation, and communication of meaningful patterns in data. It also entails applying data patterns towards effective decision making. In other words, analytics can be understood as the connective tissue between data and effective decision making within an organization. Especially valuable in areas rich with recorded information, analytics relies on the simultaneous application of statistics, computer programming and operations research to quantify performance.

Organizations may apply analytics to business data to describe, predict, and improve business performance. Specifically, areas within analytics include predictive analytics, prescriptive analytics, enterprise decision management, descriptive analytics, cognitive analytics, Big Data Analytics, retail analytics, supply chain analytics, store assortment and stock-keeping unit optimization, marketing optimization and marketing mix modeling, web analytics, call analytics, speech analytics, sales force sizing and optimization, price and promotion modeling, predictive science, credit risk analysis, and fraud analytics. Since analytics can require extensive computation, the algorithms and software used for analytics harness the most current methods in computer science, statistics, and mathematics.

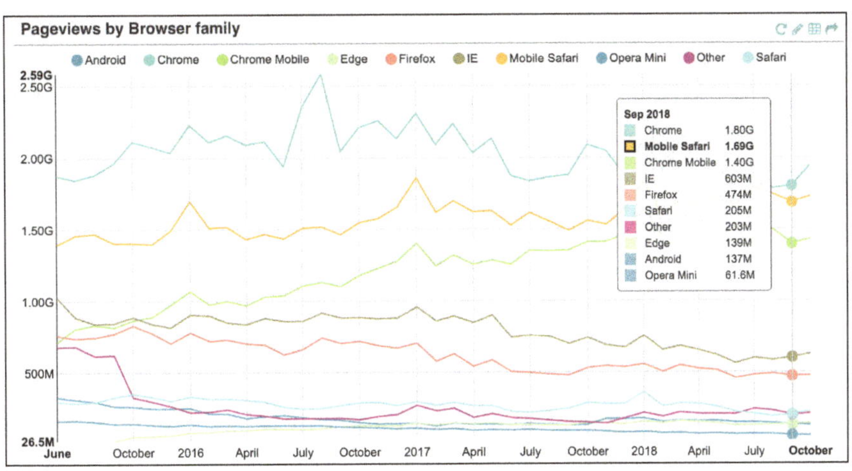


Traffic analysis of English.

## Analytics vs. Analysis

Analysis is focused on understanding the past; what happened and why it happened. Analytics focuses on why it happened and what will happen next.

Data analytics is a multidisciplinary field. There is extensive use of computer skills, mathematics, statistics, the use of descriptive techniques and predictive models to gain valuable knowledge from data while analyzing data. The insights from data are used to recommend action or to guide decision making rooted in business context. Thus, analytics is not so much concerned with individual analyses or analysis steps, but with the entire methodology There is a pronounced tendency to use the term *analytics* in business settings e.g. text analytics vs. the more generic text mining to emphasize this broader perspective. There is an increasing use of the term *advanced analytics*, typically used to describe the technical aspects of analytics, especially in the emerging fields such as the use of machine learning techniques like neural networks, Decision Tree, Logistic Regression, linear to multiple regression analysis, Classification to do predictive modeling. It also includes Unsupervised Machine learning techniques like cluster analysis, Principal Component Analysis, segmentation profile analysis and association analysis.

## Applications

### Marketing Optimization

Marketing has evolved from a creative process into a highly data-driven process. Marketing organizations use analytics to determine the outcomes of campaigns or efforts and to guide decisions for investment and consumer targeting. Demographic studies, customer segmentation, conjoint analysis and other techniques allow marketers to use large amounts of consumer purchase, survey and panel data to understand and communicate marketing strategy.

Marketing analytics consists of both qualitative and quantitative, structured and unstructured data used to drive strategic decisions in relation to brand and revenue outcomes. The process involves predictive modeling, marketing experimentation, automation and real-time sales communications. The data enables companies to make predictions and alter strategic execution to maximize performance results.

Web analytics allows marketers to collect session-level information about interactions on a website using an operation called sessionization. Google Analytics is an example of a popular free analytics tool that marketers use for this purpose. Those interactions provide web analytics information systems with the information necessary to track the referrer, search keywords, identify IP address, and track activities of the visitor. With this information, a marketer can improve marketing campaigns, website creative content, and information architecture.

Analysis techniques frequently used in marketing include marketing mix modeling, pricing and promotion analyses, sales force optimization and customer analytics e.g.: segmentation. Web analytics and optimization of web sites and online campaigns now frequently work hand in hand with the more traditional marketing analysis techniques. A focus on digital media has slightly changed the vocabulary so that marketing mix modeling is commonly referred to as attribution modeling in the digital or marketing mix modeling context.

These tools and techniques support both strategic marketing decisions (such as how much overall to spend on marketing, how to allocate budgets across a portfolio of brands and the marketing mix) and more tactical campaign support, in terms of targeting the best potential customer with the optimal message in the most cost effective medium at the ideal time.

## People Analytics

People Analytics is using behavioral data to understand how people work and change how companies are managed.

People analytics is also known as workforce analytics, HR analytics, talent analytics, people insights, talent insights, colleague insights, human capital analytics, and HRIS analytics. HR analytics is the application of analytics to help companies manage human resources. The aim is to discern which employees to hire, which to reward or promote, what responsibilities to assign, and similar human resource problems. HR analytics is becoming increasingly important to understand what kind of behavioral profiles would succeed and fail. For example, an analysis may find that individuals that fit a certain type of profile are those most likely to succeed at a particular role, making them the best employees to hire.

## Portfolio Analytics

A common application of business analytics is portfolio analysis. In this, a bank or lending agency has a collection of accounts of varying value and risk. The accounts may differ by the social status (wealthy, middle-class, poor, etc.) of the holder, the geographical location, its net value, and many other factors. The lender must balance the return on the loan with the risk of default for each loan. The question is then how to evaluate the portfolio as a whole.

The least risk loan may be to the very wealthy, but there are a very limited number of wealthy people. On the other hand, there are many poor that can be lent to, but at greater risk. Some balance must be struck that maximizes return and minimizes risk. The analytics solution may combine time series analysis with many other issues in order to make decisions on when to lend money to these different borrower segments, or decisions on the interest rate charged to members of a portfolio segment to cover any losses among members in that segment.

## Risk Analytics

Predictive models in the banking industry are developed to bring certainty across the risk scores for individual customers. Credit scores are built to predict individual's delinquency behavior and widely used to evaluate the credit worthiness of each applicant. Furthermore, risk analyses are carried out in the scientific world and the insurance industry. It is also extensively used in financial institutions like Online Payment Gateway companies to analyse if a transaction was genuine or fraud. For this purpose they use the transaction history of the customer. This is more commonly used in Credit Card purchase, when there is a sudden spike in the customer transaction volume the customer gets a call of confirmation if the transaction was initiated by him/her. This helps in reducing loss due to such circumstances.

## Digital Analytics

Digital analytics is a set of business and technical activities that define, create, collect, verify or transform digital data into reporting, research, analyses, recommendations, optimizations, predictions, and automations. This also includes the SEO (search engine optimization) where the keyword search is tracked and that data is used for marketing purposes. Even banner ads and clicks come under digital analytics. A growing number of brands and marketing firms rely on digital analytics for their digital marketing assignments, where MROI (Marketing Return on Investment) is an important key performance indicator (KPI).

### Security Analytics

Security analytics refers to information technology (IT) to gather and analyze security events to understand and analyze events that pose the greatest risk. Products in this area include security information and event management and user behavior analytics.

### Software Analytics

Software analytics is the process of collecting information about the way a piece of software is used and produced.

## Challenges

In the industry of commercial analytics software, an emphasis has emerged on solving the challenges of analyzing massive, complex data sets, often when such data is in a constant state of change. Such data sets are commonly referred to as big data. Whereas once the problems posed by big data were only found in the scientific community, today big data is a problem for many businesses that operate transactional systems online and, as a result, amass large volumes of data quickly.

The analysis of unstructured data types is another challenge getting attention in the industry. Unstructured data differs from structured data in that its format varies widely and cannot be stored in traditional relational databases without significant effort at data transformation. Sources of unstructured data, such as email, the contents of word processor documents, PDFs, geospatial data, etc., are rapidly becoming a relevant source of business intelligence for businesses, governments and universities. For example, in Britain the discovery that one company was illegally selling fraudulent doctor's notes in order to assist people in defrauding employers and insurance companies, is an opportunity for insurance firms to increase the vigilance of their unstructured data analysis. The McKinsey Global Institute estimates that big data analysis could save the American health care system $300 billion per year and the European public sector €250 billion.

These challenges are the current inspiration for much of the innovation in modern analytics information systems, giving birth to relatively new machine analysis concepts such as complex event processing, full text search and analysis, and even new ideas in presentation. One such innovation is the introduction of grid-like architecture in machine analysis, allowing increases in the speed of massively parallel processing by distributing the workload to many computers all with equal access to the complete data set.

Analytics is increasingly used in education, particularly at the district and government office levels. However, the complexity of student performance measures presents challenges when educators try to understand and use analytics to discern patterns in student performance, predict graduation likelihood, improve chances of student success, etc. For example, in a study involving districts known for strong data use, 48% of teachers had difficulty posing questions prompted by data, 36% did not comprehend given data, and 52% incorrectly interpreted data. To combat this, some analytics tools for educators adhere to an over-the-counter data format (embedding labels, supplemental documentation, and a help system, and making key package/ display and content decisions) to improve educators' understanding and use of the analytics being displayed.

One more emerging challenge is dynamic regulatory needs. For example, in the banking industry, Basel III and future capital adequacy needs are likely to make even smaller banks adopt internal risk models. In such cases, cloud computing and open source programming language R can help smaller banks to adopt risk analytics and support branch level monitoring by applying predictive analytics.

## Risks

The main risk for the people is discrimination like price discrimination or statistical discrimination.

There is also the risk that a developer could profit from the ideas or work done by users, like this example: Users could write new ideas in a note taking app, which could then be sent as a custom event, and the developers could profit from those ideas. This can happen because the ownership of content is usually unclear in the law.

If a user's identity is not protected, there are more risks; for example, the risk that private information about users is made public on the internet.

In the extreme, there is the risk that governments could gather too much private information, now that the governments are giving themselves more powers to access citizens' information.

## Role of Analytics in Business

The role of Analytics in Business Intelligence are as follows:

- Business analytics is a methodology or tool to make a sound commercial decision. Hence it impacts functioning of the whole organization. Therefore, business analytics can help improve profitability of the business, increase market share and revenue and provide better return to a shareholder.
- Facilitates better understanding of available primary and secondary data, which again affect operational efficiency of several departments.
- Provides a competitive advantage to companies. In this digital age flow of information is almost equal to all the players. It is how this information is utilized makes the company competitive. Business analytics combines available data with various well thought models to improve business decisions.
- Converts available data into valuable information. This information can be presented in any required format, comfortable to the decision maker.

# Business Reporting

Business reporting or enterprise reporting refers to both "the public reporting of operating and financial data by a business enterprise," and "the regular provision of information to decision-makers within an organization to support them in their work." It is a fundamental part of the larger movement towards improved business intelligence and knowledge management. Implementation often involves extract, transform, and load (ETL) procedures in coordination with a data warehouse and then using one or more reporting tools. Reports can be distributed in print form, via email or accessed via a corporate intranet.

With the expansion of information technology there has been an increase in the production of unified reports which join different views of an organization in one place. This reporting process involves querying data sources with different logical models to produce a human readable report. For example, a decision maker may need to query a human resources databases and a capital improvements databases to show how efficiently space is being used across an entire corporation.

Reporting can also be used for verification and cross-checks. Audit teams like FINRA and SEC adhere to reports for all business firms. Standard Business Reporting is a group of international programs instigated by a number of governments with the end of make business the centre when it comes to managing business-to-government reporting obligations.

## The Goal of Reporting in BI

Any business intelligence goal should be defined as enabling the ability to see, analyze, understand, and make critical decisions on data. The goal of business intelligence reporting is to enable end-users to observe detail level data in a way that it can be analyzed and understood giving users the ability to turn data into actionable information.

An example of this in action would be a simple sales report. A sales report may include rows that present the different names of account managers or sales representatives, and columns which present different sales data such as total orders to date, units sold, units shipped, total revenue, a percentage of quota attained to date. If a report is created in a way which allows for easy analysis the data presented in this report can be analyzed for decision-making purposes, allowing for a sales manager, for example, to discuss potential future orders with reps that have low revenue to date.

Reporting is an early step in the process of data processing. It presents data in an interactive fashion to turn it into actionable information. There can be many levels of interactivity within a report such as the ability to drill down, sort, and filter, as well as additional capabilities such as self-service editing which allows you to further explore your data for more insights. Business intelligence reporting is most beneficial when it is designed to help track and measure your strategic business goals. Other use cases for reporting tools include tracking key performance indicators, maintaining regulatory compliance, or even measuring goals between different departments or applications.

## The Benefits of BI Reporting

As mentioned the main goal of business intelligence reporting is to make data easy to understand so that accurate analysis can be efficiently carried out. Reporting is a necessary prerequisite of the analysis stage. BI collects and presents data that is ready to be analyzed. Data also includes historical information that cannot be traced over time. Business Intelligence reporting empowers the end-users with the information to become experts in their corresponding area of business. Also, underlying figures in reports can be presented to backup actions and explain decision making behaviors.

### Working of Business Intelligence Reporting

Report developers and report writers use tools such as JReport Designer, our report design tool, to distinguish elements such as data sources, display formats, graphics, filters, and other options that are essential for report presentation. Enterprise reporting solutions, such as JReport, also allow end-users to create reports and dashboards directly from web application interfaces using ad-hoc data resources specified by developers. Users are therefore given the ability to generate speedy data-driven decisions through building report components, collecting various data, and designing ad hoc reports. Reports can be published to a reporting engine, such as JReport Server, which extracts data and generates reports.

## Electronic Data Interchange

Electronic Data Interchange (EDI) is the electronic interchange of business information using a standardized format; a process which allows one company to send information to another company electronically rather than with paper. Business entities conducting business electronically are called trading partners.

Many business documents can be exchanged using EDI, but the two most common are purchase orders and invoices. At a minimum, EDI replaces the mail preparation and handling associated with traditional business communication. However, the real power of EDI is that it standardizes the information communicated in business documents, which makes possible a "paperless" exchange.

The traditional invoice illustrates what this can mean. Most companies create invoices using a computer system, print a paper copy of the invoice and mail it to the customer. Upon receipt, the customer frequently marks up the invoice and enters it into its own computer system. The entire process is nothing more than the transfer of information from the seller's computer to the customer's computer. EDI makes it possible to minimize or even eliminate the manual steps involved in this transfer.

The process improvements that EDI offers are significant and can be dramatic. For example, consider the difference between the traditional paper purchase order and its electronic counterpart:

| A Traditional Document Exchange of a Purchase Order | An EDI Document Exchange of a Purchase Order |
|---|---|
| This process normally takes between three and five days. | This process normally occurs overnight and can take less than an hour. |

| | |
|---|---|
| Buyer makes a buying decision, creates the purchase order and prints it.<br><br>Buyer mails the purchase order to the supplier.<br><br>Supplier receives the purchase order and enters it into the order entry system.<br><br>Buyer calls supplier to determine if purchase order has been received, or supplier mails buyer an acknowledgment of the order. | Buyer makes a buying decision, creates the purchase order but does not print it.<br><br>EDI software creates an electronic version of the purchase order and transmits it automatically to the supplier.<br><br>Supplier's order entry system receives the purchase order and updates the system immediately on receipt.<br><br>Supplier's order entry system creates an acknowledgment an transmits it back to confirm receipt. |

## Role of Electronic Data Interchange in BI

There are many different reasons that companies continue to use EDI within their enterprise. From saving countless amounts of money to improving speed, accuracy, and efficiency, EDI remains an incredibly useful tool.

### Cost Savings

Through the use of an EDI service, companies can execute workflows that reduce costs. Previous paper expenses, ranging from printing, reproduction, storage, and postage, are gone. A streamlined documentation process helps companies comply with EDI service standards, which helps to avoid fines due to SLA violations, delays, and other performance gaps.

### Speed

EDI allows enterprises to cut processing time remarkably through automation, speeding up business cycles. Order-to-shipment cycles in particular can be cut by 50 percent to 60 percent. There is also a tremendous difference in a transaction that is exchanged in minutes instead of days or weeks, as is common with many forms of manual transfer.

### Accuracy

Nobody wants to make errors, and that's exactly what EDI helps organizations avoid. When employees are forced to manually enter data into enterprise resource planning (ERP) software or order systems, odds are that a mistake will happen eventually. EDI solutions are designed to automate that cumbersome process and eliminate human-caused errors.

### Efficiency

EDI is proven to be fast and accurate, which is why it's such a popular integration and automation method to enterprises everywhere. No longer are companies expected to perform hands-on processing, so customer relationships are improved, errors happen less, and the delivery of goods and services are expedited.

### Security

Companies can feel safe and secure when they have an EDI model in place. In fact, EDI solutions are designed to ensure security and only allow strict access to authorized users and are usually equipped with archive tracking and audit trail capabilities. Companies are also able to share data securely across many communication protocols and security standards, to ensure compliance with mandates in global business.

## Data Sharing

Each piece of information in your business has people and purposes to serve. And for your data to serve its right purpose, you can share data with: people within your organization and people outside. And so there are two ways in which you need to share business information: with people within your organization, and people outside.

Sharing within your business is often interdepartmental and on a need-to-know basis. For example, the business owner shares information with managers, who is turn share it with subordinates, team leaders with team members, etc.

In case of sharing data with external stake holders, think of the owner sharing the information with customers or partners, or managers sharing with dealers and freelance hires, etc.

The type of data you share depends on whether it's internal or external sharing.

Some examples of internal sharing:

- If you run a service business or a journalistic practice, you may have employees on the field all the time. They will report back to the central office, sharing links, photographs, voice and video recordings they've gathered.
- Though functioning as separate departments, the sales and marketing teams of a business share assets like collateral, documents, presentations, customer life cycle information, contact information, etc.
- If you run a retail business or have a manufacturing unit, you may share details of your inventory with your packaging and delivery teams so that they're aware of the current status of stock.

In all these scenarios the origin and the destination of the information are limited to those involved in the business.

In external sharing, however, you share with people who are not directly involved in your business. Although they participate in your business, your everyday processes don't depend on them.

Here are some examples of sharing data externally:

- Sharing inventory details with the suppliers of your raw material. This information can help them know when you need a refill.

- Sharing knowledge and business assets like product catalogues, explainer documents, and brochures with external analysts and market researchers. If you run a product- or service-based company, you might need share such information about your business with third-party stakeholders as a way to extend your reach.
- Sharing your database of resources with customers. If you offer healthcare services, for example, you can offer potential customers personalized recommendations.
- If you manage a nonprofit organization, you may share the status of your fundraisers with donors.

## Ways to Share Data

There are many ways a business can share its information. While some methods are time-tested and proven, some of them are new and upcoming.

- Third-party app or software: This refers to the process of extracting information from your central database system and duplicating it before sharing. Spreadsheets like MS Excel and Google Sheets fall under this category. Though online spreadsheets are more collaborative than offline ones, data redundancy is still an issue.
- Application Programming Interfaces (APIs): Some businesses integrate sharing capability into their existing system. They either program it using an API or adopt an enterprise knowledge sharing management system.
- Print outs like brochures and leaflets: While a long-standing and often effective way to distribute information, physical copies of data can compromise data security.
- Personal communication tools: Telephone calls, messaging services, and face-to-face interactions are common when offering personal recommendations, as with healthcare practice.

Before you share anything in any way, consider the following questions. The answers will dictate how you share business data.

- What are you sharing? Storing of and sharing information about customers, students, and medical records often require compliance. Stock and inventory details, on the other hand, don't.
- Who are you sharing it with? Determine the roles and designations of those who will access the data you share. Make sure the right person sees the right information. Think about what the managers see and what the subordinates see.
- How much are you sharing? Data is the lifeblood of your business, so it's important to restrict access when necessary. You don't want everyone meddling with your data. Consider using permissions around the ability to modify, access, and consume information.

## References


- lukem (2016-11-04). "People Analytics: Transforming Management with Behavioral Data". Programs for Professionals | MIT Professional Education. Retrieved 2018-04-03
- this-is-the-role-of-benchmarking-in-driving-business-excellence, jason-albanese: inc.com

- Kohavi, Rothleder and Simoudis (2002). "Emerging Trends in Business Analytics". Communications of the ACM. 45 (8): 45–48. CiteSeerX 10.1.1.13.3005. doi:10.1145/545151.545177
- business-analytics: managementstudyguide.com, Retrieved 17 May, 2019
- Moeller, Robert (2007). COSO Enterprise Risk Management: Understanding the New Integrated ERM Framework. Wiley. ISBN 0-471-74115-9
- knowledge-base-edi-integration: cleo.com, Retrieved 14 July, 2019
- data-sharing: zoho.com, Retrieved 31 March, 2019

# 3

# Business Analytics and its Types

Business analytics deals with exploration of past business information by the substantial use of analytical modeling and numerical analysis, including explanatory and predictive modeling. Some of its types are decision analytics, descriptive analytics, predictive analytics, etc. All these diverse types of business analytics have been carefully explained in this chapter.

## Business Analytics

Business analytics (BA) is the iterative, methodical exploration of an organization's data, with an emphasis on statistical analysis. Business analytics is used by companies that are committed to making data-driven decisions. Data-driven companies treat their data as a corporate asset and actively look for ways to turn it into a competitive advantage. Successful business analytics depends on data quality, skilled analysts who understand the technologies and the business, and an organizational commitment to using data to gain insights that inform business decisions.

Specific types of business analytics include:

- Descriptive analytics, which tracks key performance indicators (KPIs) to understand the present state of a business;
- Predictive analytics, which analyzes trend data to assess the likelihood of future outcomes;
- Prescriptive analytics, which uses past performance to generate recommendations about how to handle similar situations in the future.

### Working Principle of Business Analytics

Once the business goal of the analysis is determined, an analysis methodology is selected and data is acquired to support the analysis. Data acquisition often involves extraction from one or more business systems, cleansing and integration into a single repository such as a data warehouse or data mart.

Initial analysis is typically performed against a smaller sample set of data. Analytic tools range from spreadsheets with statistical functions to complex data mining and predictive modeling applications. As patterns and relationships in the data are uncovered, new questions are asked and the analytic process iterates until the business goal is met.

Deployment of predictive models involves scoring data records - typically in a database - and using the scores to optimize real-time decisions within applications and business processes. BA also supports tactical decision-making in response to unforeseen events. And, in many cases, the decision-making is automated to support real-time responses.

### Business Analytics vs. Business Intelligence

While the terms business intelligence and business analytics are often used interchangeably, there are some key differences:

| BI vs BA | Business Intelligence | Business Analytics |
|---|---|---|
| Answers the questions: | What Happened?<br>When?<br>Who?<br>How Many? | Why Did it Happen?<br>Will it Happen again?<br>What will happen If we Change x?<br>What else does the data tell us that never thought to ask? |
| Includes: | Reporting (KPIs, metrics)<br>Automated Monitoring/Alerting (Thresholds)<br>Dashboard<br>Scoreboard<br>OLAP ( Cubes, Slice & Dice, Drilling)<br>Ad hoc query | Statistical/ Quantitative analysis<br>Data Mining<br>Predictive Modeling<br>Multivariate testing |

## Operational Intelligence

Operational intelligence (OI) is an approach to data analysis that enables decisions and actions in business operations to be based on real-time data as it's generated or collected by companies. Typically, the data analysis process is automated, and the resulting information is integrated into operational systems for immediate use by business managers and workers.

OI applications are primarily targeted at front-line workers who, hopefully, can make better-informed business decisions or take faster action on issues if they have access to timely business intelligence (BI) and analytics data. Examples include call-center agents, sales representatives, online marketing teams, logistics planners, manufacturing managers and medical professionals. In addition, operational intelligence can be used to automatically trigger responses to specified events or conditions.

What is now known as OI evolved from operational business intelligence, an initial step focused more on applying traditional BI querying and reporting. OI takes the concept to a higher analytics level, but operational BI is sometimes still used interchangeably with operational intelligence as a term.

## Working of Operational Intelligence

In most OI initiatives, data analysis is done in tandem with data processing or shortly thereafter, so workers can quickly identify and act on problems and opportunities in business operations. Deployments often include real-time business intelligence systems set up to analyze incoming data, plus real-time data integration tools to pull together different sets of relevant data for analysis.

Stream processing systems and big data platforms, such as Hadoop and Spark, can also be part of the OI picture, particularly in applications that involve large amounts of data and require advanced analytics capabilities. In addition, various IT vendors have combined data streaming, real-time monitoring and data analytics tools to create specialized operational intelligence platforms.

As data is analyzed, organizations often present operational metrics, key performance indicators (KPIs) and business insights to managers and other workers in interactive dashboards that are embedded in the systems they use as part of their jobs; data visualizations are usually included to help make the information easy to understand. Alerts can also be sent to notify users of developments and data points that require their attention, and automated processes can be kicked off if predefined thresholds or other metrics are exceeded, such as stock trades being spurred by prices hitting particular levels.

## Operational Intelligence uses and Examples

Stock trading and other types of investment management are prime candidates for operational intelligence initiatives because of the need to monitor huge volumes of data in real time and respond rapidly to events and market trends. Customer analytics is another area that's ripe for OI. For example, online marketers use real-time tools to analyze internet clickstream data, so they can better target marketing campaigns to consumers. And cable TV companies track data from set-top boxes in real time to analyze the viewing activities of customers and how the boxes are functioning.

The growth of the internet of things has sparked operational intelligence applications for analyzing sensor data being captured from manufacturing machines, pipelines, elevators and other equipment; that enables predictive maintenance efforts designed to detect potential equipment failures before they occur. Other types of machine data also fuel OI applications, including server, network and website logs that are analyzed in real time to look for security threats and IT operations issues.

There are less grandiose operational intelligence use cases, as well. That includes the likes of call-center applications that provide operators with up-to-date customer records and recommend promotional offers while they're on the phone with customers, as well as logistics ones that help calculate the most efficient driving routes for fleets of delivery vehicles.

## OI Benefits and Challenges

The primary benefit of OI implementations is the ability to address operational issues and opportunities as they arise - or even before they do, as in the case of predictive maintenance. Operational intelligence also empowers business managers and workers to make more informed - and hopefully better - decisions on a day-by-day basis. Ultimately, if managed successfully, the increased visibility and insight into business operations can lead to higher revenue and competitive advantages over rivals.

But there are challenges. Building operational intelligence architecture typically involves piecing together different technologies, and there are numerous data processing platforms and analytics tools to choose between, some of which may require new skills in organizations. High performance and sufficient scalability are also needed to handle the real-time workloads and large volumes of data common in OI applications without choking the system.

Also, most business processes at a typical company don't require real-time data analysis. With that in mind, a key part of operational intelligence projects involves determining which end users need up-to-the-minute data and then training them to handle the information once it starts being delivered to them in that fashion.

## Operational Intelligence vs. Business Intelligence

### Key Differences between BI and OI

| Business Intelligence | Operational Intelligence |
|---|---|
| Run queries and create data visualizations | Search and investigate operational data |
| Analysis of historical data | Real-time data monitoring and alerts |
| Visibility into revenues, profits and other KPIs | Visibility into business operations |
| Reactive Process | Proactive Process |
| BI involves collecting data from internal systems and external sources, preparing it for analysis, ad hoc querying, reporting, and building dashboards and data visualizations | OI applications include predictive maintenance, real- time product recommendations and promotional offers, and calculating the most efficient driving routes for delivery vehicles. |

Conventional BI systems support the analysis of historical data that has been cleansed and consolidated in a data warehouse or data mart before being made available for business analytics uses. BI applications generally aim to tell corporate executives and business managers what happened in the past on revenues, profits and other KPIs to aid in budgeting and strategic planning.

Early on, BI data was primarily distributed to users in static operational reports. That's still the case in some organizations, although many have shifted to dashboards with the ability to drill down into data for further analysis. In addition, self-service BI tools let users run their own queries and create data visualizations on their own, but the focus is still mostly on analyzing data from the past.

Operational intelligence systems let business managers and front-line workers see what's currently happening in operational processes and then immediately act upon the findings, either on their own or through automated means. The purpose is not to facilitate planning, but to drive operational decisions and actions in the moment.

# Decision Analytics

Decision analysis (DA) is a systematic, quantitative, and visual approach to addressing and evaluating the important choices that businesses sometimes face. Ronald A. Howard, a professor of Management Science and Engineering at Stanford University, is credited with originating the term in 1964. The idea is used by large and small corporations alike when making various types of decisions, including management, operations, marketing, capital investments, or strategic choices.

Decision analysis uses a variety of tools to evaluate all relevant information to aid in the decision-making process and incorporates aspects of psychology, management techniques, training, and economics. It is often used to assess decisions that are made in the context of multiple variables and that have many possible outcomes or objectives. The process can be used by individuals or groups attempting to make a decision related to risk management, capital investments, and strategic business decisions.

A graphical representation of alternatives and possible solutions, as well as challenges and uncertainties, can be created on a decision tree or influence diagram. More sophisticated computer models have also been developed to aid in the decision-analysis process.

The goal behind such tools is to provide decision-makers with alternatives when attempting to achieve objectives for the business, while also outlining uncertainties involved and providing measures of how well objectives will be reached if final outcomes are achieved. Uncertainties are typically expressed as probabilities, while frictions between conflicting objectives are viewed in terms of trade-offs and utility functions. That is, objectives are viewed in terms of how much they are worth or, if achieved, their expected value to the organization.

Despite the helpful nature of decision analysis, critics suggest that a major drawback to the approach is "analysis paralysis," which is the overthinking of a situation to the point that no decision can be made. In addition, some researchers who study the methodologies used by decision-makers argue that this type of analysis is not often utilized.

### Examples of Decision Analysis

If a real estate development company is deciding on whether or not to build a new shopping center in a location, they might examine several pieces of input to aid in their decision-making process. These might include traffic at the proposed location on various days of the week at different times, the popularity of similar shopping centers in the area, financial demographics, local competition, and preferred shopping habits of the area population. All of these items can be put into a decision-analysis program and different simulations are run that help the company make a decision about the shopping center.

As another example, a company has a patent for a new product that is expected to see rapid sales for two years before becoming obsolete. The company is confronted with a choice of whether to sell the patent now or build the product in-house. Each option has opportunities, risks, and trade-offs, which can be analyzed with a decision tree that considers the benefits of selling the patent verses making the product in-house. Within those two branches of the tree, another group of decision trees can be created to consider such things as the optimal selling price for the patent or the costs and benefits of producing the product in-house.

## Descriptive Analytics

Descriptive analytics is the interpretation of historical data to better understand changes that have occurred in a business. Descriptive analytics describes the use of a range of historic data to draw comparisons. Most commonly reported financial metrics are a product of descriptive analytics—for example, year-over-year pricing changes, month-over-month sales growth, the number of users, or the total revenue per subscriber. These measures all describe what has occurred in a business during a set period.

Descriptive analytics takes raw data and parses that data to draw conclusions that are useful and understandable by managers, investors, and other stakeholders. A report showing sales of $1 million may sound impressive, but it lacks context. If that figure represents a 20% month-over-month decline, it is a concern. If it is a 40% year-over-year increase, then it suggests something is going right with the sales strategy. However, the larger context including targeted growth is required to obtain an informed view of the company's sales performance.

Descriptive analytics uses a full range of data to give an accurate picture of what has happened in a business and how that differs from other comparable periods. These performance metrics can be used to flag areas of strength and weakness to inform management strategies.

Descriptive analytics is one of the most basic pieces of business intelligence a company will use. Although descriptive analytics can be industry specific—such as the seasonal variation in shipment completion times—analytics use broadly accepted measures common throughout the finance industry.

Return on invested capital (ROIC) is a descriptive analytic created by taking three data points—net income, dividends, and total capital—and turning those data points into an easy-to-understand percentage that can be used to compare one company's performance to others. Generally speaking, the larger and more complex a company is, the more descriptive analytics it will use to measure its performance.

### Special Considerations

Descriptive analytics provides important information in an easy-to-grasp format. There will always be a need for descriptive analytics. However, more effort is going towards newer fields of analytics such as predictive and prescriptive analytics.

These types of analytics use descriptive analytics and integrate additional data from diverse sources to model likely outcomes in the near term. These forward-looking analytics go beyond informing to decision-making. These types of analytics can also suggest courses of action that can maximize positive outcomes and minimize negative ones.

## Predictive Analytics

Predictive analytics encompasses a variety of statistical techniques from data mining, predictive modeling, and machine learning, that analyze current and historical facts to make predictions about future or otherwise unknown events.

In business, predictive models exploit patterns found in historical and transactional data to identify risks and opportunities. Models capture relationships among many factors to allow assessment of risk or potential associated with a particular set of conditions, guiding decision-making for candidate transactions.

The defining functional effect of these technical approaches is that predictive analytics provides a predictive score (probability) for each individual (customer, employee, healthcare patient, product SKU, vehicle, component, machine, or other organizational unit) in order to determine, inform, or influence organizational processes that pertain across large numbers of individuals, such as in marketing, credit risk assessment, fraud detection, manufacturing, healthcare, and government operations including law enforcement.

Predictive analytics is used in actuarial science, marketing, financial services, insurance, telecommunications, retail, travel, mobility, healthcare, child protection, pharmaceuticals, capacity planning, social networking and other fields.

One of the best-known applications is credit scoring, which is used throughout financial services. Scoring models process a customer's credit history, loan application, customer data, etc., in order to rank-order individuals by their likelihood of making future credit payments on time.

Predictive analytics is an area of statistics that deals with extracting information from data and using it to predict trends and behavior patterns. The enhancement of predictive web analytics calculates statistical probabilities of future events online. Predictive analytics statistical techniques include data modeling, machine learning, AI, deep learning algorithms and data mining. Often the unknown event of interest is in the future, but predictive analytics can be applied to any type of unknown whether it be in the past, present or future. For example, identifying suspects after a crime has been committed, or credit card fraud as it occurs. The core of predictive analytics relies on capturing relationships between explanatory variables and the predicted variables from past occurrences, and exploiting them to predict the unknown outcome. It is important to note, however, that the accuracy and usability of results will depend greatly on the level of data analysis and the quality of assumptions.

Predictive analytics is often defined as predicting at a more detailed level of granularity, i.e., generating predictive scores (probabilities) for each individual organizational element. This distinguishes it from forecasting. For example, "Predictive analytics—Technology that learns from experience (data) to predict the future behavior of individuals in order to drive better decisions." In future industrial systems, the value of predictive analytics will be to predict and prevent potential issues to achieve near-zero break-down and further be integrated into prescriptive analytics for decision optimization. Furthermore, the converted data can be used for closed-loop product life cycle improvement which is the vision of the Industrial Internet Consortium.

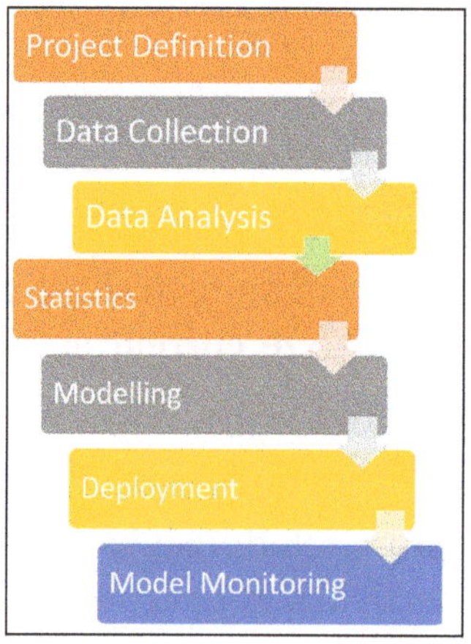


Predictive Analytics Process.

## Predictive Analytics Process

1. Define project: Define the project outcomes, deliverable, scope of the effort, business objectives, identify the data sets that are going to be used.
2. Data collection: Data mining for predictive analytics prepares data from multiple sources for analysis. This provides a complete view of customer interactions.
3. Data analysis: Data Analysis is the process of inspecting, cleaning and modeling data with the objective of discovering useful information, arriving at conclusion
4. Statistics: Statistical Analysis enables to validate the assumptions, hypothesis and test them using standard statistical models.
5. Modeling: Predictive modeling provides the ability to automatically create accurate predictive models about future. There are also options to choose the best solution with multi-modal evaluation.
6. Deployment: Predictive model deployment provides the option to deploy the analytical results into everyday decision making process to get results, reports and output by automating the decisions based on the modeling.
7. Model monitoring: Models are managed and monitored to review the model performance to ensure that it is providing the results expected.

## Types

Generally, the term predictive analytics is used to mean predictive modeling, "scoring" data with predictive models, and forecasting. However, people are increasingly using the term to refer to related analytical disciplines, such as descriptive modeling and decision modeling or optimization. These disciplines also involve rigorous data analysis, and are widely used in business for segmentation and decision making, but have different purposes and the statistical techniques underlying them vary.

## Predictive Models

Predictive modeling uses predictive models to analyze the relationship between the specific performance of a unit in a sample and one or more known attributes or features of the unit. The objective of the model is to assess the likelihood that a similar unit in a different sample will exhibit the specific performance. This category encompasses models in many areas, such as marketing, where they seek out subtle data patterns to answer questions about customer performance, or fraud detection models. Predictive models often perform calculations during live transactions, for example, to evaluate the risk or opportunity of a given customer or transaction, in order to guide a decision. With advancements in computing speed, individual agent modeling systems have become capable of simulating human behaviour or reactions to given stimuli or scenarios.

The available sample units with known attributes and known performances is referred to as the "training sample". The units in other samples, with known attributes but unknown performances, are referred to as "out of (training) sample" units. The out of sample units do not necessarily bear a chronological relation to the training sample units. For example, the training sample may consist of literary attributes of writings by Victorian authors, with known attribution, and the out-of sample unit may be newly found writing with unknown authorship; a predictive model may aid in attributing a work to a known author. Another example is given by analysis of blood splatter in simulated crime scenes in which the out of sample unit is the actual blood splatter pattern from a crime scene. The out of sample unit may be from the same time as the training units, from a previous time, or from a future time.

## Descriptive Models

Descriptive models quantify relationships in data in a way that is often used to classify customers or prospects into groups. Unlike predictive models that focus on predicting a single customer behavior (such as credit risk), descriptive models identify many different relationships between customers or products. Descriptive models do not rank-order customers by their likelihood of taking a particular action the way predictive models do. Instead, descriptive models can be used, for example, to categorize customers by their product preferences and life stage. Descriptive modeling tools can be utilized to develop further models that can simulate large number of individualized agents and make predictions.

## Decision Models

Decision models describe the relationship between all the elements of a decision—the known data (including results of predictive models), the decision, and the forecast results of the decision—in order to predict the results of decisions involving many variables. These models can be used in optimization, maximizing certain outcomes while minimizing others. Decision models are generally used to develop decision logic or a set of business rules that will produce the desired action for every customer or circumstance.

## Applications

Although predictive analytics can be put to use in many applications, we outline a few examples where predictive analytics has shown positive impact in recent years.

## Analytical Customer Relationship Management (CRM)

Analytical customer relationship management (CRM) is a frequent commercial application of predictive analysis. Methods of predictive analysis are applied to customer data to pursue CRM objectives, which involve constructing a holistic view of the customer no matter where their information resides in the company or the department involved. CRM uses predictive analysis in applications for marketing campaigns, sales, and customer services to name a few. These tools are required in order for a company to posture and focus their efforts effectively across the breadth of their customer base. They must analyze and understand the products in demand or have the potential for high demand, predict customers' buying habits in order to promote relevant products at multiple touch points, and proactively identify and mitigate issues that have the potential to lose customers or reduce their ability to gain new ones. Analytical customer relationship management can be applied throughout the customers' lifecycle (acquisition, relationship growth, retention, and win-back). Several of the application areas described below (direct marketing, cross-sell, customer retention) are part of customer relationship management.

## Collection Analytics

Many portfolios have a set of delinquent customers who do not make their payments on time. The financial institution has to undertake collection activities on these customers to recover the amounts due. A lot of collection resources are wasted on customers who are difficult or impossible to recover. Predictive analytics can help optimize the allocation of collection resources by identifying the most effective collection agencies, contact strategies, legal actions and other strategies to each customer, thus significantly increasing recovery at the same time reducing collection costs.

## Cross-sell

Often corporate organizations collect and maintain abundant data (e.g. customer records, sale transactions) as exploiting hidden relationships in the data can provide a competitive advantage. For an organization that offers multiple products, predictive analytics can help analyze customers' spending, usage and other behavior, leading to efficient cross sales, or selling additional products to current customers. This directly leads to higher profitability per customer and stronger customer relationships.

## Customer Retention

With the number of competing services available, businesses need to focus efforts on maintaining continuous customer satisfaction, rewarding consumer loyalty and minimizing customer attrition. In addition, small increases in customer retention have been shown to increase profits disproportionately. One study concluded that a 5% increase in customer retention rates will increase profits by 25% to 95%. Businesses tend to respond to customer attrition on a reactive basis, acting only after the customer has initiated the process to terminate service. At this stage, the chance of changing the customer's decision is almost zero. Proper application of predictive analytics can lead to a more proactive retention strategy. By a frequent examination of a customer's past service usage, service performance, spending and other behavior patterns, predictive models can determine the likelihood of a customer terminating service sometime soon. An intervention with lucrative offers can increase the chance of retaining the customer. Silent attrition, the behavior of a customer to slowly but steadily reduce usage, is another problem that many companies face. Predictive analytics can also predict this behavior, so that the company can take proper actions to increase customer activity.

## Direct Marketing

When marketing consumer products and services, there is the challenge of keeping up with competing products and consumer behavior. Apart from identifying prospects, predictive analytics can also help to identify the most effective combination of product versions, marketing material, communication channels and timing that should be used to target a given consumer. The goal of predictive analytics is typically to lower the cost per order or cost per action.

## Fraud Detection

Fraud is a big problem for many businesses and can be of various types: inaccurate credit applications, fraudulent transactions (both offline and online), identity thefts and false insurance claims. Some examples of likely victims are credit card issuers, insurance companies, retail merchants, manufacturers, business-to-business suppliers and even services providers. A predictive model can help weed out the "bads" and reduce a business's exposure to fraud.

Predictive modeling can also be used to identify high-risk fraud candidates in business or the public sector. Mark Nigrini developed a risk-scoring method to identify audit targets. He describes the use of this approach to detect fraud in the franchisee sales reports of an international fast-food chain. Each location is scored using 10 predictors. The 10 scores are then weighted to give one final overall risk score for each location. The same scoring approach was also used to identify high-risk check kiting accounts, potentially fraudulent travel agents, and questionable vendors. A reasonably complex model was used to identify fraudulent monthly reports submitted by divisional controllers.

The Internal Revenue Service (IRS) of the United States also uses predictive analytics to mine tax returns and identify tax fraud.

Recent advancements in technology have also introduced predictive behavior analysis for web fraud detection. This type of solution utilizes heuristics in order to study normal web user behavior and detect anomalies indicating fraud attempts.

## Predicting Outcomes of Legal Decisions

The predicting of the outcome of juridical decisions can be done by AI programs. These programs can be used as assistive tools for professions in this industry.

## Portfolio, Product or Economy-level Prediction

Often the focus of analysis is not the consumer but the product, portfolio, firm, industry or even the economy. For example, a retailer might be interested in predicting store-level demand for inventory management purposes. Or the Federal Reserve Board might be interested in predicting the unemployment rate for the next year. These types of problems can be addressed by predictive analytics using time series techniques. They can also be addressed via machine learning approaches which transform the original time series into a feature vector space, where the learning algorithm finds patterns that have predictive power.

## Project Risk Management

When employing risk management techniques, the results are always to predict and benefit from a future scenario. The capital asset pricing model (CAP-M) "predicts" the best portfolio to maximize return. Probabilistic risk assessment (PRA) when combined with mini-Delphi techniques and statistical approaches yields accurate forecasts. These are examples of approaches that can extend from project to market, and from near to long term. Underwriting and other business approaches identify risk management as a predictive method.

## Underwriting

Many businesses have to account for risk exposure due to their different services and determine the cost needed to cover the risk. For example, auto insurance providers need to accurately determine the amount of premium to charge to cover each automobile and driver. A financial company needs to assess a borrower's potential and ability to pay before granting a loan. For a health insurance provider, predictive analytics can analyze a few years of past medical claims data, as well as lab, pharmacy and other records where available, to predict how expensive an enrollee is likely to be in the future. Predictive analytics can help underwrite these quantities by predicting the chances of illness, default, bankruptcy, etc. Predictive analytics can streamline the process of customer acquisition by predicting the future risk behavior of a customer using application level data. Predictive analytics in the form of credit scores have reduced the amount of time it takes for loan approvals, especially in the mortgage market where lending decisions are now made in a matter of hours rather than days or even weeks. Proper predictive analytics can lead to proper pricing decisions, which can help mitigate future risk of default.

## Technology and Big Data Influences

Big data is a collection of data sets that are so large and complex that they become awkward to work with using traditional database management tools. The volume, variety and velocity of big data have introduced challenges across the board for capture, storage, search, sharing, analysis, and visualization. Examples of big data sources include web logs, RFID, sensor data, social networks, Internet search indexing, call detail records, military surveillance, and complex data in astronomic, biogeochemical, genomics, and atmospheric sciences. Big Data is the core of most predictive analytic services offered by IT organizations. Thanks to technological advances in computer hardware—faster CPUs, cheaper memory, and MPP architectures—and new technologies such as Hadoop, MapReduce, and in-database and text analytics for processing big data, it is now feasible to collect, analyze, and mine massive amounts of structured and unstructured data for new insights. It is also possible to run predictive algorithms on streaming data. Today, exploring big data and using predictive analytics is within reach of more organizations than ever before and new methods that are capable for handling such datasets are proposed.

## Analytical Techniques

The approaches and techniques used to conduct predictive analytics can broadly be grouped into regression techniques and machine learning techniques.

## Regression Techniques

Regression models are the mainstay of predictive analytics. The focus lies on establishing a mathematical equation as a model to represent the interactions between the different variables in consideration. Depending on the situation, there are a wide variety of models that can be applied while performing predictive analytics.

## Linear Regression Model

The linear regression model analyzes the relationship between the response or dependent variable and a set of independent or predictor variables. This relationship is expressed as an equation that predicts the response variable as a linear function of the parameters. These parameters are adjusted so that a measure of fit is optimized. Much of the effort in model fitting is focused on minimizing the size of the residual, as well as ensuring that it is randomly distributed with respect to the model predictions.

The goal of regression is to select the parameters of the model so as to minimize the sum of the squared residuals. This is referred to as ordinary least squares (OLS) estimation and results in best linear unbiased estimates (BLUE) of the parameters if and only if the Gauss-Markov assumptions are satisfied.

Once the model has been estimated we would be interested to know if the predictor variables belong in the model—i.e. is the estimate of each variable's contribution reliable? To do this we can check the statistical significance of the model's coefficients which can be measured using the t-statistic. This amounts to testing whether the coefficient is significantly different from zero. How well the model predicts the dependent variable based on the value of the independent variables can be assessed by using the $R^2$ statistic. It measures predictive power of the model i.e. the proportion of the total variation in the dependent variable that is "explained" (accounted for) by variation in the independent variables.

## Discrete Choice Models

Multiple regression (above) is generally used when the response variable is continuous and has an unbounded range. Often the response variable may not be continuous but rather discrete. While mathematically it is feasible to apply multiple regression to discrete ordered dependent variables, some of the assumptions behind the theory of multiple linear regression no longer hold, and there are other techniques such as discrete choice models which are better suited for this type of analysis. If the dependent variable is discrete, some of those superior methods are logistic regression, multinomial logit and probit models. Logistic regression and probit models are used when the dependent variable is binary.

## Logistic Regression

In a classification setting, assigning outcome probabilities to observations can be achieved through the use of a logistic model, which is basically a method which transforms information about the binary dependent variable into an unbounded continuous variable and estimates a regular multivariate model.

The Wald and likelihood-ratio test are used to test the statistical significance of each coefficient *b* in the model (analogous to the t tests used in OLS regression. A test assessing the goodness-of-fit of a classification model is the "percentage correctly predicted".

## Multinomial Logistic Regression

An extension of the binary logit model to cases where the dependent variable has more than 2 categories is the multinomial logit model. In such cases collapsing the data into two categories might not make good sense or may lead to loss in the richness of the data. The multinomial logit model is the appropriate technique in these cases, especially when the dependent variable categories are not ordered (for examples colors like red, blue, green). Some authors have extended multinomial regression to include feature selection/importance methods such as random multinomial logit.

## Probit Regression

Probit models offer an alternative to logistic regression for modeling categorical dependent variables. Even though the outcomes tend to be similar, the underlying distributions are different. Probit models are popular in social sciences like economics.

A good way to understand the key difference between probit and logit models is to assume that the dependent variable is driven by a latent variable z, which is a sum of a linear combination of explanatory variables and a random noise term.

We do not observe z but instead observe y which takes the value 0 (when z < 0) or 1 (otherwise). In the logit model we assume that the random noise term follows a logistic distribution with mean zero. In the probit model we assume that it follows a normal distribution with mean zero. Note that in social sciences (e.g. economics), probit is often used to model situations where the observed variable y is continuous but takes values between 0 and 1.

## Logit versus Probit

The probit model has been around longer than the logit model. They behave similarly, except that the logistic distribution tends to be slightly flatter tailed. One of the reasons the logit model was formulated was that the probit model was computationally difficult due to the requirement of numerically calculating integrals. Modern computing however has made this computation fairly simple. The coefficients obtained from the logit and probit model are fairly close. However, the odds ratio is easier to interpret in the logit model.

Practical reasons for choosing the probit model over the logistic model would be:

- There is a strong belief that the underlying distribution is normal.
- The actual event is not a binary outcome (*e.g.*, bankruptcy status) but a proportion (*e.g.*, proportion of population at different debt levels).

## Time Series Models

Time series models are used for predicting or forecasting the future behavior of variables. These models account for the fact that data points taken over time may have an internal structure (such as auto correlation, trend or seasonal variation) that should be accounted for. As a result, standard regression techniques cannot be applied to time series data and methodology has been developed to decompose the trend, seasonal and cyclical component of the series. Modeling the dynamic path of a variable can improve forecasts since the predictable component of the series can be projected into the future.

Time series models estimate difference equations containing stochastic components. Two commonly used forms of these models are autoregressive models (AR) and moving-average (MA) models. The Box–Jenkins methodology developed by George Box and G.M. Jenkins combines the AR and MA models to produce the ARMA (autoregressive moving average) model, which is the cornerstone of stationary time series analysis. ARIMA (autoregressive integrated moving average models), on the other hand, are used to describe non-stationary time series. Box and Jenkins suggest differencing a non-stationary time series to obtain a stationary series to which an ARMA model can be applied. Non-stationary time series have a pronounced trend and do not have a constant long-run mean or variance.

Box and Jenkins proposed a three-stage methodology involving model identification, estimation and validation. The identification stage involves identifying if the series is stationary or not and the presence of seasonality by examining plots of the series, autocorrelation and partial autocorrelation functions. In the estimation stage, models are estimated using non-linear time series or maximum likelihood estimation procedures. Finally the validation stage involves diagnostic checking such as plotting the residuals to detect outliers and evidence of model fit.

In recent years time series models have become more sophisticated and attempt to model conditional heteroskedasticity with models such as ARCH (autoregressive conditional heteroskedasticity) and GARCH (generalized autoregressive conditional heteroskedasticity) models frequently used for financial time series. In addition time series models are also used to understand inter-relationships among economic variables represented by systems of equations using VAR (vector autoregression) and structural VAR models.

## Survival or Duration Analysis

Survival analysis is another name for time-to-event analysis. These techniques were primarily developed in the medical and biological sciences, but they are also widely used in the social sciences like economics, as well as in engineering (reliability and failure time analysis).

Censoring and non-normality, which are characteristic of survival data, generate difficulty when trying to analyze the data using conventional statistical models such as multiple linear regression. The normal distribution, being a symmetric distribution, takes positive as well as negative values, but duration by its very nature cannot be negative and therefore normality cannot be assumed when dealing with duration/survival data. Hence the normality assumption of regression models is violated.

The assumption is that if the data were not censored it would be representative of the population of interest. In survival analysis, censored observations arise whenever the dependent variable of interest represents the time to a terminal event, and the duration of the study is limited in time.

An important concept in survival analysis is the hazard rate, defined as the probability that the event will occur at time t conditional on surviving until time t. Another concept related to the hazard rate is the survival function which can be defined as the probability of surviving to time t.

Most models try to model the hazard rate by choosing the underlying distribution depending on the shape of the hazard function. A distribution whose hazard function slopes upward is said to have positive duration dependence, a decreasing hazard shows negative duration dependence whereas constant hazard is a process with no memory usually characterized by the exponential distribution. Some of the distributional choices in survival models are: F, gamma, Weibull, log normal, inverse normal, exponential etc. All these distributions are for a non-negative random variable.

Duration models can be parametric, non-parametric or semi-parametric. Some of the models commonly used are Kaplan-Meier and Cox proportional hazard model (non parametric).

## Classification and Regression Trees (CART)

Globally-optimal classification tree analysis (GO-CTA) (also called hierarchical optimal discriminant analysis) is a generalization of optimal discriminant analysis that may be used to identify the statistical model that has maximum accuracy for predicting the value of a categorical dependent variable for a data-set consisting of categorical and continuous variables. The output of HODA is a non-orthogonal tree that combines categorical variables and cut points for continuous variables that yields maximum predictive accuracy, an assessment of the exact Type I error rate, and an evaluation of potential cross-generalizability of the statistical model. Hierarchical optimal discriminant analysis may be thought of as a generalization of Fisher's linear discriminant analysis. Optimal discriminant analysis is an alternative to ANOVA (analysis of variance) and regression analysis, which attempt to express one dependent variable as a linear combination of other features or measurements. However, ANOVA and regression analysis give a dependent variable that is a numerical variable, while hierarchical optimal discriminant analysis gives a dependent variable that is a class variable.

Classification and regression trees (CART) are a non-parametric decision tree learning technique that produces either classification or regression trees, depending on whether the dependent variable is categorical or numeric, respectively.

Decision trees are formed by a collection of rules based on variables in the modeling data set:

- Rules based on variables' values are selected to get the best split to differentiate observations based on the dependent variable.
- Once a rule is selected and splits a node into two, the same process is applied to each "child" node (i.e. it is a recursive procedure).
- Splitting stops when CART detects no further gain can be made, or some pre-set stopping rules are met. (Alternatively, the data are split as much as possible and then the tree is later pruned).

Each branch of the tree ends in a terminal node. Each observation falls into one and exactly one terminal node, and each terminal node is uniquely defined by a set of rules.

A very popular method for predictive analytics is Leo Breiman's random forests.

## Multivariate Adaptive Regression Splines

Multivariate adaptive regression splines (MARS) is a non-parametric technique that builds flexible models by fitting piecewise linear regressions.

An important concept associated with regression splines is that of a knot. Knot is where one local regression model gives way to another and thus is the point of intersection between two splines.

In multivariate and adaptive regression splines, basis functions are the tool used for generalizing the search for knots. Basis functions are a set of functions used to represent the information contained in one or more variables. Multivariate and Adaptive Regression Splines model almost always creates the basis functions in pairs.

Multivariate and adaptive regression spline approach deliberately overfits the model and then prunes to get to the optimal model. The algorithm is computationally very intensive and in practice we are required to specify an upper limit on the number of basis functions.

## Machine Learning Techniques

Machine learning, a branch of artificial intelligence, was originally employed to develop techniques to enable computers to learn. Today, since it includes a number of advanced statistical methods for regression and classification, it finds application in a wide variety of fields including medical diagnostics, credit card fraud detection, face and speech recognition and analysis of the stock market. In certain applications it is sufficient to directly predict the dependent variable without focusing on the underlying relationships between variables. In other cases, the underlying relationships can be very complex and the mathematical form of the dependencies unknown. For such cases, machine learning techniques emulate human cognition and learn from training examples to predict future events.

## Neural Networks

Neural networks are nonlinear sophisticated modeling techniques that are able to model complex functions. They can be applied to problems of prediction, classification or control in a wide spectrum of fields such as finance, cognitive psychology/neuroscience, medicine, engineering, and physics.

Neural networks are used when the exact nature of the relationship between inputs and output is not known. A key feature of neural networks is that they learn the relationship between inputs and output through training. There are three types of training used by different neural networks: supervised and unsupervised training and reinforcement learning, with supervised being the most common one.

Some examples of neural network training techniques are backpropagation, quick propagation, conjugate gradient descent, projection operator, Delta-Bar-Delta etc. Some unsupervised network architectures are multilayer perceptrons, Kohonen networks, Hopfield networks, etc.

## Multilayer Perceptron (MLP)

The multilayer perceptron (MLP) consists of an input and an output layer with one or more hidden layers of non linearly-activating nodes or sigmoid nodes. This is determined by the weight vector and it is necessary to adjust the weights of the network. The backpropagation employs gradient fall to minimize the squared error between the network output values and desired values for those outputs. The weights adjusted by an iterative process of repetitive present of attributes. Small changes in the weight to get the desired values are done by the process called training the net and is done by the training set (learning rule).

## Radial Basis Functions

A radial basis function (RBF) is a function which has built into it a distance criterion with respect to a center. Such functions can be used very efficiently for interpolation and for smoothing of data. Radial basis functions have been applied in the area of neural networks where they are used as a replacement for the sigmoidal transfer function. Such networks have 3 layers, the input layer, the hidden layer with the RBF non-linearity and a linear output layer. The most popular choice for the non-linearity is the Gaussian. RBF networks have the advantage of not being locked into local minima as do the feed-forward networks such as the multilayer perceptron.

## Support Vector Machines

Support vector machines (SVM) are used to detect and exploit complex patterns in data by clustering, classifying and ranking the data. They are learning machines that are used to perform binary classifications and regression estimations. They commonly use kernel based methods to apply linear classification techniques to non-linear classification problems. There are a number of types of SVM such as linear, polynomial, sigmoid etc.

### Naïve Bayes

Naïve Bayes based on Bayes conditional probability rule is used for performing classification tasks. Naïve Bayes assumes the predictors are statistically independent which makes it an effective classification tool that is easy to interpret. It is best employed when faced with the "curse of dimensionality" problem, i.e. when the number of predictors is very high.

### *k*-nearest Neighbours

The nearest neighbour algorithm (KNN) belongs to the class of pattern recognition statistical methods. The method does not impose a priori any assumptions about the distribution from which the modeling sample is drawn. It involves a training set with both positive and negative values. A new sample is classified by calculating the distance to the nearest neighbouring training case. The sign of that point will determine the classification of the sample. In the k-nearest neighbour classifier, the k nearest points are considered and the sign of the majority is used to classify the sample. The performance of the kNN algorithm is influenced by three main factors: (1) the distance measure used to locate the nearest neighbours, (2) the decision rule used to derive a classification from the k-nearest neighbours, and (3) the number of neighbours used to classify the new sample. It can be proved that, unlike other methods, this method is universally asymptotically convergent, i.e. as the size of the training set increases, if the observations are independent and identically distributed (i.i.d.), regardless of the distribution from which the sample is drawn, the predicted class will converge to the class assignment that minimizes misclassification error.

### Geospatial Predictive Modeling

Conceptually, geospatial predictive modeling is rooted in the principle that the occurrences of events being modeled are limited in distribution. Occurrences of events are neither uniform nor random in distribution—there are spatial environment factors (infrastructure, sociocultural, topographic, etc.) that constrain and influence where the locations of events occur. Geospatial predictive modeling attempts to describe those constraints and influences by spatially correlating occurrences of historical geospatial locations with environmental factors that represent those constraints and influences. Geospatial predictive modeling is a process for analyzing events through a geographic filter in order to make statements of likelihood for event occurrence or emergence.

## Prescriptive Analytics

Prescriptive analytics is the third and final phase of business analytics, which also includes descriptive and predictive analytics.

Referred to as the "final frontier of analytic capabilities," prescriptive analytics entails the application of mathematical and computational sciences and suggests decision options to take advantage of the results of descriptive and predictive analytics. The first stage of business analytics is descriptive analytics, which still accounts for the majority of all business analytics today. Descriptive analytics looks at past performance and understands that performance by mining historical data to look for the reasons behind past success or failure. Most management reporting – such as sales, marketing, operations, and finance – uses this type of post-mortem analysis.

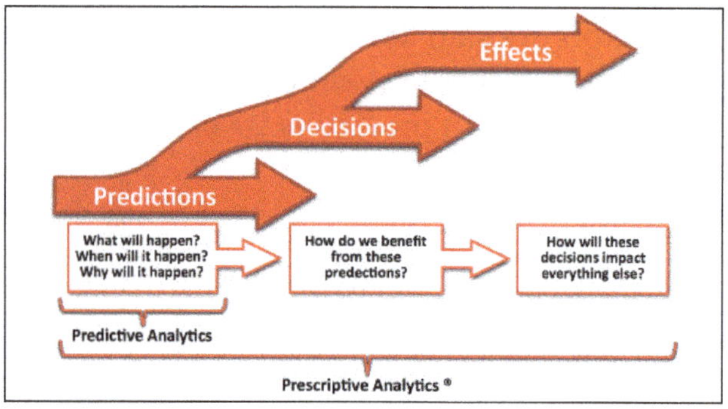


Prescriptive Analytics extends beyond predictive analytics by specifying both the actions necessary to achieve predicted outcomes, and the interrelated effects of each decision.

The next phase is predictive analytics. Predictive analytics answers the question what is likely to happen. This is when historical data is combined with rules, algorithms, and occasionally external data to determine the probable future outcome of an event or the likelihood of a situation occurring. The final phase is prescriptive analytics, which goes beyond predicting future outcomes by also suggesting actions to benefit from the predictions and showing the implications of each decision option.

Prescriptive analytics not only anticipates what will happen and when it will happen, but also why it will happen. Further, prescriptive analytics suggests decision options on how to take advantage of a future opportunity or mitigate a future risk and shows the implication of each decision option. Prescriptive analytics can continually take in new data to re-predict and re-prescribe, thus automatically improving prediction accuracy and prescribing better decision options. Prescriptive analytics ingests hybrid data, a combination of structured (numbers, categories) and unstructured data (videos, images, sounds, texts), and business rules to predict what lies ahead and to prescribe how to take advantage of this predicted future without compromising other priorities.

All three phases of analytics can be performed through professional services or technology or a combination. In order to scale, prescriptive analytics technologies need to be adaptive to take into account the growing volume, velocity, and variety of data that most mission critical processes and their environments may produce.

One criticism of prescriptive analytics is that its distinction from predictive analytics is ill-defined and therefore ill-conceived.

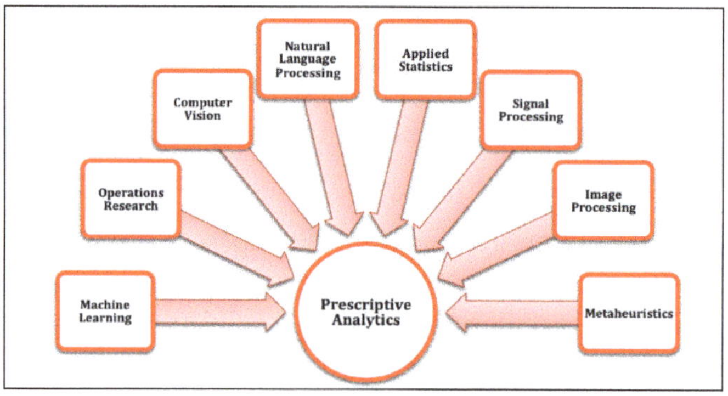


The scientific disciplines that comprise Prescriptive Analytics.

Prescriptive analytics incorporates both structured and unstructured data, and uses a combination of advanced analytic techniques and disciplines to predict, prescribe, and adapt. While the term prescriptive analytics was first coined by IBM and later trademarked by Ayata, the underlying concepts have been around for hundreds of years. The technology behind prescriptive analytics synergistically combines hybrid data, business rules with mathematical models and computational models. The data inputs to prescriptive analytics may come from multiple sources: internal, such as inside a corporation; and external, also known as environmental data. The data may be structured, which includes numbers and categories, as well as unstructured data, such as texts, images, sounds, and videos. Unstructured data differs from structured data in that its format varies widely and cannot be stored in traditional relational databases without significant effort at data transformation. More than 80% of the world's data today is unstructured, according to IBM.

In addition to this variety of data types and growing data volume, incoming data can also evolve with respect to velocity, that is, more data being generated at a faster or a variable pace. Business rules define the business process and include objectives constraints, preferences, policies, best practices, and boundaries. Mathematical models and computational models are techniques derived from mathematical sciences, computer science and related disciplines such as applied statistics, machine learning, operations research, natural language processing, computer vision, pattern recognition, image processing, speech recognition, and signal processing. The correct application of all these methods and the verification of their results implies the need for resources on a massive scale including human, computational and temporal for every Prescriptive Analytic project. In order to spare the expense of dozens of people, high performance machines and weeks of work one must consider the reduction of resources and therefore a reduction in the accuracy or reliability of the outcome. The preferable route is a reduction that produces a probabilistic result within acceptable limits.

## Applications in Oil and Gas

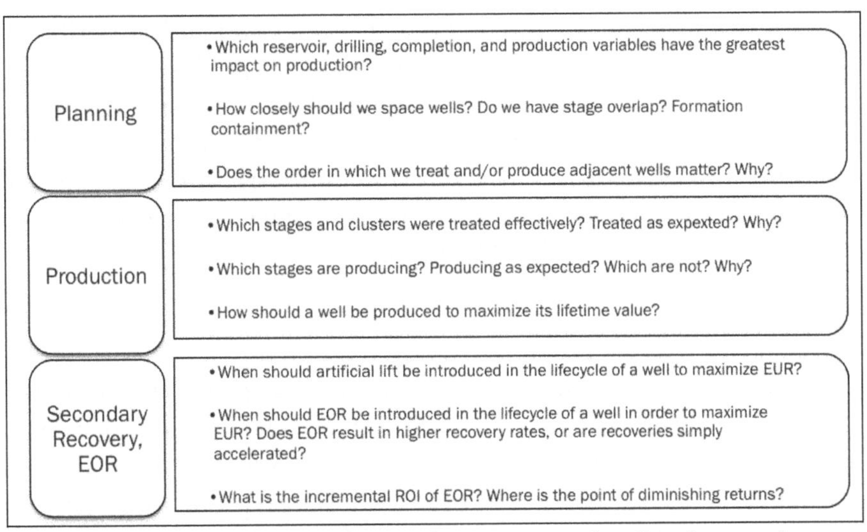


Key Questions Prescriptive Analytics software answers for oil and gas producers.

Energy is the largest industry in the world ($6 trillion in size). The processes and decisions related to oil and natural gas exploration, development and production generate large amounts of data. Many types of captured data are used to create models and images of the Earth's structure and layers 5,000 - 35,000 feet below the surface and to describe activities around the wells themselves, such as depositional characteristics, machinery performance, oil flow rates, reservoir temperatures and pressures. Prescriptive analytics software can help with both locating and producing hydrocarbons by taking in seismic data, well log data, production data, and other related data sets to prescribe specific recipes for how and where to drill, complete, and produce wells in order to optimize recovery, minimize cost, and reduce environmental footprint.

## Unconventional Resource Development

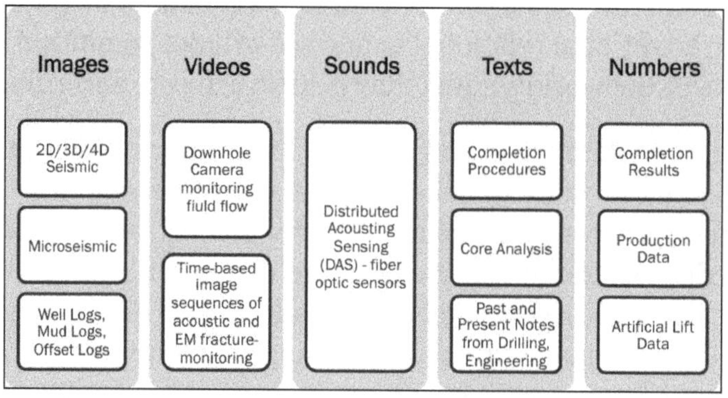


Examples of structured and unstructured data sets generated and by the oil and gas companies and their ecosystem of service providers that can be analyzed together using Prescriptive Analytics software.

With the value of the end product determined by global commodity economics, the basis of competition for operators in upstream E&P is the ability to effectively deploy capital to locate and extract resources more efficiently, effectively, predictably, and safely than their peers. In unconventional resource plays, operational efficiency and effectiveness is diminished by reservoir inconsistencies, and decision-making impaired by high degrees of uncertainty. These challenges manifest themselves in the form of low recovery factors and wide performance variations.

Prescriptive Analytics software can accurately predict production and prescribe optimal configurations of controllable drilling, completion, and production variables by modeling numerous internal and external variables simultaneously, regardless of source, structure, size, or format. Prescriptive analytics software can also provide decision options and show the impact of each decision option so the operations managers can proactively take appropriate actions, on time, to guarantee future exploration and production performance, and maximize the economic value of assets at every point over the course of their serviceable lifetimes.

## Oilfield Equipment Maintenance

In the realm of oilfield equipment maintenance, Prescriptive Analytics can optimize configuration, anticipate and prevent unplanned downtime, optimize field scheduling, and improve maintenance planning. According to General Electric, there are more than 130,000 electric submersible pumps (ESP's) installed globally, accounting for 60% of the world's oil production. Prescriptive Analytics has been deployed to predict when and why an ESP will fail, and recommend the necessary actions to prevent the failure.

In the area of Health, Safety, and Environment, prescriptive analytics can predict and preempt incidents that can lead to reputational and financial loss for oil and gas companies.

### Pricing

Pricing is another area of focus. Natural gas prices fluctuate dramatically depending upon supply, demand, econometrics, geopolitics, and weather conditions. Gas producers, pipeline transmission companies and utility firms have a keen interest in more accurately predicting gas prices so that they can lock in favorable terms while hedging downside risk. Prescriptive analytics software can accurately predict prices by modeling internal and external variables simultaneously and also provide decision options and show the impact of each decision option.

### Applications in Healthcare

Multiple factors are driving healthcare providers to dramatically improve business processes and operations as the United States healthcare industry embarks on the necessary migration from a largely fee-for service, volume-based system to a fee-for-performance, value-based system. Prescriptive analytics is playing a key role to help improve the performance in a number of areas involving various stakeholders: payers, providers and pharmaceutical companies.

Prescriptive analytics can help providers improve effectiveness of their clinical care delivery to the population they manage and in the process achieve better patient satisfaction and retention. Providers can do better population health management by identifying appropriate intervention models for risk stratified population combining data from the in-facility care episodes and home based telehealth.

Prescriptive analytics can also benefit healthcare providers in their capacity planning by using analytics to leverage operational and usage data combined with data of external factors such as economic data, population demographic trends and population health trends, to more accurately plan for future capital investments such as new facilities and equipment utilization as well as understand the trade-offs between adding additional beds and expanding an existing facility versus building a new one.

Prescriptive analytics can help pharmaceutical companies to expedite their drug development by identifying patient cohorts that are most suitable for the clinical trials worldwide - patients who are expected to be compliant and will not drop out of the trial due to complications. Analytics can tell companies how much time and money they can save if they choose one patient cohort in a specific country vs. another.

In provider-payer negotiations, providers can improve their negotiating position with health insurers by developing a robust understanding of future service utilization. By accurately predicting utilization, providers can also better allocate personnel.

## Challenges of Business Analytics

### Strategic Alignment

Most organizations today already have some element of business analytics in place, often in the BI/data warehousing area. Unfortunately analytics are often viewed by top executives as esoteric research at best, and irrelevant fringe experiments at worst. The issue surrounds not a lack of appreciation for the usefulness of information but a lack of alignment, availability, and trust.

Review the business goals that support the main strategies for the company, and for each major business process that underpins the goals, ask the following questions:

- "Would we be able to govern and optimize this process more effectively if we could predict how modifications to it would affect the result?"
- "Would we be able to adapt the process more readily to changes in the external environment if we could more accurately assess the nature and causes of those changes?"

If the answers to either of those questions is "yes", then the process (and therefore the goal it underpins, and the strategy the goal supports) would benefit from the application of analytics.

## Agility

Typically in the organizations, the analysts are organized by business domains. Findings working with top-tier, information-driven companies demonstrate that domain-based organizations are not the most effective approach for analytics. Analysts often work independently and create models in ad-hoc environments based on a patchwork of extracts and sources. The results, while advanced and valid, are not easily communicated to the business users for whom they would provide the greatest value.

Liberate the organization's analytical capabilities by pooling analysts into a Center of Excellence highly focused on "analytics-as-a-skill". Combine members of the CoE with business domain experts into teams who employ agile methods for development of analytical models, enabling your business users to gain real- or right-time insight into complex, data-demanding questions.

## Commitment

Analytics software packages often come as prefabricated solution and are not particularly difficult to implement; however they can be costly, and the ROI is not immediate. By their nature, analytical models will improve in accuracy over time as the predicted results are compared with actual events hitting the warehouse. But this is a complex endeavor that requires dedication to the solution during an extended tuning period. Here is where many deployments fail. Business users do not immediately see the promised results and lose interest, and executives lose trust in the solution and refuse to rely on what the models tell them.

By addressing key challenge 1, stakeholders in analytics will naturally be identified (the process and goal owners). These business owners must take responsibility for establishing the productive analytics environment described in key challenge 2. Realistic timelines that allow the models to take form should be set based on industry standard and best practice.

## Information Maturity

For an analytics solution to succeed, the "nails" need to be plentiful and not consistently bent or misshapen. Implementations often fail because of the lack or low quality of underlying transactional data. Either data are not available, data sources are too complex, or data are poorly mastered.

Even bleeding-edge, sentiment- and context-analysis tools require some level of trust in the data, and for any analytical model the rule is consistent: the more trustworthy the data the more trustworthy the result.

## Benefits of Business Analytics

For a business, the top concern is offering valuable products and services to customers. To do this, they need to stay innovative and ahead of their competition.

Traditionally, companies have used error-ridden, time-consuming models to define how the business operates and works toward its goals. However, as increasing amounts of data become available to companies today, these models are no longer effective at keeping businesses moving in the right direction.

Processes stagnate when businesses make the wrong move. That wrong move could mean delaying a decision because there was not enough information to make it, or powering forward with a big new idea because there was too little information. That's why analytics has become such a key tool in guiding business decisions. How exactly does it work? Here are five things that analytics can do for a business:

### Analytics Helps Quantify Company Values

Most businesses have a mission statement. Most companies teach new hires and retrain long-term employees on the fundamental values that drive the company to success. What many companies fail to do, however, is quantify these values.

With business analytics, companies can measure how these values translate into numbers. By using quantifiable numbers, broad value and mission statements can be quantified too, rather than just left to interpretation. Companies can use data to focus on operating with processes that keep in line with company values.

For example, a business might identify what its measures of return look like, both tangible returns (such as profits) and intangible returns (such as giving back to the community). These can then be quantified to clearly define expectations for employees. This should improve processes because everyone will be working toward the same clear goal.

### Analytics can be used to Ingrain Smart Decision-making into Company Culture

With more information at companies' fingertips, it's easier to empower a team to make quick decisions. Fast movement and development is important for a business if it wants to stay ahead of the competition. Equally important is careful consideration of each decision.

Nothing can derail a company faster than jetting off in the wrong direction. Making fast decisions is easy, but what is more important is to make smart decisions in a short period of time.

With so much data at hand, it's possible for everyone – not just higher-level employees – to make informed decisions. That's why every department needs access to analytics. It should be ingrained in corporate culture.

Fuel your team's success by offering access to vital data. This way, it's possible to ensure that each new idea, direction or project will build the business, rather than set it back.

### Analytics Provides Greater, Faster Insight through Data Visualization

Using visual data can make companies more agile, and can help them find revealing insights faster and make decisions without having to take as much time to understand what's really happening in the market.

With charts, graphs and other visual aids, decision-makers make speedier choices. This puts each team in motion faster. By keeping an organization fluid and constantly moving, processes improve.

### Analytics Helps Companies Avoid being Left Behind

Today's world moves faster than ever before. The way people purchase consumer goods is changing. The way businesses communicate is changing. The way companies reach clients is changing. With so much change happening at such a rapid pace, it's easy for even the largest, smartest companies to get left behind.

Business analytics can help companies avoid falling into that trap. Using analytics allows businesses to create rolling forecasts of the business and of the market. These offer valuable insight into what's happening internally and externally. Staying abreast of the latest new forecasts can spark innovative ideas, bringing more depth to a company's brand. Improving processes paves the way to releasing innovative new products, services and information.

## Business Analytics Techniques

Business analytics techniques have evolved at a rapid pace, completely changing the manner in which brands and companies are functioning in almost all areas. It is therefore considered an important and essential element of all profitable and successful modern business around the globe. A major aspect of business analytics techniques is that it has an ever-evolving definition, making it difficult to implement and sustain. In a nutshell, business analytics tools is a complex combination of practices, techniques, applications, skills, and technologies that are aimed at understanding and it is also useful for analyzing business performance so that they can achieve better results and strategic goals. At the same time, it is important to remember that business analytics process is not a universal approach and is not used by all companies and organizations in the same effect and manner.

Brands, in turn, can develop and create new strategies so that they do not just achieve their results but also increase their brand power and profits in a successful manner. And it goes without saying that such strategies are not set in stone and each company will have a unique way of functioning so that they can realize both their internal and external goals in a comprehensive manner. Business analytics techniques are, therefore, evolving at every stage so that it can help companies to achieve their goals in a manner that is individualistic but at the same time global as well. That being said, business analytics process will continue to remain an integral part of business marketing plans as business analytics tools is a decisive tool through brands can reach a much wider market in a successful yet cost-effective way.

Many of Business analytics, especially among the top rung believe that the field of big analytics posed for great change, especially in the coming years. But with so many developments taking place in the field of business analytics, many companies are opening their eyes to this advanced and technical field. This means it is set to change the face of business and brands around the world. Business analytics techniques are changing the way that brands are functioning by helping them to take more strategic decisions that have overreaching implications. Most of these predictions are based on four main categories which include faster processing capabilities. mobile related apps, powerful social decision-making models, and greater solutions provider.

Today, brands are growing in size and creating a dent in the market is becoming a really challenging task. Business analytics is, therefore, an important ingredient in the growth and development story of a brand. Business intelligence and analytics is today a mainstream technology that is helping to expand the horizon of the brand, which is to say that even small and mid-level brands are opening their eyes to the impact that this business analytics can create in their story. With advanced business analytics techniques and strategies, business analytics is the new face of business growth and evolution.

Business analytics process is therefore rapidly expanding in various ways. There is today multiple business analytics tools that brands can use in order to empower their strategies and goals in the true sense. With faster processing times and intuitively designed databases, business analytics techniques are helping brands to address challenges and make use of opportunities, both big and small.

## Effect of Business Analytics Techniques on Industry

Everyone knows that the mobile industry is expanding at a rapid pace. Mobile apps have completely changed the manner we conduct our affairs, both personal and professional. From marriage to banking needs, we have an application for all these tasks. This means mobile apps have created multiple opportunities for brands across a lot of spectrum. Even more importantly, these apps have changed customer and brand relationship and in turn changed the manner in which brands communicate, engage and connect not just within but also outside the organization.

The digital revolution has led to a new rise in business analytics, business analytics that are helping them reach an audience that is extremely big, both on a national and global stage. With brands and companies depending on mobile devices to remain connected, business analytics process deals with the mobile technology are gaining immense popularity and traction. In short, investing in mobile business analytics techniques is, therefore, one of the prime requirements of companies, irrespective of their size and expertise. With time it is but obvious that analytical companies will begin to focus more on the technology that will integrate analytics with mobile technology so that brand managers will have at their disposal all those tools to connect with their customer and vendors, through just their mobile devices or smartphones.

### Social Media and Business Analytics

Today social media is one of the most powerful business analytics in the world, which is transforming every way in which human beings live their life. In order for brands to completely make use of social media, it is important to create business analytics tools that can combine the power of social media with business analytics. This means that a collaborative approach is needed in such a situation. By integrating business analytics with social networking, brands can reach new levels of engagement, connect and reach. Integrating social media networking into the existing business intelligence models and analytical tools of the brand might be a challenging task but with the right skills, brands stand to gain a lot from this method.

## Business Analytics Tools

### Open Source Software

A programming language and software technology that is used for graphics and computing, Open Source Software is very popular and used by a lot of people. While this is generally used by a lot of individuals, the brand needs to readapt this tool for their use. At the same time, brands need to know that that there a number of graphic user interface professionals who can improve its efficiencies in order to make it adaptable for brands and companies.

### Weka

In business analytics techniques a favored and popular suite dedicated to machine learning software, the Weka tool was developed by the University of Waikato in New Zealand. Along with Weka, R is extremely common and prominent among a lot of brands and companies. Written in the Java language, this tools also contains a graphic user interface, which helps brand managers to not just interact with data files but also produce insights and results that are visual as well as dynamic.

### KXEN

Products offered by KXEN is a company that produces products that are based on automated analytics. Most of their products are based on algorithms that were created by Vladimir Vapnik, a mathematician of Russian origin. A tool that is relatively easy to use and relatively fast in nature, KXEN business analytics tools are able to work with vast amounts of data in an effective fashion. As this tool work like a black box, many users may not like the tool so much.

### Angoss

Angoss company has created products and tools that are based on classification and regression decision tree algorithms. A major advantage of this tool is that it is extremely simple to use and learn during the business analytics process. These tools are even simpler to explain to others, making it an incredible tool. With a graphic user interface that is extremely user-friendly, along with a host of features that are updated at regular intervals, making it a really comprehensive and intelligent business analytics tools.

## MATLAB

Developed by MathWorks, MATLAB is a statistical software based on computers that are used for plotting of functions and data, matrix manipulation, the creation of user interfaces and implementation of algorithms. With many add-on toolboxes, MATLAB is able to address major areas of functionality like finance, image processing, bioinformatics among other things. Though this is not a free software, there are many other business analytics tools that offer the same functionality.

## Tableau

By democratizing visualization in a professionally classic manner, Tableau provides brand managers with a great playground for personal use. Though the free trial is available for as long as the user is hooked, there are some alternatives available to this business analytics tool as well. By allowing brand managers to quickly assess their data, understand it and infer great insights from it before they implement any new and important strategy.

## Open Refine

Early referred to as Google Refine, Open refine tool allows brand managers to clean raw data and make it available for analysis as well. When data is available in different formats, say for example they have different formats like different spellings and capitalization, then this tool can help data to clear out and make their formatting simpler.

## KNIME

By allowing brand managers to manipulate and analyze data in an intuitive manner, KNIME drops nodes on a canvas and at the same time creates a connection between activities. A visual programming tool, KNIME can be extended so as to run R, chemistry data among other things, allowing brand users to use code driven analysis as well.

## RapidMiner

Similar to KNIME, RapidMiner tool operates through the process of visual programming. This business analytics tools are capable of manipulating and analyzing data, and it allows brand managers to understand that data science is not a counterintuitive endeavor that is related to coding.

## Google Fusion Tables

The larger and cooler version of Google Spreadsheet, Google Fusion table is indeed a versatile tool that is used for data analysis, mapping, and visualization. By putting in a location, this tool can easily tell the longitude and latitude data of the said place, making it a really great tool for brands that are working with a lot of data that is related to places and locations.

### NodeXL

A visualization and analysis software, NodeXL is based on relationships and networks. This business analytics process allows you to create connections between individuals on LinkedIn and Facebook, especially when they connected on these social networks. In addition, this business analytics process allows brands to make calculations that are right and exact. In case brand managers are looking for something that is a less technical, they can look to invest in node graph on Google Fusion tables or even a tool called Gephi.

### Io

Sometimes pulling off a lot of data from the internet can seem to be extremely difficult and time-consuming. With import.io, users can harvest a lot of information from forums and websites of their choices. By highlighting data that they want, the import.io tool can understand the information that you are looking for and help brand managers to gain the insights that they require in a simple manner, thereby saving a lot of time and hard work.

### Google Search Operators

A great powerful resource, Google search operators takes search duties one step ahead. By quickly allowing brand managers to filter data to what they find useful and relevant, this business analytics process saves a lot of effort or time. For instance, if someone is looking for a report published in a particular year, this business analytics process can easily locate the same. In addition to discovering new insights, this business analytics process can help brands can gain even deeper and valuable insights than ever before.

### Solver

An optimization and linear programming techniques used in Excel, Solver allows you set certain boundaries like budget, days of a campaign, etc among other things. A unique tool, Solver can help brand managers to deal with a lot of problems in a simple and easy manner.

### Wolfram Alpha

A hidden gem available on the net, Wolfram Alpha is a business analytics process that can help to power Siri on Apple. A nerdy Google, this business analytics techniques provide a lot of details to technical searches and also allows brand managers to gain a lot of visual information as well about a wide range of topics including commodities and prices.

Business analytics tools are some of the best advancements made in this field during the last decade or so. However, brands have to understand that having access to technology is not sufficient but the concerned people need to know how to use the same in an effective manner. That is why it is extremely important that brand managers create a strategic and comprehensive plan so that they can put these tools to good use. By collaborating with customers, employees, and customers, professionals can create a plan that is comprehensive and able to reach their goals in a successful manner and at the same time build their brand power and engagement.

## References


- Operational-business-intelligence, definition: techtarget.com, Retrieved 19 April, 2019
- Coker, frank (2014). Pulse: understanding the vital signs of your business (1st ed.). Bellevue, wa: ambient light publishing. Pp. 30, 39, 42, more. Isbn 978-0-9893086-0-1
- Four-key-challenges-for-business-analytics: capgemini.com, Retrieved 5 February, 2019
- Finlay, steven (2014). Predictive analytics, data mining and big data. Myths, misconceptions and methods (1st ed.). Basingstoke: palgrave macmillan. P. 237. Isbn 978-1137379276
- Business-intelligence-bi/the-4-key-benefits-of-business-analytics, it-business: techopedia.com, Retrieved 26 July, 2019
- Nigrini, mark (june 2011). Forensic analytics: methods and techniques for forensic accounting investigations. Hoboken, nj: john wiley & sons inc. Isbn 978-0-470-89046-2
- Business-analytics-techniques: educba.com, Retrieved 21 May, 2019

# 4

# Basic Domain in Business Analytics

There are numerous domains in which applications of business analytics can be applied. Behavioral analytics, cohort analysis, collection analytics, financial analytics, market analytics, pricing analytics, retail analytics, supply chain analytics, etc. are some of the examples. This chapter closely examines these business analytics domains to provide an extensive understanding of the subject.

## Behavioral Analytics

Behavioral analytics is a tool that reveals the actions users take within a digital product. It organizes raw event data such as clicks into a timeline of each user's behavior, also known as a user journey. Teams use behavioral analytics to determine what users like and don't like and, by inference, what adjustments can make the product more valuable.

### Behavioral Data

Behavioral data is the raw event data that's generated when users click, swipe, and navigate a site or app. Teams can view the data in aggregate to understand which behaviors are most common, or look at journeys, also called user flows, which show the order in which users took the actions. Behavioral analysis relies on behavioral data.

### Need of Behavioral Data for Companies

Most product, marketing, and analytics teams live in constant pursuit of the question, "How are customers using the product, if at all?" Behavioral analytics software provides concrete answers with a visual interface where teams can segment users, run reports, and deduce customers' needs and interests.

Without behavioral analytics, teams are stuck using insufficiently detailed demographic data and so-called vanity metrics. If a company wants to personalize its service to users, it needs their behavior data. A streaming movie platform can't know that a user loves horror films, for instance, simply based on their age, gender, or nationality.

Behavioral analytics can provide user-level data so teams can answer questions like:

- What do users click within the product?
- Where do users get stuck?
- How do users react to feature changes?
- How long do users take from first click to conversion?
- How do users react to marketing messages?
- Which ads are the most effective?
- Can the team nudge users to be more successful?

Conducting behavioral analysis is more complicated than simply running reports in the analytics tool. "Analyzing generic data doesn't magically produce answers to unidentified problems," Teams must first identify what they want to achieve and write down the paths they expect users to take. Only with preset expectations can teams identify whether users are deviating from the ideal path and redirect them.

The tech-driven insurance provider Lemonade, for instance, adjusted its user paths to increase revenue. The team knew their goal was to convert more website and app visitors into paying customers and with Mixpanel analytics, they noticed a "staggering drop-off" in user flow right before the point of purchase. By analyzing the page where the drop-off occurred, the team realized it was due to a technical error and a weak call-to-action (CTA). They fixed the bug and reworded the CTA, which led to a 50 percent increase in the number of users who purchased additional coverage.

What sets behavioral analytics apart from other types of business analytics is that it combines two technologies: user segmentation and event tracking. While some analytics vendors only offer one or the other—user data or event data—behavioral analytics unites the two for a complete customer view. It ties users to the events they trigger to produce a map of their actions, also known as a user flow, or customer journey.

Viewed either alone or in aggregate, user journeys tell stories that teams can use to tweak and improve their product development, marketing, and launch strategies.

## Steps to Successful Behavioral Analysis

Customer behavioral analysis requires careful planning and each team's success is a function of how carefully they implement the analytics tool and how seriously they take their tracking plan.

Behavioral analysis is not a race. The first half of the implementation process should be spent planning and all teams who will eventually benefit from user intelligence need to have a hand in selecting and deploying the tool.

Teams can prepare themselves to conduct user behavior analysis in five steps:

## Select Goals, KPIs and Metrics

To determine whether users are reaching the right goals, such as purchases or conversions, teams must select the KPIs and metrics that indicate progress toward those goals. A fitness app that makes money through monthly subscriptions, for instance, can track paid subscriber growth. An enterprise resource planning (ERP) software that relies on annual contracts, on the other hand, can track users that complete the onboarding sequence.

## Define the most Desirable user Journeys

Based on the service or app's design, what are the most common paths for users to reach their goals? If the product has already been launched, teams can use actual user data to answer this question. If the product is pre-launch, the team can use the design team's wireframes of the suspected or intended flow.

All user journeys should end in some type of a desirable outcome for the customer or the business. An e-commerce website, for instance, can track a user from their first page visit to adding an item to their shopping cart to checkout because that flow leads to purchases. Alternatively, a streaming music app can track users as they move from its homepage to playing a song and, hopefully, purchasing that song.

## Create a Tracking Plan

Based on the user flow, teams can decide which events they'll need to track within the product. It can seem appealing to track everything but this is a mistake—too much data can clutter the analytics and make useful information more difficult to find. Track events and users based on whether the data is actually useful.

Some events contain, within them, multiple properties. The event for playing a song within a music app, for instance, could contain properties for the song title, genre, and artist.

To keep events and properties organized, companies typically create a tracking plan in a spreadsheet. This acts as a directory of all events and serves as a map for implementing the analytics tool. A tracking plan is a mutable document that should be revised and updated as the product, team, and goals change. To reduce the burden of trying to share and control access to the spreadsheet, Mixpanel offers a feature called Lexicon which stores the event name taxonomy for all to see.

Involve all teams—analytics, product, marketing, and engineering—in drafting the tracking plan. Members of each will need to understand how the users and events are named and organized if they're going to run reports and understand the results.

## Set a Unique Identifier for Users

Most digital products today exist across multiple platforms and this makes it difficult to track unique users. One user can appear to be multiple people unless assigned a unique identifier—either an email or string of characters—that persists across platforms and devices and connects the touch points along their journey. Teams should ensure their behavioral analytics platform vendor provides a unique identifier that won't change over time.

## Implement Analytics and begin Event Tracking

Once the tracking plan is complete, companies can deploy behavioral data analytics software and use its SDK or API to integrate it with their products. That's when they assign a unique identifier for users and set up user and event properties as outlined in the tracking plan.

It's not uncommon for teams to discover additional events they want to track during implementation. This isn't an issue as long as they update both the tracking plan and the analytics service.

Before the tracking system goes live, teams should use test devices to verify the event and user tracking is firing properly. Once working, teams are ready to begin analyzing their users.

## Applying Results of Behavioral Analytics

Most teams study their users with segmentation, which allows them to separate users based on characteristics and behaviors. An e-commerce app, for example, can create a segment for recent users who added items to a shopping cart but then abandoned. Or, they could filter for power shoppers who access the app multiple times a day.

Segmentation allows teams to learn about their users to build more complete customer profiles. They can save user segmentations, known as cohorts, and make adjustments to their product and marketing to make it more profitable with each segment.

Media and entertainment company STARZ PLAY, for instance, segmented users that signed up through its free trial offer and found that some users were gaming the system for multiple trials. By creating alerts for the negative behavior, the product team closed the loophole and saved 8x on its marketing spend.

Here are other industry applications for user behavior analytics:

- E-commerce sites can predict future trends and increase conversion rates.
- Consumer messaging apps can increase usage.
- Insurance companies can sell additional products.
- Travel sites can increase bookings.

- Online gaming platforms can attract more users.

Teams can track users' progress toward outcomes such as purchases or signups with funnel reports. Funnels display a series of stages in a user journey, as well as how many users are progressing from one stage to the next. A fitness app could use funnels to see how many users progress from download to signup and purchase. If one stage has a low conversion rate, it's a signal that that stage needs attention.

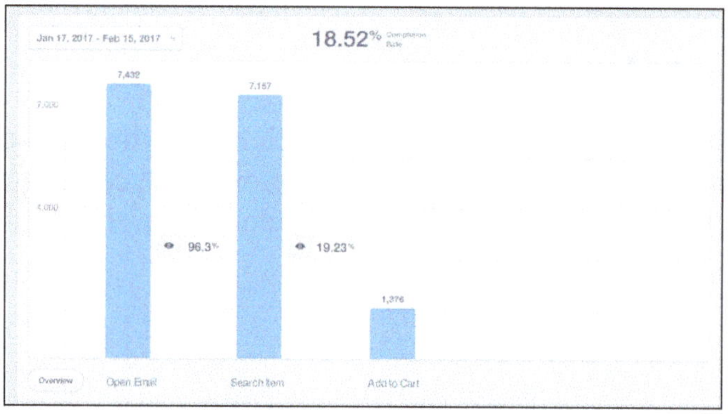


Funnel data allows teams to A/B test different buttons, messages, and images, to see if small changes improve conversions. The peer-to-peer shopping app Grabr, for instance, noticed conversions for referred users was low. The team tested new variants of the landing page and increased referral conversions 2x. The data can also be used to personalize parts of an app or website, say, to greet returning users, or present prospects with content relevant to their industry.

Teams can also use funnel data to deduce which behaviors are correlated with high retention. A media site, for instance, could look at the cohort of users that continue to return to the site eight weeks after signup to see if they share certain behaviors, such as a propensity to leave comments.

## Cohort Analysis

Cohort analysis is a subset of behavioral analytics that takes the data from a given data set (e.g. an EMRS, an e-commerce platform, web application, or online game) and rather than looking at all users as one unit, it breaks them into related groups for analysis. These related groups, or cohorts, usually share common characteristics or experiences within a defined time-span. Cohort analysis allows a company to "see patterns clearly across the life-cycle of a customer (or user), rather than slicing across all customers blindly without accounting for the natural cycle that a customer undergoes." By seeing these patterns of time, a company can adapt and tailor its service to those specific cohorts. While cohort analysis is sometimes associated with a cohort study, they are different and should not be viewed as one and the same. Cohort analysis is specifically the analysis of cohorts in regards to big data and business analytics, while in cohort study, data is broken down into similar groups.

Examples:

The goal of a business analytic tool is to analyze and present actionable information. In order for a company to act on such information it must be relevant to the situation under analysis. A database full of thousands or even millions of entries of all user data makes it tough to gain actionable data, as that data spans many different categories and time periods. Actionable cohort analysis allows for the ability to drill down to the users of each specific cohort to gain a better understanding of their behaviors, such as if users checked out, and how much did they pay. In cohort analysis "each new group (cohort) provides the opportunity to start with a fresh set of users," allowing the company to look at only the data that is relevant to the current query and act on it.

In eCommerce, a firm may only be interested in customers who signed up in the last two weeks and who made a purchase, which is an example of a specific cohort. A software developer may only care about the data from users who sign up after a certain upgrade, or who use certain features of the platform.

An example of cohort analysis of gamers on a certain platform: Expert gamers, cohort 1, will care more about advanced features and lag time compared to new sign-ups, cohort 2. With these two cohorts determined, and the analysis run, the gaming company would be presented with a visual representation of the data specific to the two cohorts. It could then see that a slight lag in load times has been translating into a significant loss of revenue from advanced gamers, while new sign-ups have not even noticed the lag. Had the company simply looked at its overall revenue reports for all customers, it would not have been able to see the differences between these two cohorts. Cohort analysis allows a company to pick up on patterns and trends and make the changes necessary to keep both advanced and new gamers happy.

## Deep Actionable Cohort Analytics

"An actionable metric is one that ties specific and repeatable actions to observed results (like user registration, or checkout). The opposite of actionable metrics are vanity metrics (like web hits or number of downloads) which only serve to document the current state of the product but offer no insight into how we got here or what to do next." Without actionable analytics the information that is being presented may not have any practical application, as the only data points represent vanity metrics that do not translate into any specific outcome. While it is useful for a company to know how many people are on their site, that metric is useless on its own. For it to be actionable it needs to relate a "repeatable action to an observed result".

## Performing Cohort Analysis

In order to perform a proper cohort analysis, there are four main stages:

- Determine what question you want to answer: The point of the analysis is to come up with actionable information on which to act in order to improve business, product, user experience, turnover, etc. To ensure that happens, it is important that the right question is asked. In the gaming example above, the company was unsure why they were losing revenue as lag time increased, despite the fact that users were still signing up and playing games.
- Define the metrics that will be able to help you answer the question: A proper cohort analysis requires the identification of an event, such as a user checking out, and specific properties, like how much the user paid. The gaming example measured a customer's willingness to buy gaming credits based on how much lag time there was on the site.
- Define the specific cohorts that are relevant. In creating a cohort, one must either analyze all the users and target them or perform attribute contribution in order to find the relevant

differences between each of them, ultimately to discover and explain their behavior as a specific cohort. The above example splits users into "basic" and "advanced" users as each group differs in actions, pricing structure sensitivities, and usage levels.

- Perform the cohort analysis: The analysis above was done using data visualization which allowed the gaming company to realize that their revenues were falling because their higher-paying advanced users were not using the system as the lag time increased. Since the advanced users were such a large portion of the company's revenue, the additional basic user signups were not covering the financial losses from losing the advanced users. In order to fix this, the company improved their lag times and began catering more to their advanced users.

# Collections Analytics

Debt collection companies are now turning to speech analytics in order to help them reduce delinquencies and mitigate losses allowing businesses to maximize their accounts receivable recovery. Collection analytics aids to understand customer preferences and behavior patterns, which in turn helps in developing better collection strategies.

Collection strategies are primarily needed to improve productivity. It is not feasible to hire agents (which costs money) to keep making collection calls from a list of payments due. Collection strategies help to determine which accounts have a higher probability of losses, categorize the different types of customers, and prioritize and target customers.

## Working of Collection Analytics

Collection analytics gives valuable information about the customer which can help develop varied collection strategies in different stages of obtaining due payment. There are primarily three stages of collection, which can be broadly classified as the early stage, the mid-stage and the final stage of collection.

In the early stage of consumer default, there is a higher chance of self-cure (i.e., customers are likely to pay by themselves without the need to make collection calls). Analytics play a vital role in identifying which customers, based on their behavior pattern (such as payments made before or after due date) are likely to pay on their own.

The mid-stage deals with customers that the collection agencies need to focus their efforts on. Here again, analytics can help segment the customers as high, medium or low risk. A risk score is a metric indicating how likely a consumer is to make payments on time, while a collection score is a metric indicating the most probable amount a delinquent consumer is likely to pay.

Collection strategies can then be targeted to recover maximum money from high-risk customers and to determine follow up intervals. A possible change in loan terms for the medium and high-risk groups is also determined.

The final stage normally deals with considering the account as a write-off. However, collection analytics steps in to decide whether the payment default is due to mismanaged finances, bad economy or the financial situation of the customer. These parameters help in deciding a hardship plan and renegotiation terms to retain the customer.

## Collection Analytics Helps in Developing the Following Types of Strategies

Collection analytics help in developing different strategies for maximum efficiency. Some of which are:

- Customer Segmentation: Customers and accounts are segmented and prioritized based on a score assigned to them.
- Contact Time: History of response data and outbound calls made helps determine the best time to contact the customer. It helps in initiating calls at times and places where the customer is most probable to answer. This increases contact efficiency and allows for directing efforts towards high-risk accounts.
- Contact Script: Based on the profile of the customer, analytics can help in setting the correct tone for agents to make their pitch.
- Call Rotation: Different calling strategies are set in place so that the customer is contacted at different times during the day and multiple times a week. This ensures that the customer is not expecting a collection call, which increases the likelihood of the call being answered.
- Contact Methods: Collection analytics help in making cost-effective decisions by making the right choice of contact methods. Some customers respond well to technology such as voice mail and online text/chat, while others are more likely to respond to print mail with payment options and settlement offers. Depending on the stage of delinquency, some customers might need to be contacted by phone calls.

## Benefits of Collection Analytics

Collection analytics is beneficial for organizations in developing and implementing an overall collection strategy. Key areas impacted by collection analytics include:

- Staffing Needs: Estimating the collection staff is the most important aspect of cost savings. Collection analytics helps organizations employ an accurate number of agents with the right skills.
- Accurate Penetration: Collection analytics plays an important role in penetrating targeted customers. The data correlation between attempted calls to actual contact with the customer is a valuable score given to agents when making calls.
- Bonus and Incentives: In order to increase agent efficiency, collection analytics helps in determining the rewards or incentives that need to be associated with the collection. For example, if there is an incentive attached to the dollar amount collected, agents are likely to be more aggressive when seeking payments.

Collection analytics helps increase collection efficiency, reduces costs, increases recovered amounts, enhances customer service, increases customer retention, reduces debt write-offs and maximizes account receivables.

Furthermore, collection analytics gives insights into customer behavior and delinquency that helps prepare customer profile data and create customer segments. All of these analytics help in creating flexible collection strategies.

# Financial Analytics

Financial analytics is a concept that provides different views on the business' financial data. It helps give in-depth knowledge and take strategic actions against them to improve your business' overall performance. Financial analytics is a subset of BI & EPM and has an impact on every aspect of your business. It plays a crucial role in calculating your business' profit. It helps you answer every business question related to your business while letting your forecast the future of your business.

## Importance of Financial Analytics

- Today's businesses require timely information for decision-making purposes.
- Every company needs prudent financial planning and forecasting.
- The diverse needs of the traditional financial department, and advancements in technology, all point to the need for financial analytics.
- Financial analytics can help shape up the business' future goals. It can help you improve the decision-making strategies for your business.
- Financial analytics can help you focus on measuring and managing your business' tangible assets such as cash and equipment.
- It provides an in-depth insight into the organization's financial status and improves the cash flow, profitability, and business value.

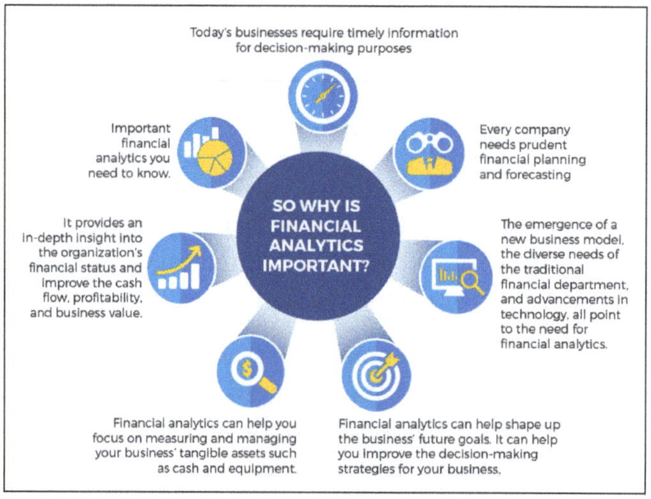


## Important Financial Analytics you Need to Know

In today's data-driven world, analytics is critical for any business that wants to remain competitive.

Financial analytics can help you understand your business' past and present performance and make strategic decisions. Here are some of the critical financial analytics that any company, size notwithstanding, should be implementing:

## Predictive Sales Analytics

Sales revenue is critical for every business. As such, accurate sales projection has essential strategic and technical implications for the organization. A predictive sales analytics involves coming up with an informed sales forecast. There are many approaches to predicting sales, such as the use of correlation analysis or use of past trends to forecast your sales. Predictive sales analytics can help you plan and manage your business' peaks and troughs.

## Client Profitability Analytics

Every business needs to differentiate between clients that make them money and clients that lose them money. Customer profitability typically falls within the 80/20 rule, where 20 percent of the clients account for 80 percent of the profits, and 20 percent of the clients account for 80 percent of customer-related expenses. Understanding of which is vital.

By understanding your customers' profitability, you will be able to analyze every client group and gains useful insight. However, the greatest challenge to customer profitability analytics comes in when you fail to analyze the client's contribution to the organization.

## Product Profitability Analytics

For organizations to remain competitive within an industry, organizations need to know where they are making, and losing money. Product profitability analytics can help you establish the profitability of every product rather than analyzing the business as a whole. To do this, you need to assess each product individually. Product profitability analytics can also help you establish profitability insights across the product range so you can make better decisions and protect your profit and growth over time.

## Cash Flow Analytics

You need a certain amount of cash to run the organization on a day-to-day basis. Cash flow is the lifeblood of your business. Understanding cash flow is crucial for gauging the health of the business. Cash flow analytics involves the use of real-time indicators like the Working Capital Ratio and Cash Conversion Cycle. You can also predict cash flow using tools like regression analysis. Besides helping with cash flow management and ensuring that you have enough money for day-to-day operations, cash flow analytics can also help you support a range of business functions.

## Value-driven Analytics

Most organizations have a sense of where they are going to and what they are hoping to achieve. These goals can be formal and listed on a strategy map that pinpoints the business' value drivers. These value drivers are the vital drivers that the organization needs to pull to realize its strategic goals. Value driver analytics assesses these levers to ensure that they can deliver the expected outcome.

### Shareholder Value Analytics

The profits and losses, and their interpretation by analysts, investors, and the media can influence your business' performance on the stock market. Shareholder value analytics calculates the value of the company by looking at the returns it is providing to shareholders. In other words, it measures the financial repercussions of a strategy and reports how much value the strategy in question is delivering to the shareholders. Shareholder value analytics is used concurrently with profit and revenue analytics. You can use tools like Economic Value Added (EVA) to measure the shareholder value analytics.

Financial analytics is a valuable tool that every organization, small and large, should use to manage and measure its progress. Done right, it can help the organization adapt to the trends that affect its operations.

## Market Analytics

A market analysis studies the attractiveness and the dynamics of a special market within a special industry. It is part of the industry analysis and thus in turn of the global environmental analysis. Through all of these analyses, the strengths, weaknesses, opportunities and threats (SWOT) of a company can be identified. Finally, with the help of a SWOT analysis, adequate business strategies of a company will be defined. The market analysis is also known as a documented investigation of a market that is used to inform a firm's planning activities, particularly around decisions of inventory, purchase, work force expansion/contraction, facility expansion, purchases of capital equipment, promotional activities, and many other aspects of a company.

### Market Segmentation

Market segmentation is the basis for a differentiated market analysis. Differentiation is important. One main reason is the saturation of consumption, which exists due to the increasing competition in offered products. Consumers ask for more individual products and services and are better informed about the range of products than before. As a consequence, market segmentation is necessary. Segmentation includes a lot of market research, since a lot of market knowledge is required to segment the market. Market research about market structures and processes must be done to define the "relevant market". The relevant market is an integral part of the whole market, on which the company focuses its activities. To identify and classify the relevant market, a market classification or segmentation has to be done.

Market segmentation is an important way to find competitive advantage with its differentiation in market analysis. Market segmentation concentrates on market energy and power to gain competitive advantage. In other words, market segmentation is the concept tool to get the force. In market analysis, market knowledge is required to analyze market structure and process. Since segmentation requires a lot of market research, various information can be extracted from it. Market segmentation can identify customer needs and wants and develop products to their satisfaction. Market segmentation can identify different products for different groups, better match customer wants and product benefits, maximize the use of available resources and focus marketing expenditures and competitive advantages.

There is no specific way to segment market. However, businesses can follow generalized rules like geographic, demographic, psychographic, and behavioral. A good market segmentation should be sustainable, accessible, actionable, measurable, and differentiable.

## Dimensions of Market Analysis

David A. Aaker outlined the following dimensions of a market analysis:

- Market size (current and future).
- Market trends.
- Market growth rate.
- Market profitability.
- Industry cost structure.
- Distribution channels.
- Key success factors.
- Key success details.

Market analysis strives to determine the attractiveness of a market, currently and in the future. Organizations evaluate future attractiveness of a market by understanding evolving opportunities, and threats as they relate to that organization's own strengths and weaknesses.

Organizations use these findings to guide the investment decisions they make to advance their success. The findings of a market analysis may motivate an organization to change various aspects of its investment strategy. Affected areas may include inventory levels, a work force expansion/ contraction, facility expansion, purchases of capital equipment, and promotional activities.

## Elements

### Market Size

The market size is defined through the market volume and the market potential. The market volume exhibits the totality of all realized sales volume of a special market. The volume is therefore dependent on the quantity of consumers and their ordinary demand. Furthermore, the market volume is either measured in quantities or qualities. The quantities can be given in technical terms, like GW for power capacities, or in numbers of items. Qualitative measuring mostly uses the sales turnover as an indicator. That means that the market price and the quantity are taken into account. Besides the market volume, the market potential is of equal importance. It defines the upper limit of the total demand and takes potential clients into consideration. Although the market potential is rather fictitious, it offers good values of orientation. The relation of market volume to market potential provides information about the chances of market growth. The following are examples of information sources for determining market size:

- Government data.
- Trade association data.

- Financial data from major players.
- Customer surveys.

## Market Trends

Market trends are the upward or downward movement of a market, during a period of time. The market size is more difficult to estimate if one is starting with something completely new. In this case, you will have to derive the figures from the number of potential customers, or customer segments.

Besides information about the target market, one also needs information about one's competitors, customers, products, etc. Lastly, you need to measure marketing effectiveness. A few techniques are:

- Customer analysis.
- Choice modeling.
- Competitor analysis.
- Risk analysis.
- Product research.
- Advertising the research.
- Marketing mix modeling.
- Simulated Test Marketing.

Changes in the market are important because they often are the source of new opportunities and threats. Moreover, they have the potential to dramatically affect the market size.

Examples include changes in economic, social, regulatory, legal, and political conditions and in available technology, price sensitivity, demand for variety, and level of emphasis on service and support.

## Market Growth Rate

A simple means of forecasting the market growth rate is to extrapolate historical data into the future. While this method may provide a first-order estimate, it does not predict important turning points. A better method is to study market trends and sales growth in complementary products. Such drivers serve as leading indicators that are more accurate than simply extrapolating historical data.

Important inflection points in the market growth rate sometimes can be predicted by constructing a product diffusion curve. The shape of the curve can be estimated by studying the characteristics of the adoption rate of a similar product in the past.

Ultimately, many markets mature and decline. Some leading indicators of a market's decline include market saturation, the emergence of substitute products, and/or the absence of growth drivers.

## Market Opportunity

A market opportunity for a product or a service, based on either one technology or several, fulfills the needs of a (preferably increasing) market better than the competition and better than substitution-technologies within the given environmental frame (e.g. society, politics, legislation, etc.).

## Market Profitability

While different organizations in a market will have different levels of profitability, they are all similar to different market conditions. Michael Porter devised a useful framework for evaluating the attractiveness of an industry or market. This framework, known as Porter five forces analysis, identifies five factors that influence the market profitability:

- Buyer power.
- Supplier power.
- Barriers to entry.
- Threat of substitute products.
- Rivalry among firms in the industry.

## Industry Cost Structure

The cost structure is important for identifying key factors for success. To this end, Porter's value chain model is useful for determining where value is added and for isolating the costs.

The cost structure also is helpful for formulating strategies to develop a competitive advantage. For example, in some environments the experience curve effect can be used to develop a cost advantage over competitors.

## Distribution Channels

Examining the following aspects of the distribution system may help with a market analysis:

- Existing distribution channels - can be described by how direct they are to the customer.
- Trends and emerging channels - new channels can offer the opportunity to develop a competitive advantage.
- Channel power structure - for example, in the case of a product having little brand equity, retailers have negotiating power over manufacturers and can capture more margin.

## Success Factors

The key success factors are those elements that are necessary in order for the firm to achieve its marketing objectives. A few examples of such factors include:

- Access to essential unique resources.
- Ability to achieve economies of scale.

- Access to distribution channels.
- Technological progress.

It is important to consider that key success factors may change over time, especially as the product progresses through its life cycle.

## Environmental Analysis

The environmental analysis can be divided into two parts which are external and internal factors. External factors. Political issues, social potential force, and local economy called external environmental factors. Internal environmental factors belongs to company's internal position such as employees, department structure, budget and so forth (Christina, n.d.). How environmental effect markets. According to the Parry, the government limit pollution emission, they mention environmental taxes to prevent company which produce pollution substance. In other words, the government drives the organization. On the contrary, the cost of products increase due to the environmental taxes. It means that company may take measure of reducing production which may grow unemployment rate by emission tax. Therefore, the environmental taxes leads an income equality. It is not an excuse ignore our serious environmental problem. Even though the higher income group also can benefit from windfall gains.

## Competitive Analysis

According to the Christina, competitive analysis is that company must know their competitors which have the same common services and products. The business can use like product cost, operational efficiency, brand recognition and market Dimensions of market analysis.

Except for David A. Aaker's 7 main dimension of a market analysis including market size, market growth rate, market profitability, industry cost structure, distribution channel, market trends, and key success factor, there is another analysis of dimension market analysis. Based on Christina Callaway, dimension of market analysis can be divided into four parts which is environmental analysis, competitive analysis, target audience analysis, and SWOT analysis. The market analysis is to help company to illustrate current trend in the market and may affect the profitability. At the same time, market analysis is also to determine the attractiveness in the market. A good marketing analysis can improve organization investment decision accurately, they can based on the attractiveness to change investment tactical.

The market analysis is to help company to illustrate current trend in the market and may affect the profitability for the business. It can be seen as a part of industry analysis with using global environmental analysis. Company can identify strengths, weakness, opportunities and threats so that the business can define the business strategy. The market analysis is also reference for company's activity, like decisions of inventory, purchase, work force, facility expansion and many aspects of company.

Penetration to find the difference or competitive advantages between two similarly companies. How can we find the competitive advantage? Kevin says that "Anticipating and reading market needs can help business leaders take significant steps towards changing the game and obtaining competitive advantage.". How can we sustain competitive advantages? In terms of Richard research, the company should focus on sustaining competitive advantage due to the swift growth global competition. Therefore, Business practice management is the follow principle to maintain competitive advantage.

## Target Audience Analysis

In the Christina contribution, target audience is for company to target their customer group who most likely to buy their products. The group can be classified with location, age, gender, income, ethnicity, and behaviors. And people who make a decision of purchase can also be divided in the target audience. How identify market in accordance with Women's enterprise centre the market can be classified in three types which are consumer market, industrial market, and reseller market. The company segment their market, research market, and identify why customer would like to buy their products.

## SWOT Analysis

SWOT is strengths, weakness, opportunities, and threats. It matches internal strengths and weaknesses up against opportunities and threats. Strengths and weakness are internal factors which we can control. And opportunities and threats are external factors that businesses cannot control, but can however impact on. When using strengths and weakness, businesses need to collect raw data to get information. Businesses can get information by customer feedback, employee surveys. Furthermore, businesses also can identify the capability if it is weakness or strengths, resources and process. Opportunities and threats are the external factors. Business can get information from secondary data like environmental information, industry information and competitive data. The purpose of the business use the SWOT analysis is to get the information from it and match each other to develop the ideas and get into goal statement to form strategic development.

Market communication has significant impact on building and maintaining the relationship of stakeholders. Market analysis elements is to form a strategic planning and the information is responsiveness, intelligence generation, and dissemination. Besides, market communication provide the information focus on the customer needs and competitive advantage. At the same time, these information spread to customers means the company spread its brand value so that customer can make awareness of the company's products. It is the communication channel between business and customers.

## Market Segmentation

Market segmentation is one of the important ways to find competitive advantage with its differentiation in market analysis. Market segmentation concentrates on market energy and power to gain competitive advantage. In other words, market segmentation is the concept tool to get the force. In the market analysis, we need a lot of market knowledge to analyse market structure and process. Since segmentation needs to do a lot of market research so that we can get the information from it. Market segmentation recommends the market strategy. Market segmentation can identify customer needs and wants and develop products to satisfy them. Market segmentation can identify different products for different groups, better match between customer wants and product benefits, maximize the use of available resources, focus marketing expenditures and competitive advantages.

There is no perfect way to segment market but business can follow some rules like geographic, demographic, psychographic, and behavioral. A good market segmentation should be sustainable, accessible, actionable, measurable, and differentiable.

## Global Market Segmentation

Since the globalization more and more developed, the global market become indispensability part of the business thinking. In order to explore global market, how market segmentation can be used in the global market. There are some aspects of defining the global market so which is more efficient to segment global market. Some researchers mention about Cross-National and Cross-Cultural Approach to segment global market. To differentiate country and culture, the company have to identify two areas which is vertical market segment existing internal area. Another area is external market segments which a group of countries has relationship of each other and share their characteristics. Compared with cross- cultural approach and cross-national approach, cross-cultural approach has its cultural stability of traditional values. cultural stability has a wide range of shared national-cultural values features, due to group solidarity, interpersonal harmony and so forth. However, cross-cultural approach has challenge of environmental changes, cultural change and some other unstable factors. Therefore, the main principle of looking at cross-cultural approach and cross- national approach base on perceive service quality. In the global service marketing, the marketing manager face a challenge of international services on account of the intangibility of services, unification standardizing services across national borders and difference of preference for customized services in different countries and culture. Therefore, it is significance for business to have a deep understanding service quality in facing across different countries, regions and cultures.

In the software market, the trend of software is the price is high and coverage is low. In order to improve the trend, there is some problems of software market. Zhang mention that "(1) What possibly discourages product differentiation in such a competitive market? (2) Why is versioning absent here? (3) How does the presence of free alternatives in this market impact its structure?". In order to improve these problems, Zhang mention that quality competition and market segmentation apply to the software market. In Zhang's research, the software company lack of developed the method of quality competition, market segmentation, and versioning. In terms of market segmentation, software company think segmentation consumer market is not useful. Therefore, even though versioning is the least costless way of spread product information, the company still ignore it.

The relationship between market segmentation and communication in marketing is interaction. For example, market segmentation is important in the social media. There is three perspectives supplier perspectives, interaction perspectives, and buyer perspectives. In order to balance these three relationships, business must do segment well. Otherwise, the buyer perspective and supplier perspective cannot interact very well may lead loss of promotion. Therefore, social media is important method of communication in the market and market segmentation also unnecessary before the business use social media channel.

## Applications

The literature defines several areas in which market analysis is important. These include: sales forecasting, market research, and marketing strategy. Not all managers will need to conduct a market analysis. Nevertheless, it would be important for managers that use market analysis data to know how analysts derive their conclusions and what techniques they use to do so.

## Pricing Analytics

In marketing, Price Analysis refers to the analysis of consumer response to theoretical prices in survey research.

In general business, price analysis is the process of examining and evaluating a proposed price without evaluating its separate cost elements and proposed profit.

Price analysis may also refer to the breakdown of a price to a unit figure, usually per square metre or square foot of accommodation or per hectare or square metre of land. The price with suitable adjustment for various differences, is then applied to the valuation problem.

Pricing Analytics enables companies, across all industries, to dramatically improve profitability & market share by defining optimal prices & pricing strategy. Pricing Solutions leverages data to understand what drives your customers' buying decisions and integrates this knowledge to meet your pricing needs.

Pricing Solutions Applies Analytics to:

1. Optimize the Trade-Off Between Price, Volume and Profit.
2. Identify Quick Wins.
3. Develop High Impact Price Strategies.
4. Increase the Confidence of the Sales Force.

## Retail Analytics

Retail analytics focuses on providing insights related to sales, inventory, customers, and other important aspects crucial for merchants' decision-making process.

The discipline encompasses several granular fields to create a broad picture of a retail business' health, and sales alongside overall areas for improvement and reinforcement. Essentially, retail analytics is used to help make better choices, run businesses more efficiently, and deliver improved customer service analytics.

The field of retail analysis goes beyond superficial data analysis, using techniques like data mining and data discovery to sanitize datasets to produce actionable BI insights that can be applied in the short-term.

Moreover, companies use these analytics to create better snapshots of their target demographics. By harnessing sales data analysis, retailers can identify their ideal customers according to diverse categories such as age, preferences, buying patterns, location, and more.

Essentially, the field is focused not just on parsing data, but also defining what information is needed, how best to gather it, and most importantly, how it will be used.

By prioritizing retail analytics basics that focus on the process and not exclusively on data itself, companies can uncover stronger insights and be in a more advantageous position to succeed when attempting to predict business and consumer needs.

### Use of Retail Analytics

There are several excellent retail analytics examples that are relevant to a variety of companies. One of the biggest benefits the field delivers to companies is optimizing their inventory and procurement. Thanks to predictive tools, businesses can use historical data and trend analysis to determine which products they should order, and in what quantities instead of relying exclusively on past orders.

In addition, they can optimize inventory management to emphasize products customers need, reducing wasted space and associated overhead costs.

Apart from inventory activities, many retailers use analytics to identify customer trends and changing preferences by combining data from different areas. By merging sales data with a variety of factors, businesses can identify emerging trends and anticipate them better. This is closely tied to marketing functions, which also benefit from analytics.

Companies can harness retail analytics to improve their marketing campaigns by building an improved understanding of individual preferences and gleaning more granular insights. By blending demographic data with information such as shopping habits, preferences, and purchase history, companies can create strategies that focus on individuals and exhibit higher success rates.

## Affinity Analysis

Affinity analysis is a data analysis and data mining technique that discovers co-occurrence relationships among activities performed by (or recorded about) specific individuals or groups. In general, this can be applied to any process where agents can be uniquely identified and information about their activities can be recorded. In retail, affinity analysis is used to perform market basket analysis, in which retailers seek to understand the purchase behavior of customers. This information can then be used for purposes of cross-selling and up-selling, in addition to influencing sales promotions, loyalty programs, store design, and discount plans.

Examples:

Market basket analysis might tell a retailer that customers often purchase shampoo and conditioner together, so putting both items on promotion at the same time would not create a significant increase in revenue, while a promotion involving just one of the items would likely drive sales of the other.

Market basket analysis may provide the retailer with information to understand the purchase behavior of a buyer. This information will enable the retailer to understand the buyer's needs and rewrite the store's layout accordingly, develop cross-promotional programs, or even capture new buyers (much like the cross-selling concept). An apocryphal early illustrative example for this was when one super market chain discovered in its analysis that male customers that bought diapers often bought beer as well, have put the diapers close to beer coolers, and their sales increased dramatically. Although this urban legend is only an example that professors use to illustrate the concept to students, the explanation of this imaginary phenomenon might be that fathers that are sent out to buy diapers often buy a beer as well, as a reward. This kind of analysis is supposedly an example of the use of data mining. A widely used example of cross selling on the web with market basket analysis is Amazon.com's use of "customers who bought book A also bought book B", e.g. "People who read History of Portugal were also interested in Naval History".

Market basket analysis can be used to divide customers into groups. A company could look at what other items people purchase along with eggs, and classify them as baking a cake (if they are buying eggs along with flour and sugar) or making omelets (if they are buying eggs along with bacon and cheese). This identification could then be used to drive other programs. Similarly, it can be used to divide products into natural groups. A company could look at what products are most frequently sold together and align their category management around these cliques.

### Business Use

Business use of market basket analysis has significantly increased since the introduction of electronic point of sale. Amazon uses affinity analysis for cross-selling when it recommends products to people based on their purchase history and the purchase history of other people who bought the same item. Family Dollar plans to use market basket analysis to help maintain sales growth while moving towards stocking more low-margin consumable goods.

## Supply Chain Analytics

Supply chain analytics is the application of mathematics, statistics, predictive modeling and machine-learning techniques to find meaningful patterns and knowledge in order, shipment and transactional and sensor data. An important goal of supply chain analytics is to improve forecasting and efficiency and be more responsive to customer needs. For example, predictive analytics on point-of-sale terminal data stored in a demand signal repository can help a business anticipate consumer demand, which in turn can lead to cost-saving adjustments to inventory and faster delivery.

Achieving true end-to-end supply chain analytics, which starts with the procurement of raw materials and extends through production, distribution and aftermarket services, depends on effective integration between the many SCM and supply chain execution platforms that make up a typical company's supply chain. The goal of such integration is supply chain visibility: the ability to view data on goods at every step in the supply chain.

### Supply Chain Analytics Software

Supply chain analytics software is generally available in two forms: embedded in supply chain software, or in a separate, dedicated business intelligence and analytics tool that has access to supply chain data. Most ERP vendors offer supply chain analytics features, as do vendors of specialized supply chain management software.

Some ERP and SCM vendors have begun applying complex event processing (CEP) to their platforms for real-time supply chain analytics. Most ERP and SCM vendors have one-to-one integrations but there is no standard. However, the Supply Chain Operations Reference (SCOR) model provides standard metrics for comparing supply chain performance to industry benchmarks.

Ideally, supply chain analytics software would be applied to the entire chain, but in practice, it is often focused on key operational subcomponents, such as demand planning, manufacturing production, inventory management or transportation management. For example, supply chain finance analytics can help identify increased capital costs or opportunities to boost working capital and procure-to-pay analytics can help identify the best suppliers and provide early warning of budget overruns in certain expense categories, and transportation analytics software can predict the impact of weather on shipments.

## Importance of Supply Chain Analytics

Supply chain analytics can help an organization make smarter, quicker and more efficient decisions. Benefits include the ability to:

- Gain a significant return on investment: A recent Gartner survey revealed that 29 percent of surveyed organizations said they have achieved high levels of ROI by using analytics, compared with only four percent that achieved no ROI.
- Better understand risks: Supply chain analytics can identify known risks and help to predict future risks by spotting patterns and trends throughout the supply chain.
- Increase accuracy in planning: By analyzing customer data, supply chain analytics can help a business better predict future demand. It helps an organization decide what products can be minimized when they become less profitable or understand what customer needs will be after the initial order.
- Achieve the lean supply chain: Companies can use supply chain analytics to monitor warehouse, partner responses and customer needs for better-informed decisions.
- Prepare for the future: Companies are now offering advanced analytics for supply chain management. Advanced analytics can process both structured and unstructured data to give organizations an edge to get alerts on time to make the optimal decisions. It can build correlation and patterns among different sources to provide alerts that minimize risks at little cost and less sustainability impact.

As technologies such as AI become more commonplace in supply chain analytics, companies may see an explosion of further benefits. Information not previously processed because of the limitations of analyzing natural language data can now be analyzed in real time. AI can rapidly and comprehensively read, understand and correlate data from disparate sources, silos and systems. It can then provide real-time analysis based on interpretation of the data. Companies will have far broader supply chain intelligence. They can become more efficient and avoid disruptions — while supporting new business models.

## Evolution of Supply Chain Analytics

In the past, supply chain analytics was limited mostly to statistical analysis and quantifiable performance indicators for demand planning and forecasting. Data was stored in spreadsheets that came from different participants in the supply chain.

By the 1990s, companies were adopting Electronic Data Interchange (EDI) and Enterprise Resource Planning (ERP) systems to connect and exchange information among the supply chain partners. These systems provided easier access to data for analysis, along with assisting businesses in their designing, planning and forecasting.

In the 2000s, businesses began turning to business intelligence and predictive analytic software solutions. These solutions helped companies gain a more in-depth knowledge of how their supply chain networks were performing, how to make better decisions and how to optimize their networks.

The challenge today is how companies can best use the huge amounts of data generated in their supply chain networks. As recently as 2017, a typical supply chain accessed 50 times more data than just five years earlier. However, less than a quarter of this data was being analyzed. Further, while approximately 20 percent of all supply chain data is structured and can be easily analyzed, 80 percent of supply chain data is unstructured or dark data. Today's organizations are looking for ways to best analyze this dark data.

Studies are pointing to cognitive technologies or artificial intelligence as the next frontier in supply chain analytics. AI solutions go beyond information retention and process automation. AI software can think, reason and learn in a human-like manner. AI can also process tremendous amounts of data and information — both structured and unstructured data — and provide summaries and analyses of that information in an instant.

IDC estimates that by 2020, 50 percent of all business software will incorporate some cognitive computing functions. AI not only provides a platform for powerfully correlating and interpreting data from across systems and sources — it also allows organizations to analyze supply chain data and intelligence in real time. Coupled with emerging blockchain technologies, companies in the future will be able to proactively forecast and predict events.

The supply chain is the most obvious face of the business for customers and consumers. The better a company can perform supply chain analytics, the better it protects its business reputation and long-term sustainability.

The five "Cs" of the effective supply chain analytics of the future:

- Connected: Being able to access unstructured data from social media, structured data from the Internet of Things (IoT) and more traditional data sets available through traditional ERP and B2B integration tools.
- Collaborative: Improving collaboration with suppliers increasingly means the use of cloud-based commerce networks to enable multi-enterprise collaboration and engagement.
- Cyber-aware: The supply chain must harden its systems from cyber-intrusions and hacks, which should be an enterprise-wide concern.

- Cognitively enabled: The AI platform becomes the modern supply chain's control tower by collating, coordinating and conducting decisions and actions across the chain. Most of the supply chain is automated and self-learning.
- Comprehensive: Analytics capabilities must be scaled with data in real time. Insights will be comprehensive and fast. Latency is unacceptable in the supply chain of the future.

In today's supply chain networks, effective analytics requires the ability to become more customer centric — responding quickly while maintaining accuracy and integrity. Businesses are looking for supply chain analytical solutions that can quickly analyze huge amounts of data from disparate data sources, including unstructured and natural language-based data. Finally, supply chain analytics are being asked to predict an increasing number of supply chain variables — including external forces such as weather, war, workers and regulations.

## References

- What-is-collection-analytics-definitions-benefits-and-more: callminer.com, Retrieved 8 January, 2019
- What-is-financial-analytics: ecapitaladvisors.com, Retrieved 13 May, 2019
- Pricing-analytics: pricingsolutions.com, Retrieved 25 February, 2019
- Retail-analytics, glossary: sisense.com, Retrieved 16 January, 2019
- Supply-chain-analytics, definition: techtarget.com, Retrieved 30 April, 2019
- Supply-chain-analytics, supply-chain: ibm.com, Retrieved 29 March, 2019

# 5

# Applications of Business Analytics

Business analytics has a wide range of applications in different fields. Such fields include finance, HR analytics, customer relationship management, manufacturing, marketing, sales forecasting, credit card companies, etc. The topics elaborated in this chapter will help in gaining a better perspective about these diverse applications of business applications.

## Finance

BA is of utmost importance to the finance sector. Data Scientists are in high demand in investment banking, portfolio management, financial planning, budgeting, forecasting, etc. For example: Companies these days have a large amount of financial data. Use of intelligent Business Analytics tools can help use this data to determine the products' prices. Also, on the basis of historical information Business Analysts can study the trends on the performance of a particular stock and advise the client on whether to retain it or sell it.

Financial analytics is the creation of ad hoc analysis to answer specific business questions and forecast possible future financial scenarios. The goal of financial analytics is to shape the strategy for business through reliable, factual insight rather than intuition. By offering detailed views of companies' financial data, financial analytics provides the tools for firms to gain deep knowledge of key trends and take action to improve their performance.

As a subset of business intelligence and enterprise performance management, financial analytics affects all parts of a business and is crucial in helping companies predict and plan for the future. Financial analytics involves using massive amounts of financial and other relevant data to identify patterns to make predictions, such as what a customer might buy or how long an employee's tenure might be. With a wealth of financial and other relevant data from various departments throughout their organizations, corporate financial teams are increasingly leveraging this data to help company leaders make informed decisions and boost the company's value. By helping businesses understand their top- and bottom-line performance (along with other indicators, including financial and macroeconomic data), measure and manage their assets, and forecast variations within the organizations and industries in which they compete, financial analytics offers insight into organizations' financial status and improves the profitability, cash flow and value of the business. Financial analytics also helps companies improve income statements and business processes.

Business transformation and advances in technology -- from big data to customer analytics software to data warehouses -- have contributed to companies' move to use financial analytics. The changing role of corporate finance department is also having an impact. Chief financial officers traditionally relied on historical data and trends to forecast future performance. However, they are changing their focus as they increasingly tap into technologies, such as advanced data analytics, machine learning and automation. As finance departments have begun adopting financial analytics to home in on what's happening in the business and what that's likely to mean going forward, their roles have changed from "information provider" to "problem solver". Having more timely access to information is helping companies make quicker, better informed business decisions.

Many experts consider predictive analytics an essential element in the digital transformation of finance. A key part of this is the ability to examine historical and new data to assess what's relevant to a specific company - be it macroeconomic data, industry trends or petroleum prices - to improve forecasting and decision-making.

The application of analytics is crucial in financial services and other data-intensive fields. Financial services businesses, including investment banks, generate and store more data than just about any other business in any other sector, mainly because finance is a transaction-heavy industry. While banks have, for many years, used data to measure and quantify risk, data analysts are now taking on the role of influential internal consultants, responsible for communicating to senior executives key insights on how to improve the organization's overall profitability. Today's financial institutions not only analyze structured data, such as market or trading data, but also unstructured data, which can include data sources from news outlets, social media and marketing materials.

## Importance of Financial Analytics

Financial analytics can help companies determine the risks they face, how to enhance and extend the business processes that make them run more effectively, and whether organizations' investments are focused on the right areas. Advanced analytics and its ability to leverage big data will enable organizations to rethink their strategies for solving problems and supporting business decisions. Analytics can also help companies examine the profitability of products across various sales channels and customers, which market segments will add more profit to the business and what could have an impact on the business in the future.

Continuous visibility into financial and operational performance will help with more than just decision-making; it will also increase visibility regarding the processes that support those decisions. So, rather than getting data on employee turnover rates and the related costs after the fact, financial analysts and HR leaders will be able to see what problems employees are having and intervene to improve performance and prevent costly turnover. Another plus is the potential for improved electronic linkage of records across the supply chain so that data will only need to be entered once.

Despite the promise of financial analytics, business experts from the academic and corporate worlds warn against automating bad processes. They note that the processes that provide financial insights based on historical data are often disconnected and leave serious data gaps. Poor-quality data can hurt business performance and lead to incomplete or inaccurate customer or prospect data, ineffective marketing and communications efforts, increased spending and bad decisions. To improve results, companies should use predictive analytics properly, improve the quality of their data and manage it effectively.

## Types of Financial Analysis

Financial analysis refers to the process of evaluating businesses, projects, budgets and other finance-related entities to determine the stability, solvency, liquidity or profitability of an organization. In addition to focusing on income statements, balance sheets and cash flow statements, financial analysis is employed for evaluating economic trends, setting financial policy, formulating long-term business plans and pinpointing projects or companies for investment.

Types of financial analysis include the following:

- Horizontal analysis refers to the side-by-side comparison of an organization's financial performance for consecutive reporting periods. The aim is to determine major shifts in the data. Later, this information could be applied to a more detailed analysis of financial results.
- Vertical analysis pertains to the proportional analysis of a financial statement. Each line item on a financial statement is listed as a percentage of another item - for example, every line item on an income statement is provided as a percentage of gross sales, while every line item on a balance sheet is given as a percentage of total assets.
- Short-term analysis provides a detailed review of working capital, involving the calculation of turnover rates for accounts receivable, inventory and accounts payable. Any differences from the long-term average turnover rate should be studied further because working capital is a significant user of cash.
- Multi-company comparison entails tallying and comparing major financial ratios of two organizations, usually in the same industry sector. The aim is to determine the companies' relative financial strengths and weaknesses.
- Industry comparison contrasts the results of a specific business and the average results of an entire industry. The purpose is to determine any unusual results in comparison to the industry average.

## Key Types of Financial Analytics

Examining financial and other relevant information, financial analytics offers various views of companies' past, present and future performance. The following are key types of analytics that can help companies of different sizes:

- Predictive sales analytics may include the use of correlation analysis or past trends to forecast corporate sales.
- Client profitability analytics helps differentiate between clients who make money for a company and those who don't.
- Product profitability analytics entails assessing each product individually, rather than establishing profitability overall at a company.

- Cash-flow analytics employs real-time indicators, including the working capital ratio and cash conversion cycle, and may include tools such as regression analysis to predict cash flow.
- Value-driven analytics assesses a business' value drivers, or the key "levers" the organization needs to pull to achieve its goals.
- Shareholder value analytics, which is used to tally the value of a company by examining the returns it provides to shareholders, is used concurrently with profit and revenue analytics.

### Financial Analytics Software Programs

As the way information is now collected and analyzed presents a significant shift - along with new challenges - software can help reduce the complexity. Financial analysis software can speed up the creation of reports and present the data in an executive dashboard, a graphical presentation that is easier to read and interpret than a series of spreadsheets with pivot tables.

Popular financial analysis software programs include:

- Oracle Financial Analytics - Modular component of Oracle's integrated family of business intelligence software applications. Enables insight into the general ledger, provides visibility into performance against budget and the way staffing costs and employee or supplier performance affects revenue and customer satisfaction.
- SAP ERP Financial Analytics - Helps organizations define financial goals, develop business plans and monitor costs and revenue during execution.
- SAS Business Analytics - Provides an integrated environment for data mining, text mining, simulation and predictive modeling - A mathematical model that predicts future outcomes - as well as descriptive modeling, a mathematical model that describes historical events and the relationships that created them.
- IBM Cognos Finance - Provides out of the box data analysis capabilities for sales, supply chain procurement and workforce management functions.
- NetSuite - Provides financial dashboards, reporting and analytic functions that allow personal key performance indicators to be monitored in real time.
- MATLAB - Allows developers to interface with programs developed in different languages, which makes it possible to harness the unique strengths of each language for various purposes.

## HR Analytics

Analytics is based on data. HR analytics is the science of gathering, organizing and analyzing the data related to HR functions like recruitment, talent management, employee engagement, performance and retention to ensure better decision making in all these areas. By using various types of HR software and technology, HR departments are creating a large amount of data every day. However, the objective of HR analytics is to actually make sense of this data and turn it into a valuable insight.

## Benefits of HR Analytics

Application of HR analytics results in a number of strategic and operational advantages to HR:

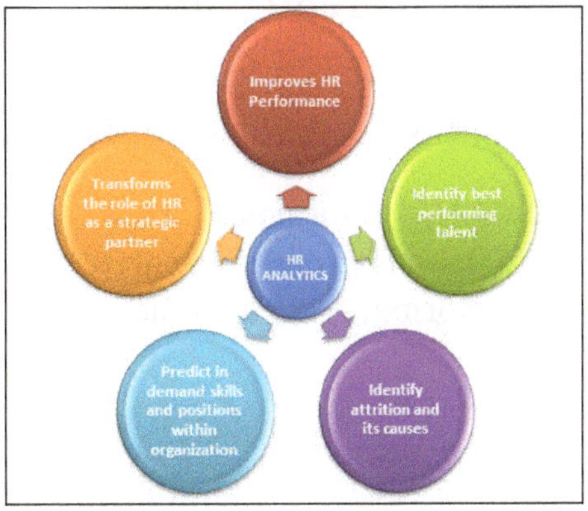


- Increased need for data and analytics tool in HR to make better HR decisions.
- Better Quality of Hire is one of the HR data analytics benefits.
- A vital benefit of HR metrics and analytics is Employee Retention.
- Transformation of HR as a strategic partner is one of the benefits of Workforce analytics.
- Business analytics in HR can help predict the hiring needs of an organization.

## Increased Need for Data and Analytics Tool in HR to make Better HR Decisions

An important role of HR analytics is to provide access to critical data and insights about the workforce which can be then analysed for making better decisions. Not only does it improve the HR performance but also provides a better understanding of what motivates employees to work productively, and how do the organizational culture affects employee performance.

## Better Quality of Hire is One of the HR Data Analytics Benefits

Running machine learning algorithms on jobseeker's data allows companies to identify the best matching talent for a vacant position, thus improving the quality of hire.

## A Vital Benefit of HR Metrics and Analytics is Employee Retention

Similarly, using employee data, recruiters can recognize a pattern of high performing employees and accordingly modify their employee hiring and retention strategy. HR analytics helps identify the departments suffering from the maximum attrition and the reasons causing it. It can also help HR in identifying the activities which have the maximum impact on employee engagement and thus allow organizations to invest in such activities.

## Transformation of HR as a Strategic Partner is one of the Benefits of Workforce Analytics

The application of HR analytics can provide a unique vantage point to HR department to validate its importance and its role as a strategic partner in a business' performance. HR professionals can provide business leaders with verifiable data to back their talent hiring, retention and engagement policies.

## Business Analytics in HR can help Predict the Hiring Needs of an Organization

HR analytics can help predict the changes that may be in the organization's future. Using HR analytics, one can predict the skills and positions which are needed to improve business performance.

With the manifestation of HR technology on a never before scale, we can assume there will be more focus areas adding to this list where HR analytics can play a role in ensuring better HR performance and improving business performance an a whole.

## Challenges of HR Analytics

It is true that the various HR tools being used today churn out huge amount of data every day, but without the clarity of how that data can be useful for a particular decision making process, it is difficult to tap into the true power of HR analytics. Although there are many local challenges that a company might face while implementing a HR analytics strategy, the major challenges that HR analytics face globally boil down to:

- Multiple sources of data: With different HR tools catering to different functions of HR, there are too many sources of data working in isolation. Whether it is your HR information system, Applicant tracking system, learning management system or an employee referral software, every tool creates its own data and integrating it with the other sources is a major challenge. You could be surprised to know that data scientists spend 85% of their time just collecting and cleaning data, i.e separating the useful data from noise. Also, you cannot use the data from one source in isolation while making a strategic business decisions. Thus a major challenge is to integrate these silo systems and make them communicate with each other.
- Lack of Skills and Training: While it's true that data scientists are at the forefront of this data & analytics revolution, hiring managers and even CHROs have a preconceived notion that HR departments have little to no role to play in analyzing the data. Considering the technicalities involved, they hesitate to learn and implement these tools, supported by a mindset which is fearful of the learning curve. The HR managers would rather rely on their human intellect and understanding than going through training for a HR analytic tool. They often fall back on a faulty argument that machine intelligence will take out human from human resources, which is not at all true.

## Methods to use HR Analytics

Despite these challenges, organizations are committed towards utilizing the benefits of HR analytics and use it in the following ways:

- Long term planning and strategic decision making: Most top performing businesses use data not to make windfall gains but to forecast and plan for future. Using data to analyze the ROI of various programs and initiatives helps make better decisions for company's future.

- Using automated tools: Using automation tools and automated processes not only reduce data errors due to human factors but also give time for more important strategic tasks. Evolving to these tools is one of the easy ways to utilize the real power of HR analytics.
- Building an analytics savvy HR team: It is good to have data but without a team which feels comfortable with data, one is still stuck with age old methods. Therefore, building a HR Tech savvy team of human resource professional, either by training or reskilling or new hiring, is going to be mandatory in future. Top performing organizations are already working towards enabling digital transformation in their human resources department.

### Disadvantages of HR Analytics

While the advantages of HR Analytics are immense, there are also a couple of disadvantages to using it in the current scenario. Since HRs deal with huge amount of sensitive and confidential data, security and privacy are two main concerns. Any HR analytics system which handles this data must be designed to prevent any unauthorized access. There have to be multiple levels of access and the system must be constantly monitored for any data theft. Maintaining such a system will obviously lead to greater costs and that's the second main disadvantage to implementing HR analytics. High acquisition and maintenance costs mostly act as a deterrent, especially for smaller companies to implement such a system. Also, operating a sophisticated HR analytics tool requires special expertise and that results in additional training costs, or the costs of hiring an IT expert to handle this system.

However, since HR analytics is still in development stage, HR are still awakening to its immense potential, there will soon be a time when using these tools will become far easier and cost effective.

## Customer Relationship Management

Customer relationship management (CRM) is an approach to manage a company's interaction with current and potential customers. It uses data analysis about customers' history with a company to improve business relationships with customers, specifically focusing on customer retention and ultimately driving sales growth.

One important aspect of the CRM approach is the systems of CRM that compile data from a range of different communication channels, including a company's website, telephone, email, live chat, marketing materials and more recently, social media. Through the CRM approach and the systems used to facilitate it, businesses learn more about their target audiences and how to best cater to their needs.

### Types

### Strategic

Strategic CRM is concentrated upon the development of a customer-centric business culture.

## Operational

The primary goal of customer relationship management systems is to integrate and automate sales, marketing, and customer support. Therefore, these systems typically have a dashboard that gives an overall view of the three functions on a single customer view, a single page for each customer that a company may have. The dashboard may provide client information, past sales, previous marketing efforts, and more, summarizing all of the relationships between the customer and the firm. Operational CRM is made up of 3 main components: sales force automation, marketing automation, and service automation.

- Sales force automation works with all stages in the sales cycle, from initially entering contact information to converting a prospective client into an actual client. It implements sales promotion analysis, automates the tracking of a client's account history for repeated sales or future sales and coordinates sales, marketing, call centers, and retail outlets. It prevents duplicate efforts between a salesperson and a customer and also automatically tracks all contacts and follow-ups between both parties.
- Marketing automation focuses on easing the overall marketing process to make it more effective and efficient. CRM tools with marketing automation capabilities can automate repeated tasks, for example, sending out automated marketing emails at certain times to customers, or posting marketing information on social media. The goal with marketing automation is to turn a sales lead into a full customer. CRM systems today also work on customer engagement through social media.
- Service automation is the part of the CRM system that focuses on direct customer service technology. Through service automation, customers are supported through multiple channels such as phone, email, knowledge bases, ticketing portals, FAQs, and more.

## Analytical

The role of analytical CRM systems is to analyze customer data collected through multiple sources and present it so that business managers can make more informed decisions. Analytical CRM systems use techniques such as data mining, correlation, and pattern recognition to analyze the customer data. These analytics help improve customer service by finding small problems which can be solved, perhaps by marketing to different parts of a consumer audience differently. For example, through the analysis of a customer base's buying behavior, a company might see that this customer base has not been buying a lot of products recently. After scanning through this data, the company might think to market to this subset of consumers differently, in order to best communicate how this company's products might benefit this group specifically.

## Collaborative

The third primary aim of CRM systems is to incorporate external stakeholders such as suppliers, vendors, and distributors, and share customer information across groups/departments and organisations. For example, feedback can be collected from technical support calls, which could help provide direction for marketing products and services to that particular customer in the future.

## Customer Data Platform

A customer data platform (CDP) is a computer system used by marketing departments that assembles data about individual people from various sources into one database, with which other software systems can interact. As of February 2017 there were about twenty companies selling such systems and revenue for them was around US$300 million.

## Components

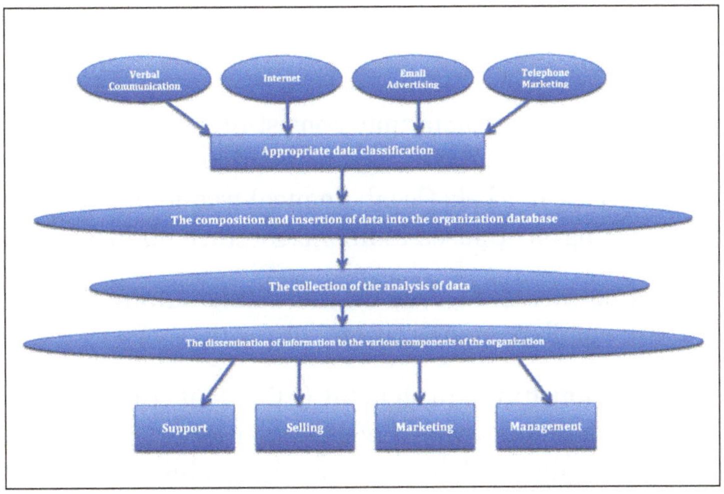


Components in the different types of CRM.

The main components of CRM are building and managing customer relationships through marketing, observing relationships as they mature through distinct phases, managing these relationships at each stage and recognizing that the distribution of value of a relationship to the firm is not homogeneous. When building and managing customer relationships through marketing, firms might benefit from using a variety of tools to help organizational design, incentive schemes, customer structures, and more to optimize the reach of its marketing campaigns. Through the acknowledgement of the distinct phases of CRM, businesses will be able to benefit from seeing the interaction of multiple relationships as connected transactions. The final factor of CRM highlights the importance of CRM through accounting for the profitability of customer relationships. Through studying the particular spending habits of customers, a firm may be able to dedicate different resources and amounts of attention to different types of consumers.

Relational Intelligence, or awareness of the variety of relationships a customer can have with a firm, is an important component to the main phases of CRM. Companies may be good at capturing demographic data, such as gender, age, income, and education, and connecting them with purchasing information to categorize customers into profitability tiers, but this is only a firm's mechanical view of customer relationships. This therefore is a sign that firms believe that customers are still resources that can be used for up-sell or cross-sell opportunities, rather than humans looking for interesting and personalized interactions.

CRM systems include:

- Data warehouse technology, used to aggregate transaction information, to merge the information with CRM products, and to provide key performance indicators.

- Opportunity management which helps the company to manage unpredictable growth and demand, and implement a good forecasting model to integrate sales history with sales projections.
- CRM systems that track and measure marketing campaigns over multiple networks, tracking customer analysis by customer clicks and sales.
- Some CRM software is available as a software as a service (SaaS), delivered via the internet and accessed via a web browser instead of being installed on a local computer. Businesses using the software do not purchase it, but typically pay a recurring subscription fee to the software vendor.
- For small businesses a CRM system may consist of a contact manager system that integrates emails, documents, jobs, faxes, and scheduling for individual accounts. CRM systems available for specific markets (legal, finance) frequently focus on event management and relationship tracking as opposed to financial return on investment (ROI).
- CRM systems for eCommerce, focused on marketing automation tasks, like: cart rescue, re-engage users with email, personalization.
- Customer-centric relationship management (CCRM) is a nascent sub-discipline that focuses on customer preferences instead of customer leverage. CCRM aims to add value by engaging customers in individual, interactive relationships.
- Systems for non-profit and membership-based organizations help track constituents, fundraising, sponsors' demographics, membership levels, membership directories, volunteering and communication with individuals.

## Effect on Customer Satisfaction

Customer satisfaction has important implications for the economic performance of firms because it has the ability to increase customer loyalty and usage behavior and reduce customer complaints and the likelihood of customer defection. The implementation of a CRM approach is likely to have an effect on customer satisfaction and customer knowledge for a variety of different reasons.

Firstly, firms are able to customize their offerings for each customer. By accumulating information across customer interactions and processing this information to discover hidden patterns, CRM applications help firms customize their offerings to suit the individual tastes of their customers. This customization enhances the perceived quality of products and services from a customer's viewpoint, and because perceived quality is a determinant of customer satisfaction, it follows that CRM applications indirectly affect customer satisfaction. CRM applications also enable firms to provide timely, accurate processing of customer orders and requests and the ongoing management of customer accounts. For example, Piccoli and Applegate discuss how Wyndham uses IT tools to deliver a consistent service experience across its various properties to a customer. Both an improved ability to customize and a reduced variability of the consumption experience enhance perceived quality, which in turn positively affects customer satisfaction. Furthermore, CRM applications also help firms manage customer relationships more effectively across the stages of relationship initiation, maintenance, and termination.

## Customer Benefits

With Customer relationship management systems customers are served better on day to day process and with more reliable information their demand of self service from companies will decrease. If there is less need to interact with the company for different problems, customer satisfaction level increases. These central benefits of CRM will be connected hypothetically to the three kinds of equity that are relationship, value and brand, and in the end to customer equity. Eight benefits were recognized to provide value drivers:

1. Enhanced ability to target profitable customers.
2. Integrated assistance across channels.
3. Enhanced sales force efficiency and effectiveness.
4. Improved pricing.
5. Customized products and services.
6. Improved customer service efficiency and effectiveness.
7. Individualized marketing messages also called campaigns.
8. Connect customers and all channels on a single platform.

In 2012, after reviewing the previous studies, someone selected some of those benefits which are more significant in customer's satisfaction and summarized them into the following cases:

1. Improve customer services: In general, customers would have some questions, concerns or requests. CRM services provide the ability to a company for producing, allocating and managing requests or something made by customers. For example, call center software, which helps to connect a customer to the manager or person who can best assist them with their existing problem, is one of the CRM abilities that can be implemented to increase efficiency.
2. Increased personalized service or one-to-one service: Personalizing customer service or one-to-one service provides companies to improve understanding and gaining knowledge of the customers and also to have better knowledge about their customers' preferences, requirements and demands.
3. Responsive to customer's needs: Customers' situations and needs can be understood by the firms focusing on customer needs and requirements.
4. Customer segmentation: In CRM, segmentation is used to categorize customers, according to some similarity, such as industry, job or some other characteristics, into similar groups. Although these characteristics, can be one or more attributes. It can be defined as a subdividing the customers based on already known good discriminator.
5. Improve customization of marketing: Meaning of customization of marketing is that, the firm or organization adapt and change its services or products based on presenting a different and unique product or services for each customer. With the purpose of ensuring that customer needs and requirements are met Customization is used by the organization.

Companies can put investment in information from customers and then customize their products or services to maintain customer interests.

6. Multichannel integration: Multichannel integration shows the point of co creation of customer value in CRM. On the other hand, a company's skill to perform multichannel integration successfully, is heavily dependent on the organization's ability getting together customer information from all channels and incorporate it with other related information.
7. Time saving: CRM will let companies to interact with customers more frequently, by personalized message and communication way which can be produced rapidly and matched on a timely basis, and finally they can better understand their customers and therefore look forward to their needs.
8. Improve customer knowledge: Firms can make and improve products and services through the information from tracking (e.g. via website tracking) customer behaviour to customer tastes and needs. CRM could contribute to a competitive advantage in improving firm's ability of customer information collecting to customize products and services according to customer needs.

Examples:

Research has found a 5% increase in customer retention boosts lifetime customer profits by 50% on average across multiple industries, as well as a boost of up to 90% within specific industries such as insurance. Companies that have mastered customer relationship strategies have the most successful CRM programs. For example, MBNA Europe has had a 75% annual profit growth since 1995. The firm heavily invests in screening potential cardholders. Once proper clients are identified, the firm retains 97% of its profitable customers. They implement CRM by marketing the right products to the right customers. The firm's customers' card usage is 52% above industry norm, and the average expenditure is 30% more per transaction. Also 10% of their account holders ask for more information on cross-sale products.

Amazon has also seen great success through its customer proposition. The firm implemented personal greetings, collaborative filtering, and more for the customer. They also used CRM training for the employees to see up to 80% of customers repeat.

## Customer Profile

Customer or consumer profiles are the essence of the data that is collected alongside core data (name, address, company) and processed through customer analytics methods, essentially a type of profiling. A customer is abstracted to information that sums up consumption habits so far and projects them into the future so that they can be grouped for marketing and advertising purposes.

## Improving CRM within a Firm

Consultants argue that it is important for companies establishing strong CRM systems to improve their relational intelligence. According to this argument, a company must recognize that people have many different types of relationships with different brands. One research study analyzed relationships between consumers in China, Germany, Spain, and the United States, with over 200 brands in 11 industries including airlines, cars and media. This information is valuable as it provides demographic, behavioral, and value-based customer segmentation. These types of relationships can be both positive and negative. Some customers view themselves as friends of the brands, while others as enemies, and some are mixed with a love-hate relationship with the brand. Some relationships are distant, intimate or anything in between.

## Analyzing the Information

Managers must understand the different reasons for the types of relationships, and provide the customer with what they are looking for. Companies can collect this information by using surveys, interviews, and more, with current customers. For example, Frito-Lay conducted many ethnographic interviews with customers to try and understand the relationships they wanted with the companies and the brands. They found that most customers were adults who used the product to feel more playful. They may have enjoyed the company's bright orange color, messiness and shape.

Companies must also improve their relational intelligence of their CRM systems. These days, companies store and receive huge amounts of data through emails, online chat sessions, phone calls, and more. Many companies do not properly make use of this great amount of data, however. All of these are signs of what types of relationships the customer wants with the firm, and therefore companies may consider investing more time and effort in building out their relational intelligence. Companies can use data mining technologies and web searches to understand relational signals. Social media such as social networking sites, blogs and forums can also be used to collect and analyze information. Understanding the customer and capturing this data allows companies to convert customer's signals into information and knowledge that the firm can use to understand a potential customer's desired relations with a brand.

It is also very important to analyze all of this information to determine which relationships prove the most valuable. This helps convert data into profits for the firm. Stronger bonds contribute to building market share. By managing different portfolios for different segments of the customer base, the firm can achieve strategic goals.

## Employee Training

Many firms have also implemented training programs to teach employees how to recognize and effectively create strong customer–brand relationships. For example, Harley Davidson sent its employees on the road with customers, who were motorcycle enthusiasts, to help solidify relationships. Other employees have also been trained in social psychology and the social sciences to help bolster strong customer relationships. Customer service representatives must be educated to value customer relationships, and trained to understand existing customer profiles. Even the finance and legal departments should understand how to manage and build relationships with customers.

## Application

Applying new technologies while using CRM systems requires changes in infrastructure of the organization as well as deployment of new technologies such as business rules, databases and information technology.

## In Practice

### Call Centers

Contact center CRM providers are popular for small and mid-market businesses. These systems codify the interactions between company and customers by using analytics and key performance indicators to give the users information on where to focus their marketing and customer service. This allows agents to have access to a caller's history to provide personalized customer communication. The intention is to maximize average revenue per user, decrease churn rate and decrease idle and unproductive contact with the customers.

Growing in popularity is the idea of gamifying, or using game design elements and game principles in a non-game environment such as customer service environments. The gamification of customer service environments includes providing elements found in games like rewards and bonus points to customer service representatives as a method of feedback for a job well done. Gamification tools can motivate agents by tapping into their desire for rewards, recognition, achievements, and competition.

### Contact-center Automation

Contact-center automation, the practice of having an integrated system that coordinates contacts between an organization and the public, is designed to reduce the repetitive and tedious parts of a contact center agent's job. Automation prevents this by having pre-recorded audio messages that help customers solve their problems. For example, an automated contact center may be able to re-route a customer through a series of commands asking him or her to select a certain number in order to speak with a particular contact center agent who specializes in the field in which the customer has a question. Software tools can also integrate with the agent's desktop tools to handle customer questions and requests. This also saves time on behalf of the employees.

### Social Media

Social CRM involves the use of social media and technology to engage and learn from consumers. Because the public, especially young people, are increasingly using social networking sites, companies use these sites to draw attention to their products, services and brands, with the aim of building up customer relationships to increase demand.

Some CRM systems integrate social media sites like Twitter, LinkedIn and Facebook to track and communicate with customers. These customers also share their own opinions and experiences with a company's products and services, giving these firms more insight. Therefore, these firms can both share their own opinions and also track the opinions of their customers.

Enterprise feedback management software platforms combine internal survey data with trends identified through social media to allow businesses to make more accurate decisions on which products to supply.

### Location-based Services

CRM systems can also include technologies that create geographic marketing campaigns. The systems take in information based on a customer's physical location and sometimes integrates it with popular location-based GPS applications. It can be used for networking or contact management as well to help increase sales based on location.

## Business-to-business Transactions

Despite the general notion that CRM systems were created for the customer-centric businesses, they can also be applied to B2B environments to streamline and improve customer management conditions. For the best level of CRM operation in a B2B environment, the software must be personalized and delivered at individual levels.

The main differences between business-to-consumer (B2C) and business-to-business CRM systems concern aspects like sizing of contact databases and length of relationships. Business-to-business companies tend to have smaller contact databases than business-to-consumer, because the volume of sales in business-to-business is relatively small. There are fewer figure propositions in business-to-business, but in some cases, they cost a lot more than business-to-consumer items and relationships in business-to-business environment are built over a longer period of time. Furthermore, business-to-business CRM must be easily integrated with products from other companies. Such integration enables the creation of forecasts about customer behavior based on their buying history, bills, business success, etc. An application for a business-to-business company must have a function to connect all the contacts, processes and deals among the customer's segment and then prepare a paper. Automation of sales process is an important requirement for business-to-business products. It should effectively manage the deal and progress it through all the phases towards signing. Finally, a crucial point is personalization. It helps the business-to-business company to create and maintain strong and long-lasting relationship with the customer.

CRM (customer relationship management) analytics comprises all programming that analyzes data about customers and presents it to help facilitate and streamline better business decisions.

CRM analytics can be considered a form of online analytical processing (OLAP) and may employ data mining. As companies have added new and often faster ways to interact with customers, the opportunity and the need to turn data collected about customers into useful information has become increasingly important. As a result, a number of software companies have developed products that perform customer data analysis, and analytics is a component of many CRM systems.

## Applications of CRM Analytics

After implementation, CRM analytics offers insights to understand and use the data that is mined. Organizations use CRM analytics in the following ways:

- Customer segmentation groupings: Dividing customers into those most and least likely to repurchase a product;
- Profitability analysis and customer value: Learning which customers contribute to the highest profits over time. This involves understanding not just how much a customer spends, but how many resources you dedicate to that customer in return;
- Personalization: The ability to market to individual customers based on the data collected about them. This requires obtaining a 360-degree customer view;

- Measuring and tracking escalation: The ability to measure how often problems arise with a product or service to eliminate that issue and quickly achieve customer satisfaction; and
- Predictive modeling: Comparing various product development plans in terms of likely future success given the customer knowledge base by measuring engagement levels through customer shares.

Data collection and analysis are viewed as a continuing and iterative process. And over time, business decisions are refined based on feedback from earlier analysis and consequent decisions.

## Benefits and Challenges of CRM analytics

CRM analytics can lead to better and more productive customer relationships through the evaluation of the organization's customer service, analyzing the customers and verifying user data. CRM analytics can lead to improvement in supply chain management - lower inventory and speedier delivery - and thus lower costs and more competitive pricing. One of the biggest benefits of CRM analytics is the ability to create target marketing campaigns from customer analysis.

A major challenge that accompanies CRM analytics is the integration of analytical software with existing systems, as well as new systems. If the software does not integrate, the collected data becomes difficult to utilize.

# Manufacturing

Manufacturing Industry is amongst the most data-intensive business vertical today. The industry is evolving and leveraging the available tools and technology like IIoT and Cloud that allow them to connect with the supply chain and customers like never before. Each and every connection and communication are delivering access to massive volumes of data, i.e., big data. Big data uncover hidden patterns, unknown correlations, market trends, customer preferences, and other useful information.

## Need of Data Analytics for Manufacturing Industry

Manufacturing is predominantly process-driven industry. These various processes involved in manufacturing create innumerable data-points that can be used for effective reporting and decision support systems. Historically, manual analysis (audits and statistical reports) was relied upon by decision-makers for various purposes. Today, business analysts use software and tools for real-time data analysis and historical trend help in making a decision for an organization.

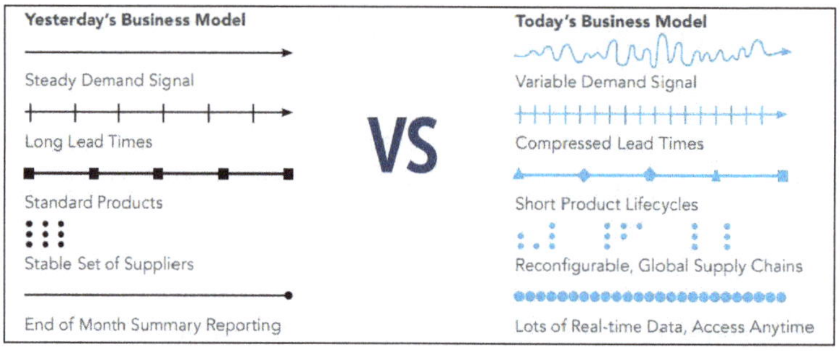

The manufacturing sector, like any other industry, also has its share of challenges that it needs to contend with — day-in and day-out. Although not all the problems could be addressed easily, a good number of those may be overcome with due application of technology wherever possible.

## The Advantage of Data Analytics

Big data is a collection of structured and unstructured data having different formats, being collected from several sources using a different type of database. Business analysts and policymakers perform data mining to get the most important information needed to achieve one or more objectives; consolidated and arranged on a single screen so the data can be monitored at a glance.

Big data analysis is primarily used to find correlations, trends, outliers (anomalies), patterns, and business conditions in data. Below we run through a series of use cases where business analysis / visual analysis performs through historical data and in some cases real-time data to enables businesses to address the existing bottlenecks and achieve a competitive edge.

## Improved Inventory Management

Pretty much every entity in manufacturing has inventory based on the nature of the business:

- Raw Materials.
- Work-In-Progress (WIP).
- Finished Goods.
- Packing Material, Etc.

The amount of profit a business obtain is considerably based on how well the inventory is managed, from procurement of inventory to inventory control & warehouse management to the shipping of goods and finally the post-sales activities, such as customer service and returns management. Whether an inventory is located in one warehouse or multiple locations, businesses should keep a tight inventory control.

Data analytics allows you to understand how much inventory you have as well as understand trends in your use. Accurate inventory can enhance ordering and lower loss, making it possible to optimize your inventory expenses fully.

## Optimized Staffing for Efficient Workforce Management

Resources, like inventory, can pose some challenges that impact the production, supply, and quality of the goods. A staff shortage implies longer hold up times and delayed production, delivery as well as might be compromised quality with the produced products. Being overstaffed means increased overhead.

Looking at historical data for resource planning and different seasons can make for better forecasting and scheduling of staff. Whereas, real-time data allows managers to move the right people to the right shifts and roles — even more efficiently than possible when analyzing past trends. With real-time data, managers have a birds-eye view of staffing across departments and functions, enabling rapid response to unexpected circumstances such as call-offs.

## Enhanced Supply Chain Practices

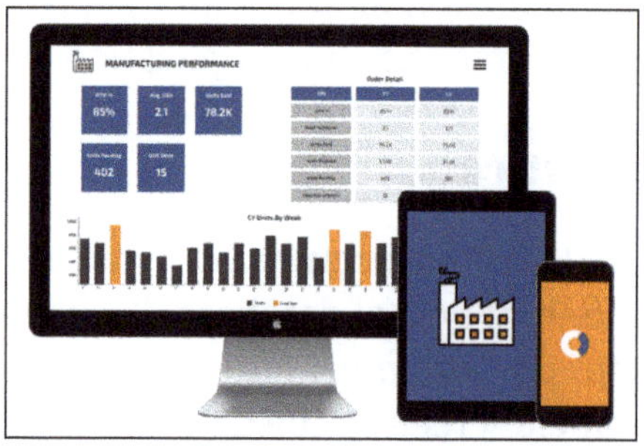

Supply chain builds building blocks for manufacturers. Connecting people, process and supply chains provide end-to-end visibility and control over superior quality and optimized utilization of resources.

Big data of this particular business process helps here for predictive analysis to plan better and set the right expectations internally and externally. Real-time data analysis enables you to determine the materials required for a master production schedule, where you easily track when what and how much to buy and make.

With changing customer expectations, you can still deliver world-class performance over shorter order lead times, last-minute order changes, custom products orders, and perfect order deliveries. Connected supply chain practices influence your financial and operational plans thus enables growth and prioritizes investments.

## More Effective Fault Prediction and Preventive Maintenance

Machines continuously generate data using sensors. Traditionally, this data was used mostly for signaling alerts to prevent misfortune. The rest of the data was ignored. Predictive analytics uses all the data the machine can ever generate. With big data tools, it is possible to extract essential correlations between fault diagnostics and operational parameters.

It provides a better understanding of the system's complexities. The insight can help plan highly accurate predictive models to reduce or eliminate downtime from maintenance. For example: If a system has already crossed certain operational thresholds, there is not much lead time left to perform preventive maintenance. Predictive analytics here enable you to perform pre-emptive maintenance that helps reduce or eliminate catastrophic failures.

## Cost Modeling and Forecasting

"What price should we quote our product to ensure profits and generate a winning bid?" Cost modeling and forecasting makes a difference in manufacturing a product. Cost modeling helps businesses to systematically capture all factor input costs including material, labor, production, administration, sales, and research and development essential in estimating the cost of the final manufactured product.

Cost modeling helps manufacturers to be confident in their ability to predict costs and enable them to get better at developing quotes for winning bids that ensure long-term profitability.

Pulling together all the data of every department costs including significant indexes, process parameters, etc. which is highly structured and help develop a useful cost model and forecast.

## Marketing

Marketing analytics is the practice of measuring, managing and analyzing marketing performance to maximize its effectiveness and optimize return on investment (ROI). Understanding marketing analytics allows marketers to be more efficient at their jobs and minimize wasted web marketing dollars.

Beyond the obvious sales and lead generation applications, marketing analytics can offer profound insights into customer preferences and trends. Despite these compelling benefits, a majority of organizations fail to ever realize the promises of marketing analytics.

*In your opinion, how effective is your company's ability to measure the financial returns (ROI) generated from marketing investments?*

| | 2005 | 2006 | 2007 | 2008 |
|---|---|---|---|---|
| A source of real leadership | 2% | 4% | 2% | 4% |
| As good as it needs to be | 6% | 12% | 7% | 13% |
| Somewhat short of where it could be | 38% | 42% | 40% | 40% |
| A long way from where it could be | 53% | 42% | 51% | 43% |

A Survey of Sr. Marketing Executives on their Marketing Analytics Effectiveness.

However, with the advent of search engines, paid search marketing, search engine optimization, and powerful new software products from WordStream, marketing analytics is more powerful and easier to implement than ever.

### The Importance of Marketing Analytics

Marketing analytics, Internet (or Web) marketing analytics in particular, allow you to monitor campaigns and their respective outcomes, enabling you to spend each dollar as effectively as possible.

The importance of marketing analyics is obvious: if something costs more than it returns, it's not a good long-term business strategy.

In search marketing in particular, one of the most powerful marketing performance metrics comes in the form of keywords. Keywords tell you exactly what is on the mind of your current and potential customers. In fact, the most valuable long-term benefit of engaging in paid and natural search marketing isn't incremental traffic to your website, it's the keyword data contained within each click which can be utliized to inform and optimize other business processes.

- Product Design: Keywords can reveal exactly what features or solutions your customers are looking for.
- Customer Surveys: By examining keyword frequency data you can infer the relative priorities of competing interests.
- Industry Trends: By monitoring the relative change in keyword frequencies you can identify and predict trends in customer behavior.
- Customer Support: Understand where customers are struggling the most and how support resources should be deployed.

## Implementing Marketing Analytics

The Web is clearly the only game in town. Statistics show that almost 90% of the entire North American population is online. The quickest and easiest way to reach out to this huge market is through paid search marketing, for example, advertising on Google AdWords or through other search engines.

Reports and information received from search marketing help in all areas of your business, including offline revenue and product development.

## Important Points for the Implementation of Market Analytics

- Start with Keyword Research: A stagnant keyword list is dangerous as it neglects trends and information on new products or developments.
- Set up some Paid Search Marketing Campaigns: Group keywords in relevant groups and write appropriate ad text to help improve your Quality Score, which will lower your bid and improve ad position.
- Analyze the Results: Displaying your keywords in ad text prove to the searcher and to Google that your ad is relevant to their search.
- Implement Natural Search: Google estimates that 80% of searchers click on an organic result over a paid advertisement. Incorporate your best performing keywords into your website and continue to generate relevant content.
- Repeat Ad Nauseum: Negative keywords are great because they prevent unnecessary clicks and spend, ensuring your advertisement displays only for applicable searches.

## References


- Applications-of-business-analytics: proschoolonline.com, Retrieved 29 June, 2019
- Columbus, louis (6 may 2014). "gartner crm market share update: 41% of crm systems are saas-based, salesforce dominating market growth". Forbes. Retrieved 22 august 2016
- Financial-analytics, definition: techtarget.com, Retrieved 14 July, 2019
- Buttle, francis; maklan, stan (11 february 2015). Customer relationship management: concepts and technologies. Isbn 9781317654766
- The-importance-of-hr-analytics: naukrirms.com, Retrieved 11 January, 2019
- Lakshman jha (2008). Customer relationship management: a strategic approach. Isbn 9788190721127. Retrieved 8 june 2017
- Crm-analytics, definition: techtarget.com, Retrieved 18 April, 2019
- Scope-of-business-analytics-in-manufacturing: medium.com, Retrieved 27 May, 2019

# 6

# Business Intelligence Technologies

Technology plays a vital role in business analytics by providing the ability to extract valuable information from business data in the most feasible way. Data warehousing, dashboards, ad-hoc reporting, data discovery, cloud business intelligence, etc. are some of the technologies that fall under this domain. All these business intelligence technologies have been carefully analyzed in this chapter.

## Data Warehousing

The purpose of a data warehouse is to establish a repository that makes operational data accessible in a form readily acceptable for analytical processing activities, such as EC applications, decision support, and other end-user applications. As part of this accessibility, detail-level operational data must be transformed into a relational form, which makes them more amenable to analytical processing. Thus, data warehousing is not a concept by itself, but is interrelated with data access, retrieval, analysis, and visualization.

The process of building and using a data warehouse is shown in the figure - Data Warehouse Framework and Views. The organization's data are stored in operational systems (left side of the figure). Not all data are transferred to the data warehouse, and frequently only a summary of the data is transferred in a process of extraction, transformation, and load (ETL). The data that are transferred are organized within the warehouse as a relational database so that it is easy for end users to access. Also, the data are organized by subject, such as by product, customer segment, or business partner. EC data also may be organized according to a business process, such as ordering, shipping, or available inventory. The data then can be optionally replicated in data marts. Data access is provided through Web browsers via middleware software. On the right side of the figure are various applications that may use the data.

The activities conducted during much of the process described in the figure - Data Warehouse Framework and Views are generally referred to as business intelligence. The major reason for the name is that these activities not only collect and process data, they also enable analysis that results in useful—intelligent—solutions to business problems. The concept of business intelligence originated from executive information system (EIS) activities, but today it is used to describe online analytical processing and data mining activities as well.

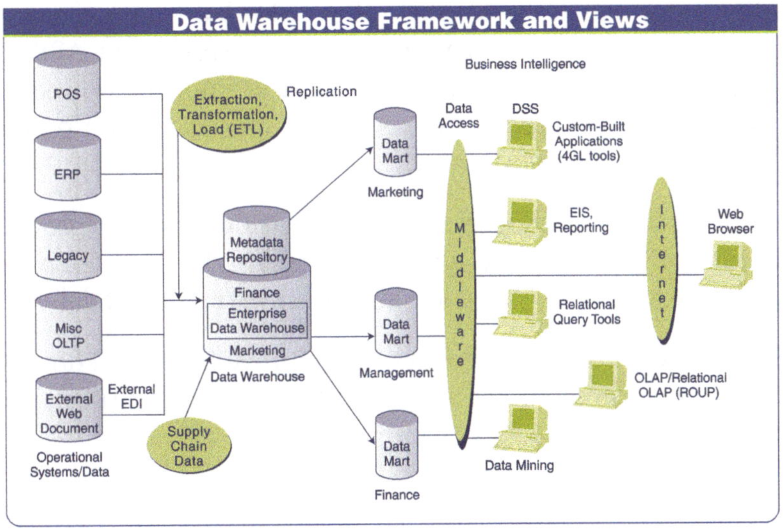


Data warehouses provide for the storage of metadata, which are data about data. Metadata include software programs about data, rules for organizing data, and data summaries that are easy to index and search, especially with Web tools.

## Characteristics of Data Warehousing

The major characteristics of data warehousing include the following:

- Organization: Data are organized by detailed subject (e.g., by customer, vendor, product, price level, and region) and only contain information relevant for decision support.
- Consistency: Data in different operational databases may be encoded differently. For example, gender data may be encoded 0 and 1 in one operational system and "m" and "f" in another. They will be coded in a consistent manner within each warehouse.
- Time variant: The data are kept for 5 to 10 years so that they can be used for trends, forecasting, and comparisons over time.
- Nonvolatile: Once entered into the warehouse, data are not updated. However, new, related data may replace or supplement old data.
- Relational: The data warehouse typically uses a relational structure (organized into tables of rows and columns).

## Benefits of Data Warehouses

The major benefits of data warehouses are (1) the ability of users to reach data quickly, because data are located in one place and organized properly, and (2) the ability to reach data easily, frequently by end users themselves, using Web browsers. Another benefit is that a data warehouse provides a consolidated view of corporate data, which is better than providing many smaller (and differently formatted) views. For example, separate production systems may track sales and coupon mailings. Combining data from these different systems may yield insights into the cost efficiency of coupon sales promotions that would not be immediately evident from the output data of either system alone. Integrated within a data warehouse, however, such information can be easily extracted.

Data warehouses allow information processing to be off-loaded from expensive operational systems onto low-cost servers (or processed by application service providers, ASPs). Once this is done, end-user tools can handle a significant number of end-user information requests. Furthermore, some operational system reporting requirements can be moved to Web-based decision support systems, thus freeing up production processing.

In addition, accessibility to data warehouse content by decision makers is provided throughout the enterprise via an intranet. Users can view, query, and analyze the data and produce reports using Web browsers. This is an extremely economical and effective method of delivering data.

The various benefits offered by data warehouses can improve business knowledge, provide competitive advantage, enhance customer service and satisfaction, facilitate decision making, and help in streamlining business processes.

## Suitability

Data warehousing is most appropriate for organizations in which some of the following apply:

- Large amounts of data need to be accessed by end users.
- The operational data are stored in different systems.
- An information-based approach to management is in use.
- The company has a large, diverse customer base (such as in a utility company or a bank).
- The same data are represented differently in different systems.
- Data are stored in highly technical formats that are difficult to decipher.
- Extensive end-user computing is performed (many end users performing many activities).

Although data warehouses offer substantial benefits, the cost of a data warehouse can be very high, both to build and to maintain. Furthermore, it may difficult and expensive to incorporate data from obsolete legacy systems. Finally, there may be a lack of incentive among departments within a company to share data. Therefore, a careful feasibility study must be undertaken before a commitment is made to data warehousing. Alternatively, one or more data marts can be used.

## Three Main Types of Data Warehouses

## Enterprise Data Warehouse

Enterprise Data Warehouse is a centralized warehouse. It provides decision support service across the enterprise. It offers a unified approach for organizing and representing data. It also provide the ability to classify data according to the subject and give access according to those divisions.

## Operational Data Store

Operational Data Store, which is also called ODS, are nothing but data store required when neither Data warehouse nor OLTP systems support organizations reporting needs. In ODS, Data warehouse is refreshed in real time. Hence, it is widely preferred for routine activities like storing records of the Employees.

## Data Mart

A data mart is a subset of the data warehouse. It specially designed for a particular line of business, such as sales, finance, sales or finance. In an independent data mart, data can collect directly from sources.

## General Stages of Data Warehouse

Earlier, organizations started relatively simple use of data warehousing. However, over time, more sophisticated use of data warehousing begun.

The following are general stages of use of the data warehouse:

### Offline Operational Database

In this stage, data is just copied from an operational system to another server. In this way, loading, processing, and reporting of the copied data do not impact the operational system's performance.

### Offline Data Warehouse

Data in the Datawarehouse is regularly updated from the Operational Database. The data in Datawarehouse is mapped and transformed to meet the Datawarehouse objectives.

### Real time Data Warehouse

In this stage, Data warehouses are updated whenever any transaction takes place in operational database. For example, Airline or railway booking system.

### Integrated Data Warehouse

In this stage, Data Warehouses are updated continuously when the operational system performs a transaction. The Datawarehouse then generates transactions which are passed back to the operational system.

## Components of Data warehouse

Four components of Data Warehouses are:

Load manager: Load manager is also called the front component. It performs with all the operations associated with the extraction and load of data into the warehouse. These operations include transformations to prepare the data for entering into the Data warehouse.

Warehouse Manager: Warehouse manager performs operations associated with the management of the data in the warehouse. It performs operations like analysis of data to ensure consistency, creation of indexes and views, generation of denormalization and aggregations, transformation and merging of source data and archiving and baking-up data.

Query Manager: Query manager is also known as backend component. It performs all the operation operations related to the management of user queries. The operations of this Data warehouse components are direct queries to the appropriate tables for scheduling the execution of queries.

## End-user Access Tools

This is categorized into five different groups like 1. Data Reporting 2. Query Tools 3. Application development tools 4. EIS tools, 5. OLAP tools and data mining tools.

## Who needs Data warehouse?

Data warehouse is needed for all types of users like:

- Decision makers who rely on mass amount of data.
- Users who use customized, complex processes to obtain information from multiple data sources.
- It is also used by the people who want simple technology to access the data.
- It also essential for those people who want a systematic approach for making decisions.
- If the user wants fast performance on a huge amount of data which is a necessity for reports, grids or charts, then Data warehouse proves useful.
- Data warehouse is a first step If you want to discover 'hidden patterns' of data-flows and groupings.

## Uses of Data Warehouse

Here, are most common sectors where Data warehouse is used:

### Airline

In the Airline system, it is used for operation purpose like crew assignment, analyses of route profitability, frequent flyer program promotions, etc.

### Banking

It is widely used in the banking sector to manage the resources available on desk effectively. Few banks also used for the market research, performance analysis of the product and operations.

### Healthcare

Healthcare sector also used Data warehouse to strategize and predict outcomes, generate patient's treatment reports, share data with tie-in insurance companies, medical aid services, etc.

### Public Sector

In the public sector, data warehouse is used for intelligence gathering. It helps government agencies to maintain and analyze tax records, health policy records, for every individual.

### Investment and Insurance Sector

In this sector, the warehouses are primarily used to analyze data patterns, customer trends, and to track market movements.

## Retain Chain

In retail chains, Data warehouse is widely used for distribution and marketing. It also helps to track items, customer buying pattern, promotions and also used for determining pricing policy.

## Telecommunication

A data warehouse is used in this sector for product promotions, sales decisions and to make distribution decisions.

## Hospitality Industry

This Industry utilizes warehouse services to design as well as estimate their advertising and promotion campaigns where they want to target clients based on their feedback and travel patterns.

Steps to Implement Data Warehouse:

The best way to address the business risk associated with a Datawarehouse implementation is to employ a three-prong strategy as below

- Enterprise strategy: Here we identify technical including current architecture and tools. We also identify facts, dimensions, and attributes. Data mapping and transformation is also passed.
- Phased delivery: Datawarehouse implementation should be phased based on subject areas. Related business entities like booking and billing should be first implemented and then integrated with each other.
- Iterative Prototyping: Rather than a big bang approach to implementation, the Datawarehouse should be developed and tested iteratively.

Here, are key steps in Datawarehouse implementation along with its deliverables:

| Step | Tasks | Deliverables |
|---|---|---|
| 1 | Need to define project scope | Scope Definition |
| 2 | Need to determine business needs | Logical Data Model |
| 3 | Define Operational Datastore requirements | Operational Data Store Model |
| 4 | Acquire or develop Extraction tools | Extract tools and Software |
| 5 | Define Data Warehouse Data requirements | Transition Data Model |
| 6 | Document missing data | To Do Project List |
| 7 | Maps Operational Data Store to Data Warehouse | D/W Data Integration Map |
| 8 | Develop Data Warehouse Database design | D/W Database Design |
| 9 | Extract Data from Operational Data Store | Integrated D/W Data Extracts |
| 10 | Load Data Warehouse | Initial Data Load |
| 11 | Maintain Data Warehouse | On-going Data Access and Subsequent Loads |

Best practices to implement a Data Warehouse:

- Decide a plan to test the consistency, accuracy, and integrity of the data.

- The data warehouse must be well integrated, well defined and time stamped.
- While designing Datawarehouse make sure you use right tool, stick to life cycle, take care about data conflicts and ready to learn you're your mistakes.
- Never replace operational systems and reports.
- Don't spend too much time on extracting, cleaning and loading data.
- Ensure to involve all stakeholders including business personnel in Datawarehouse implementation process. Establish that Data warehousing is a joint/ team project. You don't want to create Data warehouse that is not useful to the end users.
- Prepare a training plan for the end users.

## Advantages and Disadvantages of Data Warehouse

Advantages of Data Warehouse:

- Data warehouse allows business users to quickly access critical data from some sources all in one place.
- Data warehouse provides consistent information on various cross-functional activities. It is also supporting ad-hoc reporting and query.
- Data Warehouse helps to integrate many sources of data to reduce stress on the production system.
- Data warehouse helps to reduce total turnaround time for analysis and reporting.
- Restructuring and Integration make it easier for the user to use for reporting and analysis.
- Data warehouse allows users to access critical data from the number of sources in a single place. Therefore, it saves user's time of retrieving data from multiple sources.
- Data warehouse stores a large amount of historical data. This helps users to analyze different time periods and trends to make future predictions.

Disadvantages of Data Warehouse:

- Not an ideal option for unstructured data.
- Creation and Implementation of Data Warehouse is surely time confusing affair.
- Data Warehouse can be outdated relatively quickly.
- Difficult to make changes in data types and ranges, data source schema, indexes, and queries.
- The data warehouse may seem easy, but actually, it is too complex for the average users.
- Despite best efforts at project management, data warehousing project scope will always increase.
- Sometime warehouse users will develop different business rules.

- Organisations need to spend lots of their resources for training and Implementation purpose.

### The Future of Data Warehousing

- Change in Regulatory constrains may limit the ability to combine source of disparate data. These disparate sources may include unstructured data which is difficult to store.
- As the size of the databases grows, the estimates of what constitutes a very large database continue to grow. It is complex to build and run data warehouse systems which are always increasing in size. The hardware and software resources are available today do not allow to keep a large amount of data online.
- Multimedia data cannot be easily manipulated as text data, whereas textual information can be retrieved by the relational software available today. This could be a research subject.

## Dashboards

A business intelligence dashboard (BI dashboard) is a data visualization tool that displays on a single screen the status of business analytics metrics, key performance indicators (KPIs) and important data points for an organization, department, team or process.

Essential features of modern BI dashboard software include a customizable interface, interactivity and the ability to pull real-time data from multiple sources; these features represent a significant advance over older, static dashboards. BI dashboards are also now an integral component of most leading cloud-based analytics platforms. The popular self-service analytics model -- nearly always delivered from the cloud as SaaS -- is, in large part, based on BI dashboards that enable end users to quickly visualize data they have selected.

### Benefits and Limitations of BI Dashboards

BI dashboards are increasingly seen as critical tools for enterprises to derive instant and longer-term insights from their growing storehouses of big data and to enable better informed decision-making and data analysis. They enable enterprises to make number-intensive data easily comprehensible and useable for nontechnical decision-makers. Sophisticated and colorful dashboard design provides multiple visualization possibilities for critical data.

Drawbacks of BI dashboards don't necessarily result from the design of the software, but rather from how the dashboards are used, the expense and the difficulty of installing them. While most BI dashboards are relatively self-service, enterprises generally must use IT professionals to implement the technology.

Other challenges include overly flashy or cluttered design, trying to include too much information without constraining raw data enough and difficulty plumbing surface metrics for underlying data.

## BI Dashboard Design Best Practices

A good dashboard design presents business insights derived from data in a way that's easy to understand. The dashboard components provide different overall views of the data and allow users to drill down to see more granular data, as well.

In general, dashboard best practices:

- Involve end users in BI dashboard design;
- Refine design during development using iterative approach;
- Precisely identify data to be tracked;
- Allow for customization by different sections of the enterprise;
- Keep BI dashboard data current;
- Include actionable information.

## BI Dashboard Vendors

Major vendors of modern analytics and BI platforms - all of which include BI dashboards in their product lineups - include Tableau, Microsoft, Qlik, MicroStrategy, Sisense, Salesforce, SAS, SAP, Tibco and IBM. Some vendors - notably Tableau and Microsoft, with its Power BI platform - provide various levels of product licensing, including options in which users can get a view-only license that doesn't include its own analytics capability, but relies on analytics applications from third parties.

# Ad Hoc Reporting

Ad-hoc reporting is a model of business intelligence (BI) in which reports are built and distributed by nontechnical business intelligence users. In other words, with ad-hoc reporting, all the technical user does is set up the BI solution, connect it to the data-sources, establish security parameters and determine which objects end-users can see. From that point on, the actual reports are created by business end-users.

Ad-hoc means that with this BI model, users can use their reporting and analysis solution to answer their business questions "as the occasion requires," without having to request queries from IT. Naturally, ad-hoc reports can be and look as simple as a one page data table or as complex and rich as interactive tabular or cross-tab reports with drill-down and visualization features–or present themselves in the form of dashboards, heat maps, or other more advanced forms.

This depends in large part on a) the type of ad-hoc solution employed, b) the needs of the end-user and c) the user's confidence with the solution.

Ad-hoc reporting stands in contrast with managed reporting, in which it is the technical user–the report developer–who creates and distributes the report.

## The Goal of Ad-hoc Reporting

Ad-hoc reporting's goal is to empower end-users to ask their own questions of company data, without burdening IT with the task of creating a myriad of reports to serve different functions and purposes. Ad-hoc reporting therefore makes the most sense when a large number of end-users need to see, understand, and act on data more or less independently, while still being on the same page as far as which set of numbers they look at.

For example, a company with a large outside-sales force would be the perfect fit for ad-hoc reporting. Each sales rep can set up his own report for his territory, showing performance against sales goals, orders taken, number of visits to each client, etc., in a format that makes the most sense to him. And just as importantly, the numbers used are pulled from the same data sources as the rest of the company, thereby promoting consistency and minimizing surprises at the end of the quarter.

A good-quality, Web-based ad-hoc reporting solution greatly enhances the benefits of the ad-hoc reporting model for the company adopting it.

## The Benefits of Web-based Ad-hoc Reporting

- Get critical information to the right people at the right time: Self-service results plus automatic scheduling/delivery of information let you facilitate timely decision making. Users get the information they need when they need it to answer critical, real-time questions.
- Flexibility for constantly changing environments: Business needs to evolve. Answers to changing business questions become more critical. It's impossible to predict what questions and answers users may need in the future.

- Saves training costs and time: Streamlines users' access to critical information. Easy-to-use wizards allow users to get up and running quickly, requiring less time to learn the application and providing clear guidance and saving time to build reports.
- Encourages collaboration and information sharing: Users can easily create, organize, publish and make reports available to other users via the Web for on-demand viewing.
- Reduces IT workload: The Web-based reporting application itself can be deployed quickly for widespread availability to end-users. Once deployed, it empowers users to build the reports themselves anytime they need the information. No waiting for IT report developers to build them.

## What to Look for in a Good Ad-hoc Reporting Solution

A good ad-hoc reporting solution should–like all BI applications–be squarely aimed at the achievement of the company's strategy. The key here is to identify what each end-user's strategic function is within the organization, and ensure that the ad-hoc reporting solution is optimized to make that function easier and more effective, while not offsetting benefits by being too costly.

To do so, a good reporting solution will offer the following characteristics:

- Being easy to use: If it is or even appears to be complicated, many end-users will be turned off and user adoption will suffer. For this reason, some of the better ad-hoc reporting solutions available today offer a basic set of intuitive features that are wizard-driven and will look easy even to the proverbial "non-computer person," while also offering more advanced sets of tools for the user who feels confident.
- Being robust: Assuming that adoption is not an issue, the ad-hoc solution should offer end-users what they need to see, understand and act upon their data. Far from being a more hi-tech version of Excel, it should offer interactive features like ad-hoc dashboards, drill-down and drill-through, advanced sorting and filtering, rich visualization tools like heat maps, charts and graphs, etc.
- Being Web-based: For it to be truly useful, a BI solution (including ad-hoc reporting) should run on the Internet. Apart from offering the familiar navigability with which we are all familiar, a Web-based solution is available from virtually anywhere and on any device sporting Internet connection. Another benefit of a Web-based ad-hoc solution is that the system administrator won't have to set it up individually on every user's machine: installing it on the server is enough, and all the users need to access it is a simple URL.
- Being easy to set up: Today's better Web-based ad-hoc reporting solutions are data-source neutral, meaning that they can connect practically out of the box to most of today's commonly-used data-sources, including databases, Web-services, flat files, etc. This saves the IT department the burden of creating complex metadata structures as the underlying layer, which is time-consuming, cumbersome and expensive.
- Having a server-based licensing with no per-user fees. If the benefit of ad-hoc reporting is that of empowering end-users, it should not come with a "user-tax" in the form of per-seat licensing.

## Data Discovery

One of the biggest problems in business intelligence is the mismatch between those in the company who know how to prepare data for analysis, and those who need to run these analysis and use the insights, day-to-day.

Data discovery tools get around this by making it easier for non-IT staff to access complex data sets and draw out the information they need, without the technical know-how this required in the past.

Data discovery tools are great, but they aren't always able to keep up with the pace of change, especially when new data is being added to the back end all the time.

That's where the idea of governed data discovery (GDD) comes in.

It's really just a more complete and extensive approach to data discovery, which shifts power over data preparation and analysis from IT to the business side of the enterprise.

Governed data discovery systems need to do three things:

### Offer Centralized Self-service

There should be a central, built-in interface that allows users to manage business intelligence and run analyses at will, on a self-service basis.

### Provide Data Governance

It's not just the tools that need to be centralized. All data used by the company should be held in a central location that can be accessed, updated and shared by colleagues throughout the organization. This provides a "single version of truth" across the entire business, ensuring that insights are up-to-date and valuable and that there is a data governance strategy in place.

Most of your team are hitting their targets, but profits are stagnating. When you take a look at your KPI dashboard, you see that renewal rates are falling, eating into your profits. You realize your team is too focused on new sales at the expense of nurturing relationships with existing customers, so you play around with your KPIs to place more emphasis on securing renewals than bringing in new clients.

## Cloud Business Intelligence

Cloud Business Intelligence (BI) applications are hosted on a virtual network, such as the internet. They are used to provide organizations access to BI-related data such as dashboards, KPIs and other business analytics. Enterprises are increasingly turning to cloud-based tools, like Customer Relationship Management (CRM) applications (Salesforce), online file collaboration and storage (Dropbox, Box) and help desk software (UserVoice, Zendesk). This trend includes business intelligence tools embracing the agility and accessibility of the Cloud.

## Cloud Computing Meets Business Intelligence

Cloud computing and business intelligence are an ideal match. Business intelligence is about delivering the right information to the right people at the right time, and cloud computing provides a lightweight, agile way to access BI applications. The beauty of Cloud BI applications is that they are accessible on multiple devices and web browsers. This is circumventing traditional software barriers such as the requirement to access the application on-site.

## Advantages of Cloud Computing for BI Users

Cloud BI offers some significant advantages over on-premise applications. Here are a few of these advantages:

### Ease of Use

Cloud BI applications, like other cloud applications, tend to be easier for end-users to operate and set up. This means reduced IT involvement and costs.

### Deployment Speed

Cloud applications are very simple to deploy, since they require no additional hardware or software installations.

### Scalability and Elasticity

Cloud applications can be rapidly scaled to accommodate for an increase in the number of users in an organization.

### Accessibility

Cloud BI applications can be accessed on any web browser or on any mobile device.

## References


- Data-warehousing: guru99.com, Retrieved 21 July, 2019
- Business-intelligence-dashboard, definition: techtarget.com, Retrieved 13 July, 2019
- Ad-hoc-reporting, bi-encyclopedia, resources: logianalytics.com, Retrieved 24 March , 2019
- Data-discovery, glossary: sisense.com, Retrieved 1 June, 2019
- What-is-cloud-business-intelligenc, resources: klipfolio.com, Retrieved 21 March , 2019

# 7

# Modeling in Business Intelligence

Data modeling refers to the process of constructing a data model to store data in the database. Such model which deals with business data is referred to as data modeling for business intelligence. This chapter delves into concepts such as business intelligence applications and tools, business intelligence model roadmap, etc. to provide in-depth knowledge for the subject.

## Data Modeling

Data modeling (data modeling) is the process of creating a data model for the data to be stored in a Database. This data model is a conceptual representation of Data objects, the associations between different data objects and the rules. Data modeling helps in the visual representation of data and enforces business rules, regulatory compliances, and government policies on the data. Data Models ensure consistency in naming conventions, default values, semantics, security while ensuring quality of the data.

Data model emphasizes on what data is needed and how it should be organized instead of what operations need to be performed on the data. Data Model is like architect's building plan which helps to build a conceptual model and set the relationship between data items.

The two types of Data Models techniques are:

- Entity Relationship (E-R) Model.
- UML (Unified Modeling Language).

We will discuss them in detail later.

### Using Data Model

The primary goal of using data model are:

- Ensures that all data objects required by the database are accurately represented. Omission of data will lead to creation of faulty reports and produce incorrect results.

- A data model helps design the database at the conceptual, physical and logical levels.
- Data Model structure helps to define the relational tables, primary and foreign keys and stored procedures.
- It provides a clear picture of the base data and can be used by database developers to create a physical database.
- It is also helpful to identify missing and redundant data.
- Though the initial creation of data model is labor and time consuming, in the long run, it makes your IT infrastructure upgrade and maintenance cheaper and faster.

## Types of Data Models

There are mainly three different types of data models:

- Conceptual: This Data Model defines WHAT the system contains. This model is typically created by Business stakeholders and Data Architects. The purpose is to organize, scope and define business concepts and rules.
- Logical: Defines HOW the system should be implemented regardless of the DBMS. This model is typically created by Data Architects and Business Analysts. The purpose is to developed technical map of rules and data structures.
- Physical: This Data Model describes HOW the system will be implemented using a specific DBMS system. This model is typically created by DBA and developers. The purpose is actual implementation of the database.

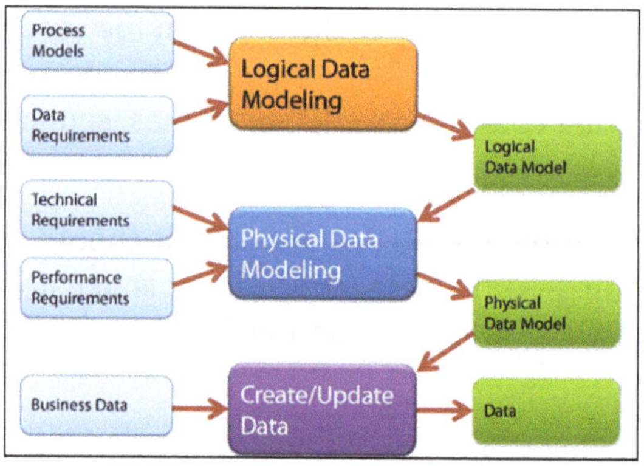


## Conceptual Model

The main aim of this model is to establish the entities, their attributes, and their relationships. In this Data modeling level, there is hardly any detail available of the actual Database structure.

The 3 basic tenants of Data Model are:

- Entity: A real-world thing.
- Attribute: Characteristics or properties of an entity.
- Relationship: Dependency or association between two entities.

For example:

- Customer and Product are two entities: Customer number and name are attributes of the Customer entity.
- Product name and price are attributes of product entity.
- Sale is the relationship between the customer and product.

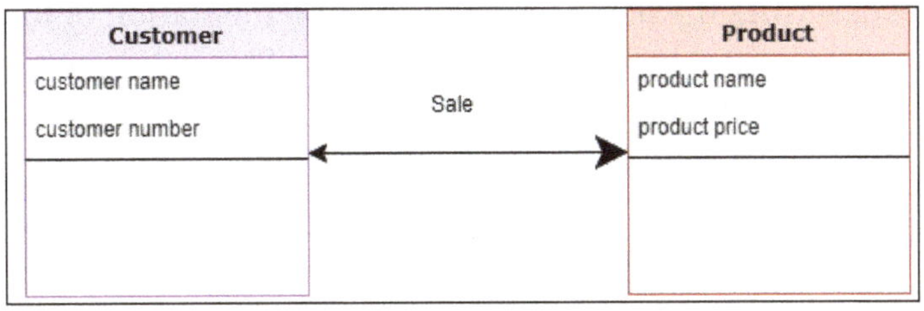


## Characteristics of a Conceptual Data Model

- Offers Organisation-wide coverage of the business concepts.
- This type of Data Models are designed and developed for a business audience.
- The conceptual model is developed independently of hardware specifications like data storage capacity, location or software specifications like DBMS vendor and technology. The focus is to represent data as a user will see it in the "real world".

Conceptual data models known as Domain models create a common vocabulary for all stakeholders by establishing basic concepts and scope.

## Logical Data Model

Logical data models add further information to the conceptual model elements. It defines the structure of the data elements and set the relationships between them.

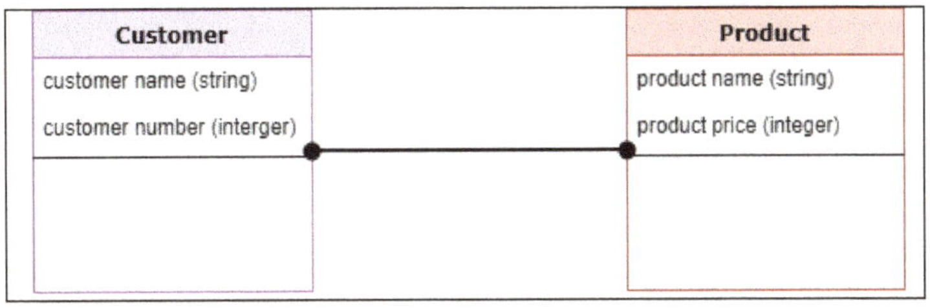


The advantage of the Logical data model is to provide a foundation to form the base for the Physical model. However, the modeling structure remains generic.

At this Data Modeling level, no primary or secondary key is defined. At this Data modeling level, you need to verify and adjust the connector details that were set earlier for relationships.

Characteristics of a logical data model:

- Describes data needs for a single project but could integrate with other logical data models based on the scope of the project.

- Designed and developed independently from the DBMS.
- Data attributes will have datatypes with exact precisions and length.
- Normalization processes to the model is applied typically till 3NF.

## Physical Data Model

A Physical Data Model describes the database specific implementation of the data model. It offers an abstraction of the database and helps generate schema. This is because of the richness of meta-data offered by a Physical Data Model.

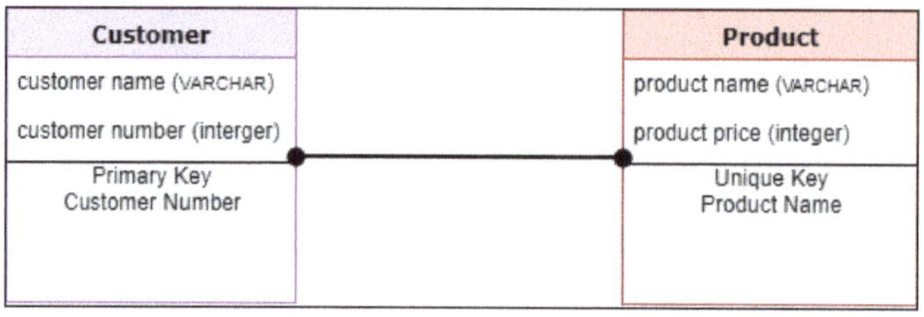


This type of Data model also helps to visualize database structure. It helps to model database columns keys, constraints, indexes, triggers, and other RDBMS features.

## Characteristics of a Physical Data Model

- The physical data model describes data need for a single project or application though it maybe integrated with other physical data models based on project scope.
- Data Model contains relationships between tables that which addresses cardinality and nullability of the relationships.
- Developed for a specific version of a DBMS, location, data storage or technology to be used in the project.
- Columns should have exact datatypes, lengths assigned and default values.
- Primary and Foreign keys, views, indexes, access profiles, and authorizations, etc. are defined.

## Advantages and Disadvantages of Data Model

Advantages of data model:

- The main goal of a designing data model is to make certain that data objects offered by the functional team are represented accurately.
- The data model should be detailed enough to be used for building the physical database.
- The information in the data model can be used for defining the relationship between tables, primary and foreign keys, and stored procedures.
- Data Model helps business to communicate the within and across organizations.
- Data model helps to documents data mappings in ETL process.

- Help to recognize correct sources of data to populate the model.

Disadvantages of data model:

- To develop Data model one should know physical data stored characteristics.
- This is a navigational system produces complex application development, management. Thus, it requires a knowledge of the biographical truth.
- Even smaller change made in structure require modification in the entire application.
- There is no set data manipulation language in DBMS.

## Data Modeling for Business Intelligence

A data model for one line of business is hardly appropriate for another line of business. Only after a thorough analysis of an organization can a data model for the business lines be established to support the Business Intelligence process for the organization.

So, to ensure a successful Business Intelligence process, a data model should exist as follows:

- Business-Specific: The data model must be developed based on the unique nature of the business, the data types and their relationships. It should represent and organize the "big data" in the particular line of the business. It should be based on how data will be searched and used in the organization.
- With Built-in "Intelligence": The data model should include built-in "intelligence" through metadata, data dictionaries, hierarchies and inheritances. With such information, much of the "manual" inference work can be taken out of the decision process, thus, making the Business Intelligence process more efficient and effective.
- Robust: The data model should be able accurately and thoroughly represent the business, the data, and the decision process. It should reach a certain level of exhaustivity and specificity. Anything short of that will not be able to effectively support the Business Intelligence process.
- Scalable: The data model should be scalable and modular to support the ever-changing business needs of the organization. For instance, a subset of the data model could be adapted to more efficiently support a small business unit within the organization. Or, the data model could be easily expanded to support future business expansion, or as new data becomes available.
- Implementable: The data model should be easily implemented, either through in-house development, or through commercial tools, such as Oracle's BI Publisher.

## Business Intelligence Model

The Business Intelligence Model (BIM) is a model that offers opportunities for businesses to transform raw data into meaningful and useful information, in order to build an effective strategic plan, as well as create tactical and operational insights for decision-making within a given timeframe.

In the end, this knowledge needs to get to the right people, at the right moment, and via the right channel. Organisations collect large quantities of information. These are often raw data, such as facts and large data chains. This information, data, needs to be processed and interpreted because it opens up new opportunities within the organisation, which may result in a competitive advantage. The purpose of Business Intelligence (BI) depends on the strategy of the organisation. This is often derived from the business goal or mission statement.

### Business Intelligence Applications and Tools

Business Intelligence (BI) is not a product or system in itself. More often, the Business Intelligence Model (BIM) is referred to as an architecture that includes a collection of integrated applications and databases which support operations and the decision-making process. These provide the business world with easy access to business and market data. Such Business Intelligence (BI) applications support activity and decision support systems (DSS), systems, reports, online analytical processing (OLAP), static data analyses, prognosis, and data mining.

### DSS

The Decision Support System (DSS) is a computer support system used by managers and planners for decision-making. DSS combines human thinking and modeling systems in order to make well-informed and considered decisions.

For instance, DSS is used in logistical solutions. A business with a large inventory list can use DSS to generate movement in the supply chain.

### OLAP

Online Analytical Processing (OLAP) is another effective IT solution that is much used in the decision-making process of the business world. With this system, it is possible to quickly make calculations for analyses and reporting, two important elements in the decision-making process. The system has access to centralised business data which it rapidly analyses. The insights formed here are used in the decision-making process. Applications such as DSS and OLAP also appear in the Business Intelligence Model (BIM).

OLAP, not to be confused with OLTP, is often accompanied by huge quantities of data, Big Data. Think of bank employees who analyse what the online banking behaviour of their customers looks like. OLAP first requests data from the bank accounts of all customers, analyses user activity, and then presents the insights in a uncomplicated way.

### Data Warehouses

The software needs to access a lot of data, centralised or decentralised, for the use described above. Data comes in different shapes and sizes. Some data comes from systems, other comes from a database that was managed by a certain department, etc. It often concerns automatically generated reports, or manually kept lists in Excel.

### Business Intelligence Model (BIM) Roadmap

Business Intelligence (BI) is often considered to be more difficult than it really is. Naturally, the collecting and processing of business or market sensitive information is a delicate process, but it becomes easier with the six-step roadmap from the Business Intelligence Model (BIM).

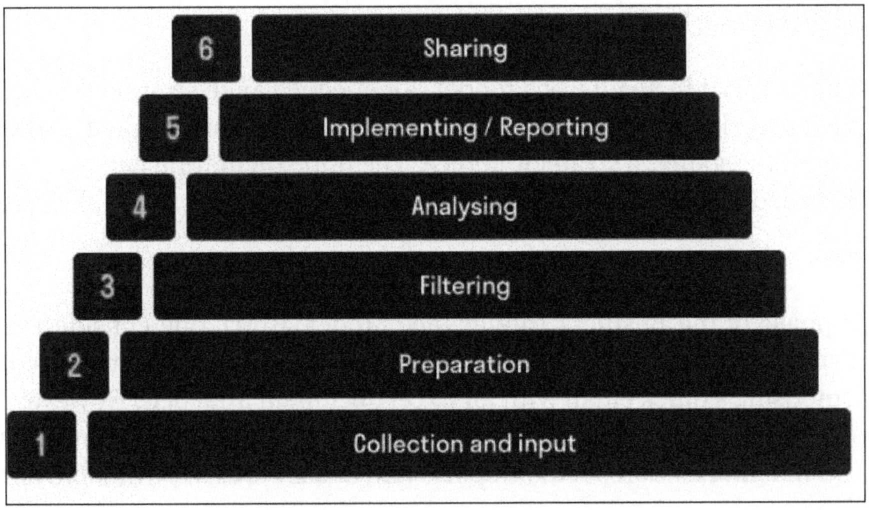


Business Intelligence Model BIM Roadmap.

## Collection and Input

The first step is collecting the data and connecting them to the Business Intelligence (BI) system. Depending on which system is used, the system can be ordered to get as much relevant data from a centralised database as possible, but Excel documents can also be added. There is a high diversity in types of sources and data and those all have their own way of requesting and input.

## Preparation

Following input, not all data is available in the correct format. This is especially the case when multiple types of data, for example qualitative and quantitative information, are to be used together. This means the data must often be prepared for the analysis. This happens in the preparation phase. Here, raw data is transformed into a clear collection of data.

This phase generally takes a lot of time, but it is essential for reliable and efficient analysis. Raw data can be logged in statistical software like IBM's SPSS, which cleans it and divides it into categories. If the data sets are large, as is the case with Big Data, other, advanced technologies are needed.

## Filtering

Now that all the data has been collected, cleaned, and entered, a selection must be made with relevant data. It may be the case that the customer behaviour data of the past five years are available, but the manager only wants to use the data of the past two years.

## Analysing

Once the data are in a workable format, actual analysis can start. This is what it is about in the Business Intelligence Model (BIM). This it where it is decided which cross-section must be made of the data. Averages per month and year, per segment, correlations between two variables, everything the organisation desires at that moment. The possibilities with data are endless and additional insights can be made by adding calculations.

### Implementing/Reporting

The analysis is summarised in an analysis model. An effective analysis model makes it possible to easily and clearly gain insight based on reports and dashboards. This is called implementation and forms the basis for, for instance, a strategic choice. The implementation can take place in different ways: professional reports, simple number lists, interactive graphic result tables, infographics, etc.

### Sharing

During the final phase of the Business Intelligence Model (BIM), one considers how the results that were given shape in the previous phase will get to the right people at the right time. This is often done by composing a quick email with an Excel document attached. However, there is a danger that different versions of the same file will get mixed up. More complex information solutions often have an internal information portal. Reports and dashboards are available here for everyone who has been given access.

## Strategic Modeling

Business intelligence (BI) consists of a range of technologies for using information within organizations to ensure compliance to strategic and tactical objectives, as well as to laws and regulations. As a research field, it encompasses data and knowledge management, modeling of processes and policies, data quality, data privacy and security, data cleaning and integration, data exchange, inconsistency management, information retrieval, data mining, analytics, and decision support.

This interest in technologies and services that improve organizational governance has caused dramatic growth for the BI market and the industry that serves it. By now, most competitive organizations have a significant investment in BI, much of it technology-related, based on software tools and artifacts. However, as summarized by Gartner, one important problem of BI technologies is that information generated by BI systems and other decision inputs are rarely linked to business decisions and outcomes. In addition, business people – be they executives, managers, consultants, or analysts – are in general agreement that what they are looking for is not new gadgets producing a dizzying array of largely useless statistics. Instead, they are interested in having their business data analyzed in their terms: strategic objectives, business models and strategies, business processes, markets, trends and risks. This gap between the worlds of business and data remains today the greatest barrier to the adoption of BI technology, and the greatest factor in the cost of applying BI technology.

We propose to bridge this gap by extending the notion of conceptual schema to include concepts beyond entities and relationships. In particular, we propose the Business Intelligence Model (BIM) as a business-level counterpart to the Entity-Relationship or Relational Model, so that strategic objectives, business processes, risks and trends can all be represented in a business schema. Users can query this schema, much like conventional database schemas but with business terms, to perform analysis, to track decisions and their impacts, or to explore suitable strategies to problems at hand. Such queries are to be translated through schema mappings into queries defined over databases and data warehouses, and the answers are to be translated back into business-level concepts.

As shown in figure, the final aim of the BIM is to represent the internal and external business and environment, and to support managers in making decisions at each level of management providing answers to questions such as "What will happen next?". Indeed, the BIM is based on the idea that you cannot measure what you cannot represent, and you cannot improve what you cannot measure.

As defined and summarized in table below, people at different levels in an organization have different types of decision-making responsibilities.

Strategic decisions, which are typically made by executive managers, affect the long-term direction of an organization and are often complex and characterized by uncertainty due to the limited availability of information. Usually, managers at this level depend on their past experiences and instincts for making a decision.

Examples of strategic decisions can be to decide whether it is time to discontinue a product line or to launch a new one.

Tactical decisions regard more intermediate-term issues and are typically made by middle managers. The decisions made at this level attempt to move the organization closer to reaching the strategic goals.

Examples of tactical decisions can be to hire an advertising agency in order to promote a new product or to create an incentive plan for encouraging employees in increasing the organization's production.

Operational decisions concentrate on day-to-day organization activities and are typically made by lower-level managers. Decisions made at this level attempt to ensure that the daily activities are conform with respect to business targets and standards in order to achieve the strategic goals.

Examples of operational decisions include scheduling employees, purchasing raw materials needed for production, or answering questions such as "Do we extend credit to this customer?".

Table: A taxonomy of management decision-making.

| Level of Management | Core Requirement | Nature of the Decision |
|---|---|---|
| Executive | Strategic Planning | Long term, unstructured, difficult to develop specific decision models. |
| Mid-level | Management Control | Shorter term, semi-structured, modeling possible. |
| Operational | Operational Control | Short term, structured, modeling possible. |

Here we focus on a particular use of the model for supporting the strategic planning process, which is the process of defining an organization's strategy (or direction) and making decisions on allocating the organization's resources in order to pursue this strategy.

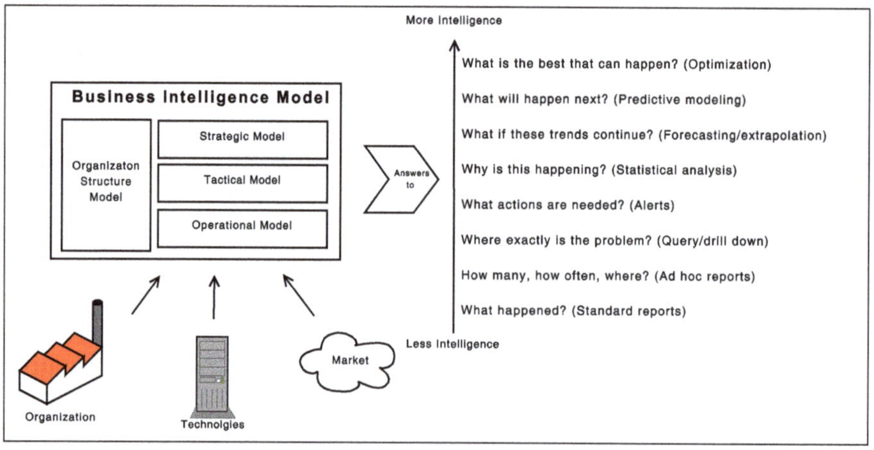


The Business Intelligence Model.

In pursue this strategy. In particular, an organization can follow different approaches for strategic planning such as the Situation-Target-Path, the Draw-See-Think-Plan, the See-Think-Draw, etc. which can be summarized by the following activities:

1. Formulate Vision & Mission: An organization must clearly define its Vision and Mission statements and the associated hierarchy of goals and objectives.
2. Situational Analysis: An analysis of the organization and its environment must be conducted in order to identify influences among external and internal factors and the organization goals, e.g., the SWOT analysis.
3. Develop Strategies: A set of alternatives for the fulfillment of goals must be formulated in terms of actions and processes to be taken to achieve goals and in terms of the resources required to execute these actions.
4. Implement Strategies: The "best" strategies must be chosen and implemented using organizational processes and resources.
5. Evaluate and Monitor Performance: The implemented strategies must be evaluated to see if they are working successfully.

## Primitive Concepts

Table introduces the primitive concepts in BIM for modeling strategic objectives and strategies.

The former (SM) is a visual representation of the strategy of an organization showing plans used to achieve missions and visions. In particular, it illustrates the cause-and effect relationships between different strategic goals and associated measures, the key performance indicators (KPIs).

These measures are included in the latter, the BSC, which represents a "balanced" range of metrics against which to measure the Organization's performance. "Balance" here means that the broader view of leading performance indicators includes also non-financial concerns, such as "learning and growth of employees" and "customer satisfaction". Both SMs and BSCs describe and measure organizational performance across four balanced perspectives: financial, customers, internal business processes, and learning and growth.

## Situations, Intentions and Processes

Primitive concepts are represented as metaclasses (having names that end in -Class). In particular, Intention can be used to define a hierarchy of Vision, Strategic/Tactical goals, etc., which represents the desired end state of an organization. Process models an organization's Mission and the different Strategies and, at tactical and operational levels, their decomposition into Business processes and Activities. Resource models what resources are required to execute such strategies.

In any strategic planning setting, a scan of the internal and external environment is a fundamental issue. Accordingly, BIM provides the Situation concept for modeling internal and external situations that can be helpful or harmful to an organization's goals. In addition, we adopt the SWOT classification in order to define the types of influence that a Situation may exercise on an Intention.

Table: BIM primitive concepts.

| Concept | Description | Example | Superclass |
|---|---|---|---|
| Thing | BIM's most general concept. This abstract metaclass has everything as an instance. | | |
| Object | Abstract metaclass whose instances persist/endure over time. | | Thing |
| Event | Instantaneous happening (perdurant) that changes an Object; can be described by a Proposition that was false before the Event and is true after. | New order received | Thing |
| Situation | Partial state of the world described by a Proposition. Situations can have structure consisting of relations and Things standing in those relations. | Christmas season | Object |
| Proposition | Describes a Situation. In general, Propositions are true/false/undefined in a Situation. | | Object |
| Intention | A Proposition an Actor wants to make true. | More products sold | Proposition |
| Domain Assumption | A Proposition assumed by an Actor to be true for purposes of fulfilling an Intention. | Market increases at least 10% annually | Proposition |
| Directive | A Proposition prescribed by an authority intended to constraint, guide, govern, or influence elements of an organization such as Actors and Processes. | Pizza delivery in 30 mins. | Proposition |
| Entity | Object whose existence does not depend on that of others. | | Object |
| Actor | Entity that carries out Actions to achieve Intentions. | Sales manager | Entity |
| Action | Entity performed by an Actor that produces Events and can have pre- and postconditions. | Deliver product | Entity |
| Process | Entity consisting of coordinated Actions to achieve an Intention. | Sales process | Entity |
| Resource | Entity of value to an Actor. | Money, information | Entity |
| Indicator | Measurable Object that gives information about the state of an associated Object. Can be used to quantify the satisfaction level of an Intention or the operational performance of an Actor, a Process or a Resource. | Number of products sold per week | Object |

| | | | |
|---|---|---|---|
| Relationship | An Object that relates two or more Things and whose existence depends on that of the Things it relates. | | Object |
| Influence | A Relationship between two Things t1 and t2, where the state of t1 constraints the state of t2 in a probabilistic or causal sense. | | Relationship |

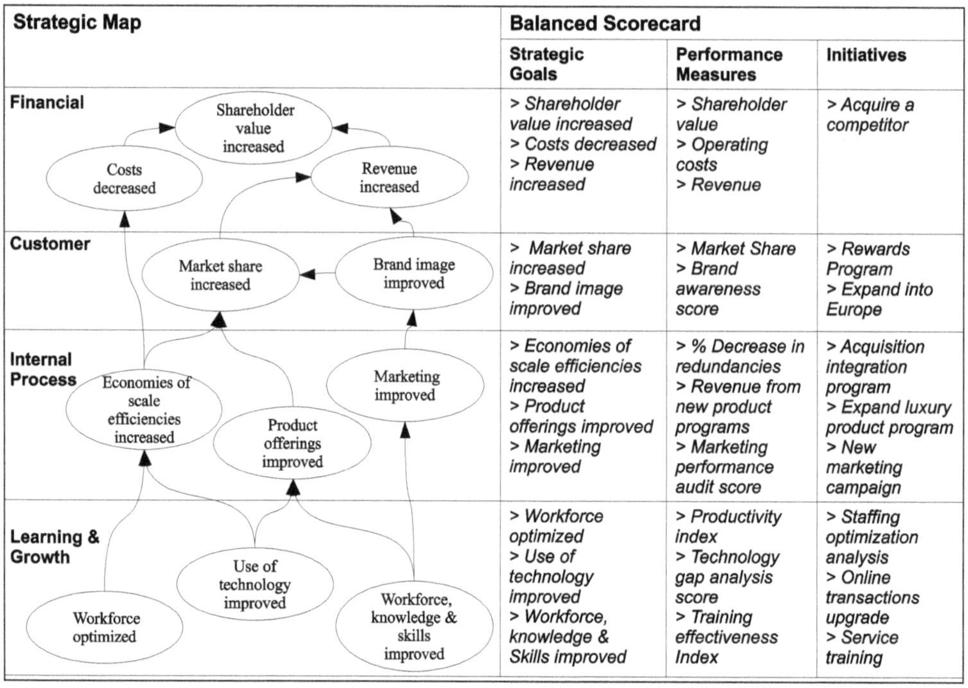


A strategic map and a balanced scorecard for BestTech Inc.

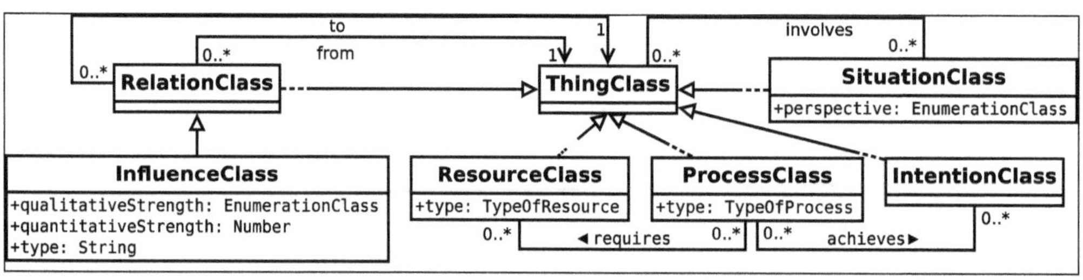


Intention, Process and Situation metaclasses and associated relationships in the BIM metamodel.

In this classification, internal factors are situations further classified into Strengths or Weaknesses while external factors are Opportunities or Threats. For example, a Threat for Wal-Mart may be "Exposure to political problems in the countries that we operate in". Notice that a strength with respect to one Intention may well be a weakness for another.

Figure shows a small example that instantiates the metaclasses of figure. Goals (i.e., Intentions), such as "Shareholder value increased" are decomposed into subgoals. Subgoals may be mandatory or optional (the notation used here is adapted from feature diagrams). Goals may be achieved by carrying out Processes. In turn, Processes require Resources; there are various types of Resources with associated icons. Situations can influence goals but also Processes, Resources, etc. Opportunities and weaknesses are particular kinds of influences. Influence relationships [3] can actually exist between any two Things and play a pivotal role in governance models.

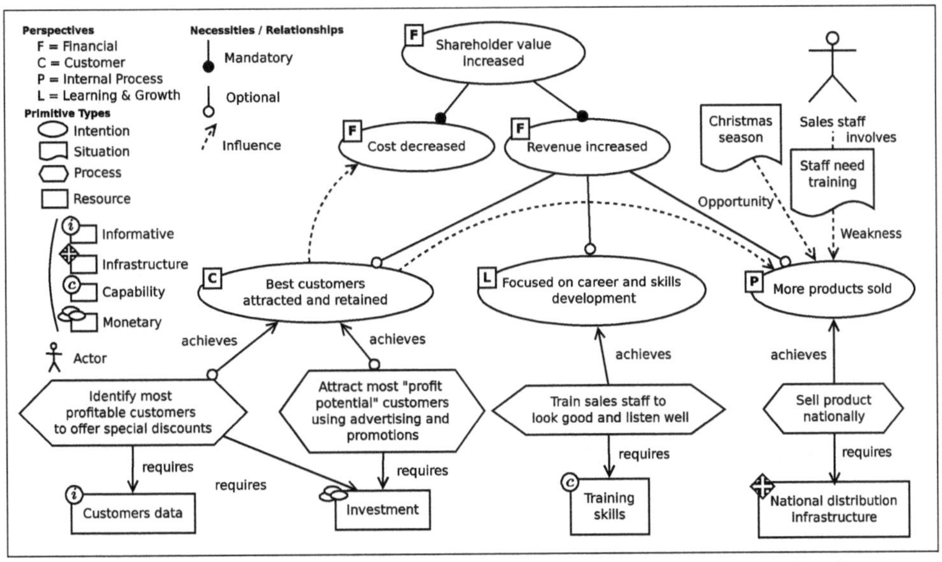

An example of Situation, Intention and Process concepts at schema level.

## Actors

Figure shows the Actor type and its relationships. An important relationship is the "responsible for" that defines which Actor is liable to be called on to (legally) answer when Intentions, Processes, Resources, and Directives are not acting in accordance with the business of an organization. For example, an Actor can be responsible for enforcing a work-site safety policy (i.e. a Directive). Indeed, if an accident occurs due to inappropriate safety conditions or there is a problem during a safety inspection, the responsibility will fall upon the Actor.

Actors must also comply with Directives, e.g., an employee must wear the protective equipments, and are able to define them, e.g., the executive board can define a policy such as "Pizza must be delivered within 20 minutes from the order or it will be free".

An Actor can desire Intentions which are satisfied by other Actors; for example, the "More products sold" Intention is desired by the executive board and is satisfied by the sales staff under the responsibility of the sales manager. An Actor is also capable of a Process (or an Action) that can actually performing or not.

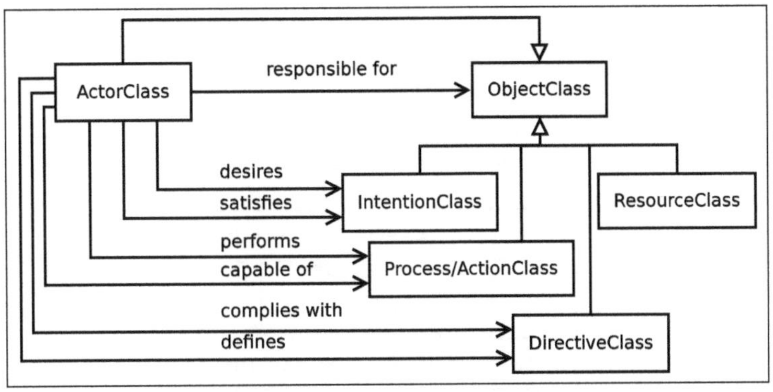

The Actor primitive type and the associated relationships.

Figure shows an example of Actors and their relationships with the business environment.

Notice how cardinality values can be used for enriching the semantic of relationships in order to describe the minimum and maximum number of associated elements within a set. For example, in the figure, the sales department is constituted by a sales manager and from a minimum of six to twelve sales employees. In particular, regarding the "Package product" Action, a minimum of three employees are capable of the "Package product" Action and at least two must perform this Action on a maximum of ten that can be allocated to such Action.

Moreover, as described in figure, an Actor can be specialized in Agent, Role, and Position. As defined in *i**, a Role is an abstract characterization of the behavior of a social Actor within some specialized context or domain of endeavor, and a Position is a set of Roles, usually played by one Agent. An Agent is an Actor with concrete, physical manifestations, such as a human individual or an artificial component of a system (hardware/software agents). Finally, an Agent can occupy a Position, while a Position covers a Role. Figure shows an example of Agent, Role and Position.

## Indicators

Indicators evaluate the quality of Objects to ensure compliance to internal policies and external directives.

Figure (a) shows the Indicator metaclass, consisting of attributes such as target, thresholds, extreme values, etc. The attributes 's description is provided in table.

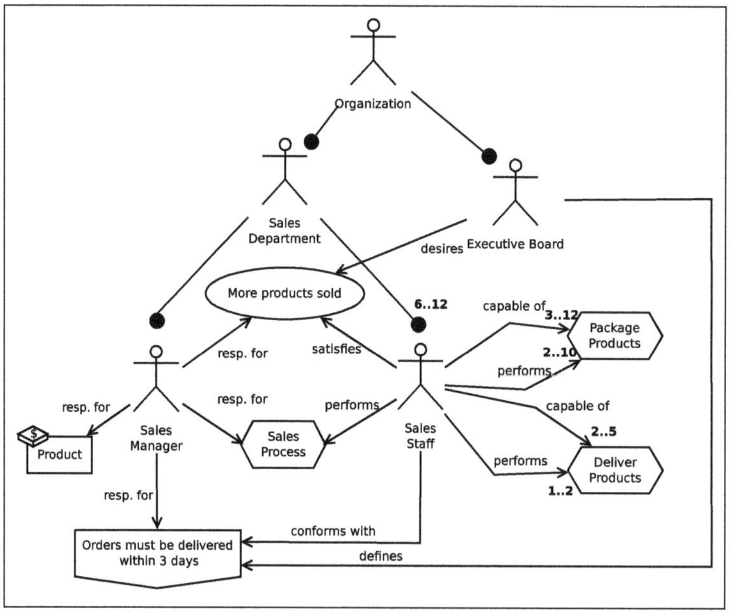


An example of Actors and their relationships with the business environment.

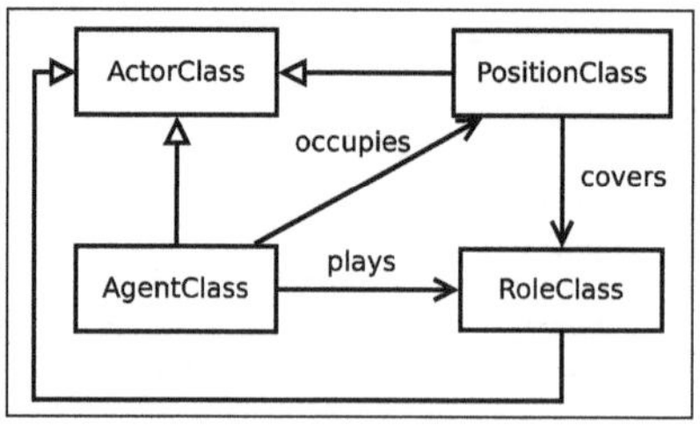


Agent, Role and Position in the BIM metamodel.

Notice that, in Table, the evaluationTime represents the timestamp associated to a specific current value instance, i.e., the time when the instance is calculated and created. This "system" time is different from the "domain" time (e.g. a Time dimension) used to navigate and calculate Indicators in a historical period of time, e.g., the Time dimension's value "March, 2009" to calculate the number of products sold in March.

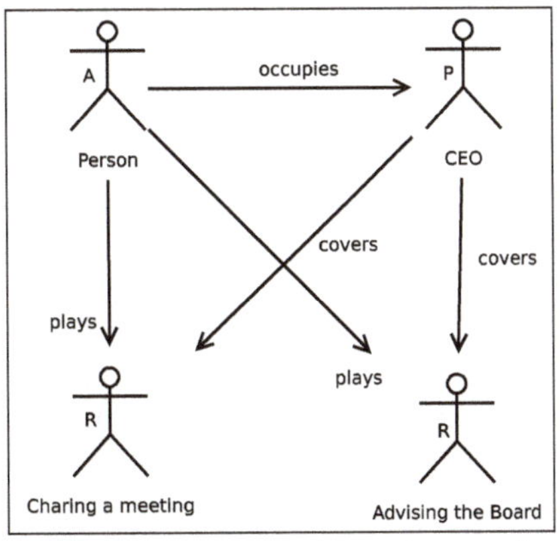


An example for Agent, Role and Position at schema level.

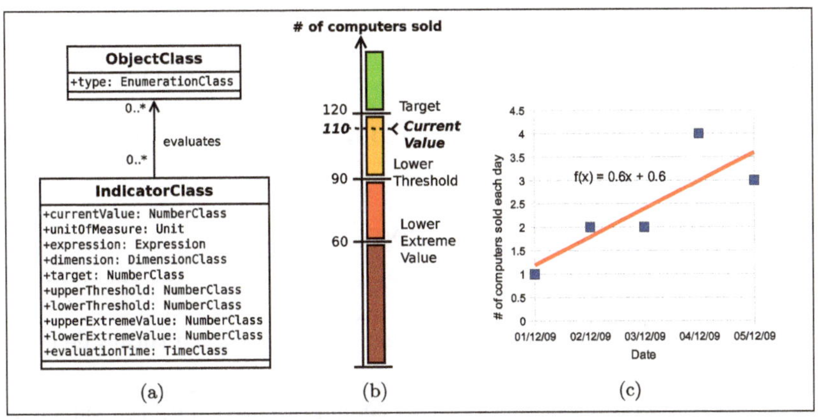


(a) The Indicator primitive type in the BIM metamodel.
(b) An example of visual notation for Indicators at instance level. (c) An Indicator 's Trend example.

An example of Indicator and the use of its attributes is shown in Figure. Notice how the current value (current Value) is found between Lower Threshold and Target; therefore, the company has almost reached its target in selling computers. The current value is calculated at evaluation Time using the metrics defined in the expression field. In general, BIM relies on the Object Constraint Language (OCL) to define such expressions. Moreover, one or more dimensions can be used to calculate and navigate an Indicator along specific directions of interest, e.g., the number of "Apple" computers sold.

Table: The description of Indicator's attributes.

| Meta-attribute's name | Description |
|---|---|
| Current Value | The current value of an Indicator which is calculated through the evaluation of a metric's expression. |
| Unit of Measure | The unit of measure associated with the current value of an Indicator. |
| Expression | The metric's expression used to calculate the current value of an Indicator. |

| | |
|---|---|
| Dimension | It allows to navigate (calculate the value of) an Indicator along specific directions of interest. |
| Target | It is a value which allows to quantify the satisfaction level of an Intention (or, more in general, a performance level desired for a property of an Object). If an Indicator reaches the Target the associated Intention is satisfied. |
| (upper & lower) threshold | It defines a threshold (upper or lower) value that can be assumed by an Indicator that represents a critical situation for the Organization's business. |
| (upper & lower) extreme Value | It defines the worst (upper or lower) value that can be assumed by an Indicator which represents a critical (extreme) situation for the Organization's business. |
| EvaluationTime | The time in which the current value of an Indicator is calculated. |

BIM also supports the definition of operations, such as Trend, Risk, Reward or Confidence, at the class level (i.e., at the schema level), which calculate additional information (meta values) for the current values assumed by an Indicator. The result is in-depth information on the subject of an Indicator. Table provides a brief description of such methods while Figure is an example of a Trend operation based on a linear regression method. The result is a trend with a slope of +0.6 which means that: i) the trend is positive, and ii) the prediction of computers sold on Dec. 6, 2009 is about four units.

In order to better understand the use of Indicators, take a look at the following example:

Suppose that a Car Dealer has in store 16 units of "Luxury car" that it desires to sell over a period of one month.

Table: The description for the Indicator's operations.

| Method's name | Description |
|---|---|
| Trend | It represents a general movement over time of a statistically detectable Indicators's change. |
| Risk | It provides the actual loss associated to the current value assumed by an Indicator. |
| Reward | It provides the actual gain associated to the current value assumed by an Indicator. |
| confidence | It provides the actual confidence associated to the current value assumed by an Indicator. The confidence is based on i) the quality of the information used to calculate the current value, ii) the reputation of the source who provided the information and iii) the reliability of the method used to calculate the current value. |

Suppose also that the actual (partial) state of the world, i.e. on December 6th,2009, is as described in table in which each car is identified by a Vehicle Identification Number (VIN).

Table: The (desired) states of the world for the "Car sold" Intention.

| (Desired) State of the world | Evaluation |
|---|---|
| Car (VIN 1HGBH41J8MN109180) Sold | True |
| Car (VIN 1HGBH41J8MN109181) Sold | False |
| Car (VIN 1HGBH41J8MN109182) Sold | True |
| Car (VIN 1HGBH41J8MN109183) Sold | False |
| Car (VIN 1HGBH41J8MN109184) Sold | True |

| | |
|---|---|
| Car (VIN 1HGBH41J8MN109185) Sold | False |
| Car (VIN 1HGBH41J8MN109186) Sold | False |
| Car (VIN 1HGBH41J8MN109187) Sold | True |
| Car (VIN 1HGBH41J8MN109188) Sold | False |
| Car (VIN 1HGBH41J8MN109189) Sold | True |
| Car (VIN 1HGBH41J8MN109190) Sold | False |
| Car (VIN 1HGBH41J8MN109191) Sold | True |
| Car (VIN 1HGBH41J8MN109192) Sold | True |
| Car (VIN 1HGBH41J8MN109193) Sold | False |
| Car (VIN 1HGBH41J8MN109194) Sold | False |
| Car (VIN 1HGBH41J8MN109195) Sold | True |

We have the following Indicator as described in Figure and in table Notice the use of the cardinality (0..16) to express the number of cars the organization desires to sell. Moreover, Figure shows the different zones defined by using the extreme, threshold and target values; and the current value for December 6th, 2009 lying on the red zone.

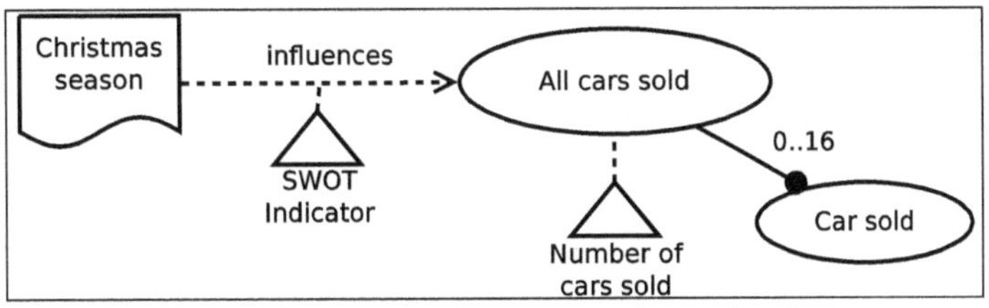


An example of Indicators at schema level.

Table: An example of an Indicator at different levels of modeling.

| Meta-Level | Schema-Level | Instance-Level |
|---|---|---|
| Indicator | Number of Cars Sold | Inst 1:Number of Cars Sold |
| currentValue | Integer | 8 |
| unitof Measure | cars sold | - |
| expression | "context Car select (car \| car.status='Sold' ∧ car.type='Luxury car') – > size()" | - |
| target | Integer | 13 |
| (Lower) threshold | Integer | 10 |
| (Lower) extreme Value | Integer | 7 |
| dimension | Type of Car | "Luxury Car" |
| Evaluation Time | Time | Dec 6, 2009 |

Below figures shows examples of Indicator's operations. In particular, the former is an example of a Trend Operation based on a linear regression method. The operation calculates the slope (or gradient) of the trend line fitting the time series provided in input, where the time series are the number of cars sold from Dec. 1st to 2009 to Dec. 6th, 2009. The result of the operation is a slope of −0.7 which means that on Dec. 6, 2009 the Trend for the number of cars sold is negative.

The latter, Figure, is an example of risk and reward operations which allow to associate specific loss or gain values to any current value. In fact, if we suppose that 30,000 USD is the total cost sustained for a car while 50,000 USD is the revenue obtained by its selling, we have that: i) a total gain of 170,000 USD is obtained when the target is reached, ii) a loss of 130,000 USD is endured when the current value assumes the extreme value and iii) a loss of 80,000 USD is endured on the current value calculated on December 6, 2009.

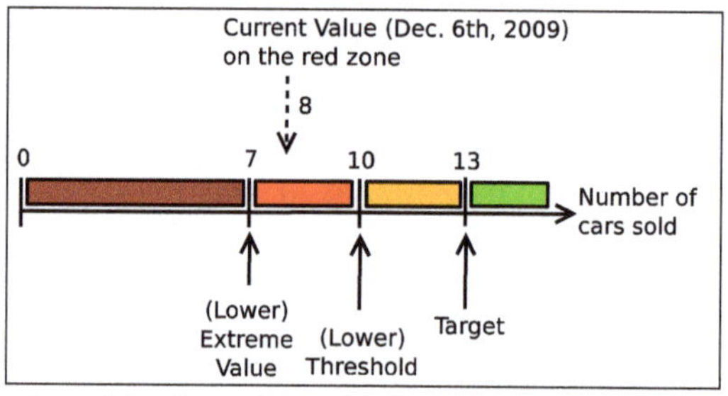


The current value of the "Number of cars sold" Indicator on December, 6th.

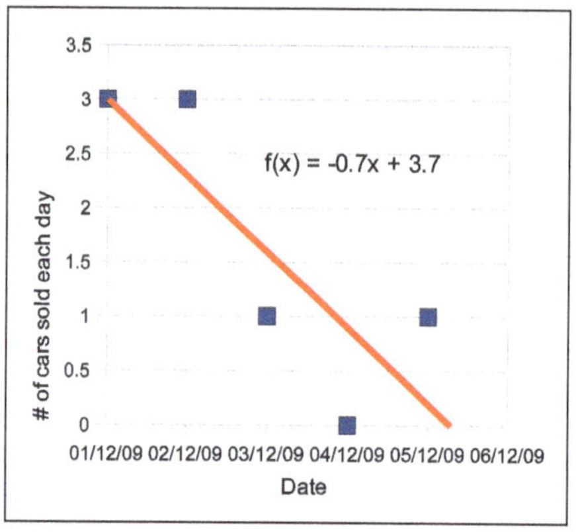


The Trend for the "Number of cars sold" Indicator.

Figure shows another Indicator, namely the SWOT Indicator, which is used to evaluate the influences among Situations and Intentions. We have four kind on influences, namely, Strength, Weakness, Threat, and Opportunity. For each type, it is possible to define a quality or quantity power scale, e.g., < high, medium, low > or [0, 100], in order to determine the degree of the influence. Therefore, a SWOT Indicator can assume a current value that ranges among values of the power scale and can have a unit of measure equal to Strength, Weakness, Threat, or Opportunity. The SWOT Indicator's current value is used by the InfluenceClass metaclass to support different kind of analysis.

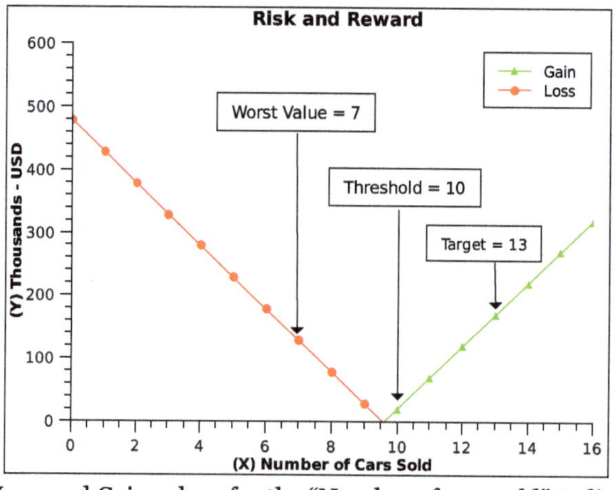


The Loss and Gain values for the "Number of cars sold" Indicator.

## Objects' Life-cycle and Behavior: A Finite State Machine Model

A Finite State Machine (FSM) provides a simple and effective means to control the life-cycle and overall behavior of BIM's Objects. In fact, a FSM is an abstract computational model which allows to define for each Object: i) a set of different states assumed by Objects' instances in the real world; ii) the transitions among these different states in order to define the (computational) behavior; iii) the events/inputs which express the stimuli taken into account; and, iv) the actions/outputs which are the possible responses that can be generated.

Formally, a FSM is a multi-tuple $FSM - (\Sigma, \Lambda, S,\ s0,\ \delta,\ \omega)$ where:

- ($\Sigma$) is the input alphabet of symbols representing external stimuli (inputs or events) that are used by transition functions;
- ($\Lambda$) is the output alphabet of symbols representing responses (outputs or actions) that are provided by output functions;
- (S) is the set of possible states which are conditions of the state machine at a certain time;
- ($so \in S$) is the start state;
- ($\delta : S \times \Sigma \rightarrow S$) is the state transition function. Based on the current state $s_c \in S$ and an input symbol $i \in \Sigma$, it computes the transition to the next state $s_n \in S$;
- ($\omega : S \times \Sigma \rightarrow \Lambda$) is the output function (as defined in the Mealy model).

The BIM also allows to associate to each state a Time attribute which stores a timestamp value representing the last time in which an Object enter in that specific state.

In general, for all Objects, it is possible to identify a START state and a (possible) END state. The START state allows to define when an instance of the real world becoming an instance of a specific type of the BIM. For example, the "Car VIN=1HGBH41J8MN109180 sold" instance stars to be an Intention's instance when the car dealer defines a clear statement to sell that specific car, i.e. the car with VIN=1HGBH41J8MN109180. Than, the car dealer will be able to pursue it, i.e., the state BEING PURSUED.

In the opposite way, the END state allows to define when the same instance stops to be an (active) instance of that type 6 . For example, the "Car VIN=1HGBH41J8MN109180 sold" Intention's instance stops to be an Intention's instance when the car dealer stops to pursued it either because it is achieved, failed or aborted (i.e., the car dealer has changed his mind).

Moreover, for each specific Object, such as the Intention, it is also possible to define specific states which have a particular semantic into the business environment. For example, the above BEING PURSUED state can be defined for Intentions to express the continuing activity by an Actor to achieve a specific Intention.

Below figures shows, respectively, possible FSM diagrams for Intention and Resource. Notice that, a Vision cannot be fitted in the diagram illustrated in Figure since, usually, it is not possible to define a SATISFIED state or an END state for such a concept. Therefore, if it is necessary, a specific FSM diagram must be defined or, alternatively, the same FSM diagram can be used in which some states will be never assumed by the instances.

Moreover, it is also important to notice the two "pass Deadline" and "pass Expiring date" events which, respectively, lead to a FAILED Intention's state and to an EXPIRED Resource's state.

These events are fired when: i) the current time in the system is greater than, respectively, the "deadline date" and the "expiring date" defined in the business environment; and, ii) the actual states of Intention's and Resource's instances are, respectively, BEING PURSED and BEING CONSUMED. FSMs allows to define these events as guards which can be expressed by using constrains.

In this way, for example, it is possible to represent situations where a goal's deadline has passed and, since it is not longer important whether or not the goal will be satisfied, we transit to a FAILED state.

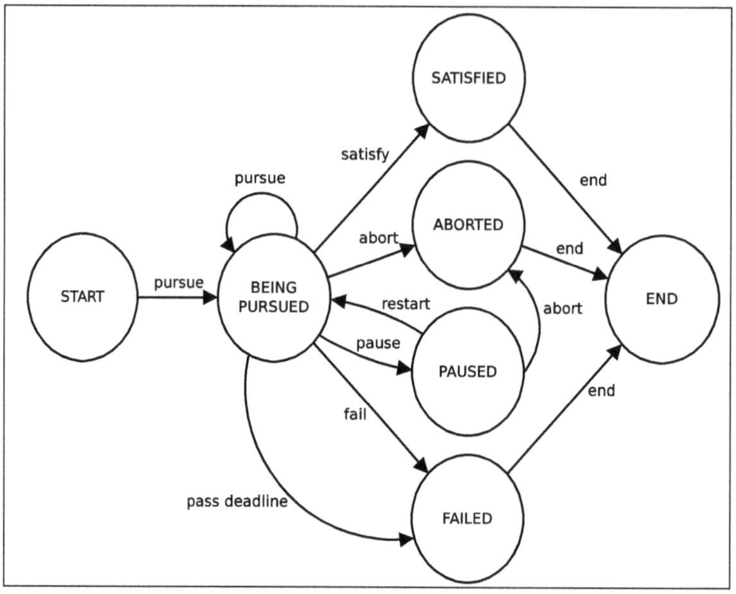


A FSM diagram for Intention.

A similar situation exists for Resources in the case we have passed the expiring date. In fact, the Resource stops to be a valid Resource loosing its intrinsic properties that make it such as a Resource in the business environment; however, we can still consume it with all the relative consequences.

The use of states and timestamps enable the definition of interesting queries over Objects belonging to a schema. For example, we can express queries such as (1)="List all goals that are not yet satisfied" or (2)="Show the time in which was satisfied" that can be defined as:

(1) = context Intention

select (intention | not (intention.state = 'SATISFIED')

(2) = context Intention

select (intention | intention.name = 'All car sold'

and intention.state = 'SATISFIED' ).time

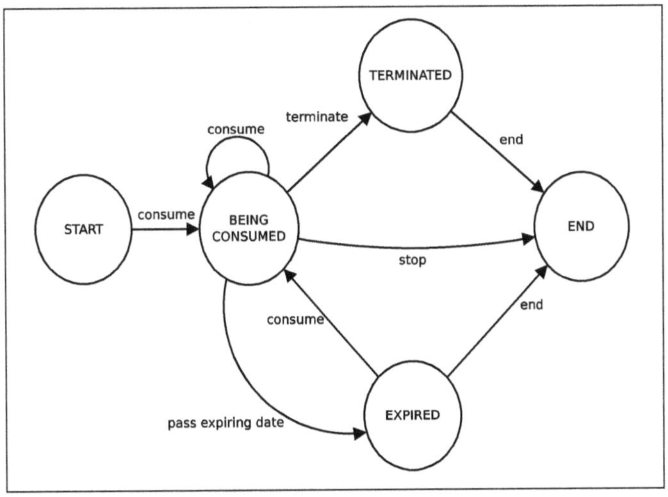


A FSM diagram for Resource.

## Evolution Timeline and Time Constrains for Objects

The previous subsection presented the concept of State to address issues related to the life cycle and behavior of Objects. However, since we want to describe the "evolution" of Objects within a business environment, we need to introduce the concept of Evolution Timeline. Figure shows the fragment of the BIM metamodel aimed to describe such aspect.

Each object can have an Evolution Timeline which represents its "lifetime". On this lifetime line, two types of Timepoints can be defined: i) time constrains for the definition of time constrains, such as a deadline for an Intention, and ii) timestamps to define when an instance enters into a specific state, such as when an Intention's instance assumes a SATISFIED state.

Notice that, for now, we are not constraining an Evolution Timeline to be associated to only one Object. In fact, as shown by the model, a same timeline can be shared among different Objects. Indeed, we think that having a unique timeline for the entire organization on which Timepoints belonging to different Objects can coexist, will be useful for analysis activities.

Finally, notice the relationship among State and Time point. Each State can have multiple Timepoints representing all the times (timestamps) an Object entered in that particular State. Moreover, a State might not have a Timepoint associated, i.e., the Object never assumed that State, and a Timepoint might not have a State associated, i.e., the Timepoint represents a time constrain for the associated Object and not a timestamp for a particular State.

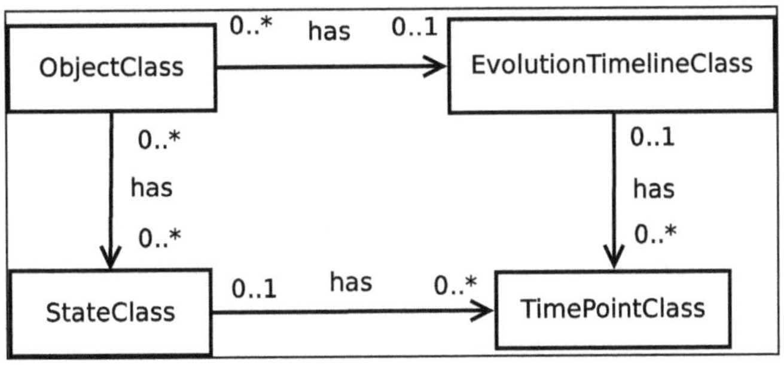


The Evolution Timeline concept.

Figure shows an example describing the above concepts with respect to the Intention primitive type.

In this example, we can see how an Intention was defined on March 1, 2009 with a deadline fixed on March 30, 2009. Moreover, the Intention was started to be pursed on March 3, 2009 to be paused on March 11, 2009 and finally satisfied on March 23, 2009 (after it was re-pursed on March 13, 2009). Notice that, all the above Timempoints represent timestamps with the exception of the deadline Timepoint constrain.

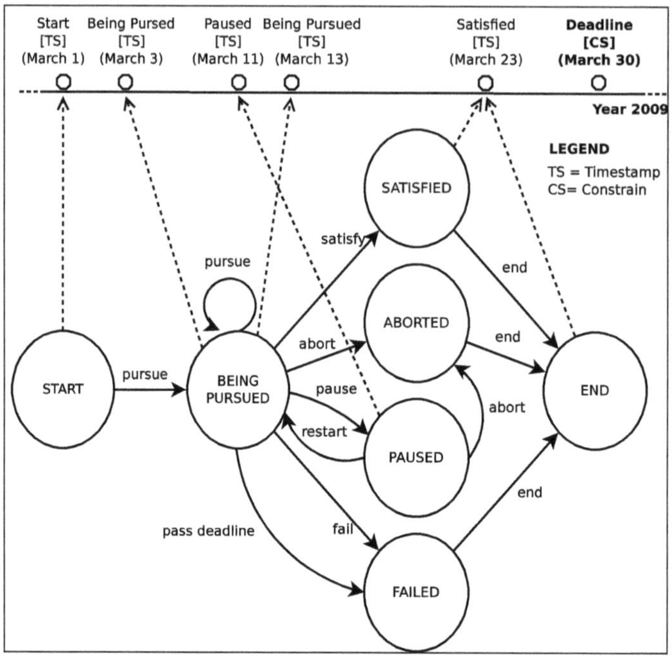


An example of Evolution Timeline for the Intention primitive type.

## The BIM Repository and the Abstraction Mechanisms

A BIM Repository is a persistent location in which organization and business data are stored and maintained in order to be fetched to perform some particular task, e.g., analytics tasks. In particular, a BIM Repository consists of structured classes(or types) and objects (or instances) which are defined using the BIM metamodel.

In general, as with other modeling languages, classes and objects can be organized along the three dimensions of aggregation, classification and generalization. The act of "abstracting a collection of units into a new unit is called aggregation"; indeed, an aggregation is a special type of association in which objects or classes are assembled or configured together to create a more complex object or class.

For example, the John object can be aggregated into the Pizza Pizza Sales Department object and respectively, the Employee class can be aggregated into the Department class. We adopt the feature model in order to allow users to be flexible during the aggregation activity.

The classification dimension calls for each object or class to be an instance of one or more generic classes or metaclasses. In fact, referring to the previous example, John is an instance of Employee while Employee is an instance of the ActorClass metaclass. The Classification dimension is also used for relationships belonging to the model; in fact, we can have an HomeAddress object which can be classified by an Address class which, similarly, can be classified by an AddressClass metaclass.

Classes and Metaclasses can be specialized along generalization or ISA hierarchies. As defined in, generalization is the act of "abstracting the commonalities among a collection of units into a new conceptual unit suppressing detailed differences". For example, an Employee class may have subclasses such as Clerk, Sales Person, etc.; similarly, an ObjectClass metaclass may have submetaclasses such as EntityClass, SituationClass, etc. Notice that ISA hierarchies are orthogonal to the classification dimension; therefore, all the above subclasses, i.e., Clerk, Sales Person, etc., should be instances of the Actor Class.

## Aggregation: Mandatory, Optional, OR and Alternative

The BIM provides a flexible way for the aggregation activity that allows to have a direct control in the choice of the parts (i.e., the "partOf" relationship) constituting an Object.

Indeed, the BIM aggregation mechanism uses the same approach described earlier in which the relationships between a parent and its children are categorized as:

- Mandatory: A child is required,
- Optional: A child is optional,
- Or: At least one of the children must be selected,
- Alternative (xor): Exact one of the children must be selected.

Figure provides an example which shows the visual notation used to aggregate different Intentions. The example, also show how cardinalities can be used to add more semantic during the aggregation activity; e.g., the "iPods produced" aggregates from one to one million "one iPod produced". Moreover, since the "one iPod produced" is mandatory the range of cardinality must start from "one".

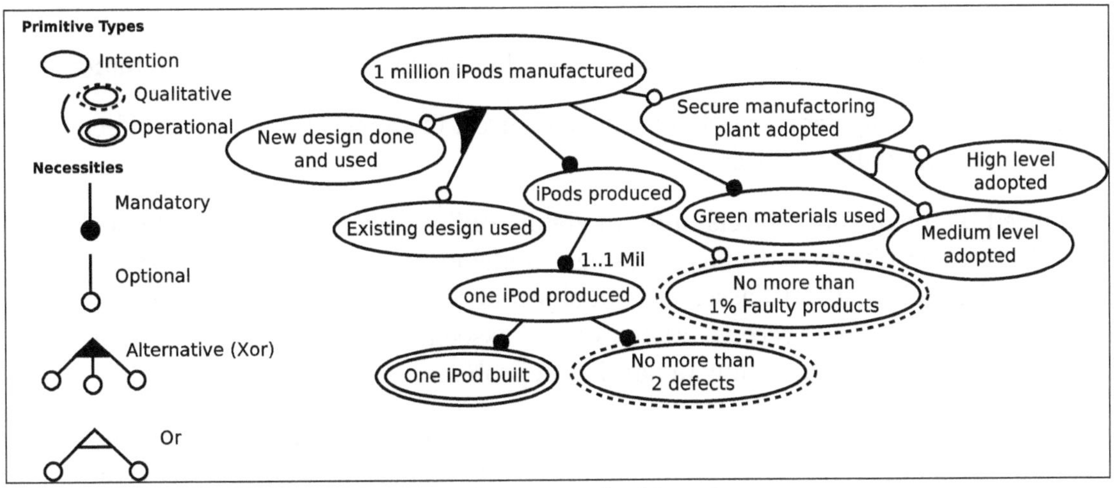


An Intention aggregation hierarchy.

## Classification: The OMG Four-layer Metamodel Architecture

The BIM metamodel is designed to be aligned with the OMG four-layer metamodel architecture which is summarized in table.

Table: The OMG four-layer metamodel architecture.

| Layer | Description | Example of model elements |
|---|---|---|
| M3: metameta-model | Defines the language for specifying metamodels. | MetaClass, MetaAttribute, MetaOperation |
| M2: metamodel | An instance of a metametamodel. Defines the language for specifying a model. | Class, Attribute, Operation, Component |
| M1: model | An instance of a metamodel. Defines a language to describe an information domain. | StockShare, askPrice, sellLimitOrder, StockQuoteServer |
| M0: user objects (user data) | An instance of a model. Defines a specific information domain. | <Acme Sof tware Share 98789>, 654.56, sell limit order, < Stock Quote Svr 32123 > |

In this architecture, a model at one layer is used to specify models belonging to the layer below. Similarly, a model at one layer can be seen as an instance of a particular model in the layer above.

Usually, models at Mn layer have an higher level of abstraction and are typically more compacts than models at $M_{n-1}$ layer. In fact, models at $M_{n-1}$ are more elaborate than the models at $M_n$ layer that describe them. Figure shows an example where the top layers M3 and M2 of the architecture are represented and specified, respectively, by the MOF meta-metamodel and by the UML metamodel.

The BIM metamodel is at the same layer of the UML metamodel, i.e, at the M2 layer. Therefore, we would consider the BIM metamodel to be an instance of the MOF meta-metamodel. We want this for two reasons: i) MOF enables the interoperability of model and metadata driven systems; and, ii) MOF is quite spread across industry. In this way, our model can exploit the interoperability provided by MOF in order to facilitate its eventual integration with industry's models and systems.

However, a major problem is that MOF (and UML) suffers from the "shallow" instantiation problem.

Basically, a class can only define the semantic of its direct instances, but it has no effect on entities created by further instantiation steps.

This is caused by the old "two-levels only" modeling philosophy which does not adequately support a multi layer architecture. In fact, although model elements in a multiple layer architecture can represent both objects and classes, i.e., an object at M2 layer can be seen as a class for objects at M1 layer, a class can never receive attributes and associations from its classifier, but only slots and links, thus leading to the shallow instantiation problem.

The BIM metamodel needs to be able to influence both the M1 layer and the M0 layer in order to constrain designers in the choice of domain concepts and relationships at M1 layer but also to propagate such "semantic" constrains (when requested) on instances at M0 layer.

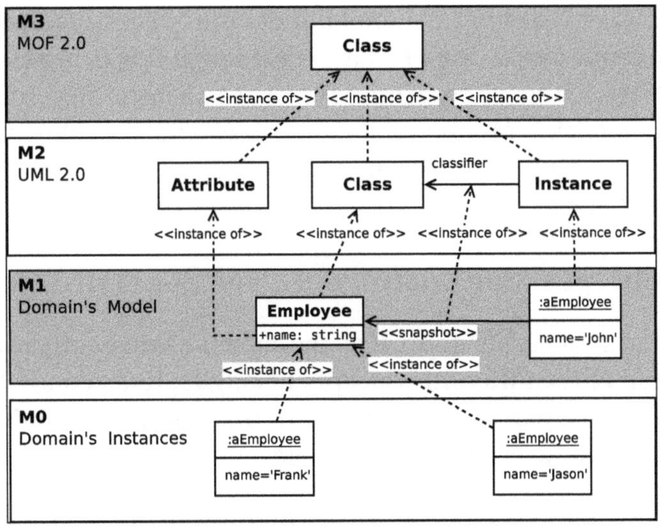


An example for the four-layer model architecture which uses MOF and UML.

Figure shows an example of such deep instantiation in which some "instance of" links are missing to simplify the illustration. Notice how:

1. Associations, such as "evaluates", can be propagated across multiple layers.
2. Some attributes, such as "currentValue", can be propagated across multiple layers while refining their types, e.g., the type of currentValue is NumberClass at M2 while is Integer at M1.
3. Some attributes, such as "metric", can be limited to specific layer, i.e., metric is instantiated at M1 while is disappearing at M0.
4. Some attributes, such as "director", can be freely defined by the designer at M1 but are not specified at M2, i.e., they are domain specific and are not mandatory by the BIM metamodel.

In order to support such deep instantiation, the BIM is inspired by the Telos language in which classes, attributes, and associations 1 are collectively referred to by the term "proposition" and are treated uniformly by the structuring mechanisms of aggregation, classification, and generalization. Therefore, as shown in Figure, we can have metaclasses, classes, objects; but also: i) metattributes, attributes, slots; and, ii) metassociations, associations, links.

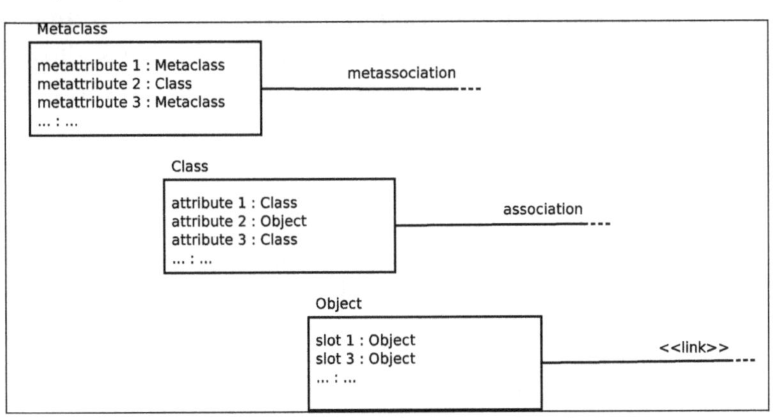


The Metaclass, Class and Objects instantiation.

A careful reader can observe that the UML metamodel introduces Instance metaclasses in order to "link" objects of different types at the M0 Layer. Although this can resolve the instantiation of associations at the M0 layer, this approach arises issues such as the "ambiguous classification" and the "replication of concepts". Moreover, it can increase the complexity of the model and lead to inconsistencies and the losing of precision; and, it does not satisfy the "need" of propagating attributes across different layers.

## Generalization: Subtypes and Business Terms Specialization

The primitive types presented earlier represent the model elements provided by the BIM metamodel for the description of the different concepts belonging to a generic business environment. Moreover, in order to describe particular instances of the real world, the BIM metamodel defines a set of subtypes whose semantic is described in table.

Moreover, in order to cover and map to business terminologies, such as a vision, mission, or strategy, we use metaproperties such as (i) short-/long-term, (ii) many/few instances, (iii) formal/informal definition, and (iv) chances of success. Clusters of terms from a business glossary, such as Vision, Strategic/Tactical goal, Softgoal, Objective are then represented in terms of a single BIM primitive concept (Intention) but each has different combinations of values for the four metaproperties. For example, a Vision is a long-term Intention without a formal definition, which is likely to only have a few instances (usually one) whose chances of success are low (depending on many uncertain factors).

To represent business terms, the BIM metamodel defines an attribute associated to the ThingClass metaclass, called type which is inherited by all the other metaclass in the metamodel to store specific terminology for each Thing. Table provides common clusters for some of BIM's primitive concepts.

Figure shows an example of subtypes and business terms specialization for the Intention primitive type.

## An UML Class Diagram for the BIM's Abstraction Mechanisms

The model is shown in Figure. The RefinementLinkClass, the NodeElementClass and the AggregationClass are parts of the aggregation mechanism. In particular, the attribute mandatory of the RefinementLinkClass allows to specify if the "refiner" component in the refinement relationship is mandatory or optional; while, the attribute type of the AggregationClass allows to specify the type of the aggregation, i.e., OR, AND, XOR, Alternative, performed on the sub-components.

Table: Subtypes belonging to the BIM metamodel.

| Primitive Type | Subtype | Subtype Description |
|---|---|---|
| Intention | Intention | An atomic Intention which has a very strict and clear logical criterion of satisfiability and can be achieved by an operational process or activity. |
| | Qualitative Intention | An atomic Intention which has not a clear-cut criterion for its satisfaction and can be claimed only when there is sufficient positive and little negative evidences (or unsatisfaction in the opposite case). |

| Actor | Agent | Actor with concrete, physical manifestations, such as a human individual. We use the term agent instead of person for generality, so that it can be used to refer to human as well as artificial (hardware/ software agents). An agent has dependencies that apply regardless of what roles he/she/it happens to be playing. These characteristics are typically not easily transferable to other individuals, e.g. its skills and experiences, and its physical limitations. |
|---|---|---|
| | Role | Abstract characterization of the behavior of a social actor within some specialized context or domain of endeavor. Its characteristics are easily transferable to other social actors. The dependencies associated with a role apply regardless of the agent who plays the role. |
| | Position | Intermediate abstraction that can be used between a role and an agent. It is a set of roles typically played by one agent (e.g., assigned jointly to that one agent). We say that an agent occupies a position. A position is said to cover a role. |

Table: An example of business terms captured with the Thing's attribute type.

| BIM Concept | Business Terms |
|---|---|
| Intention | Vision, Strategic/Tactical Goal, SoftGoal, Objective. |
| Process | Mission, Strategy, Tactic, Initiative, Business Process, Activity. |
| Actor | Organization, Business Unit, Human person, System Application. |
| Resource | Monetary/Infrastructure/Economic Good/Information/Human/Capability Resource. |
| Directive | Policy, Rule. |

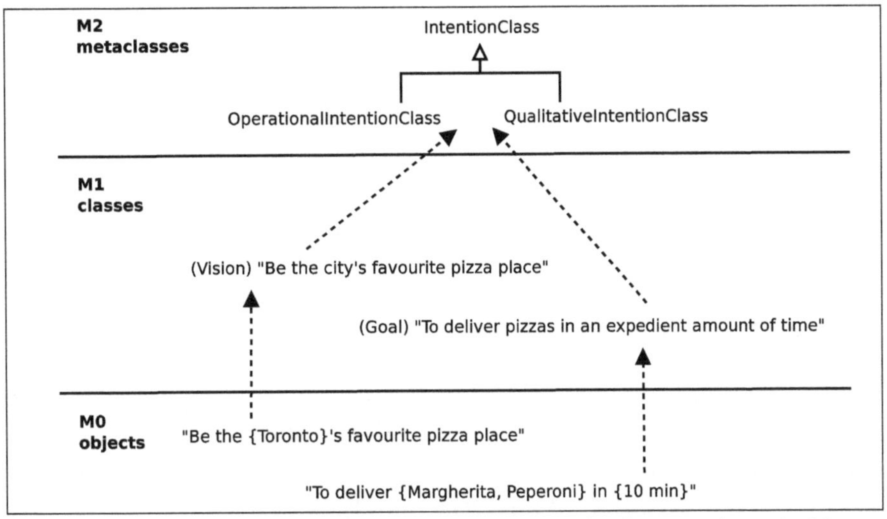


An example of subtypes and business terms specialization for the Intention primitive type.

In regard to the generalization mechanism, the class named "..." (specializing the ThingClass) represents the different primitive types. Instead, the attribute type belonging to the ThingClass is used to specify the business terminology shown in table.

Finally, the right part of the model represents the state and the evolution timeline concepts.

Figure shows an example of how the model works underlying the feature model visual notation.

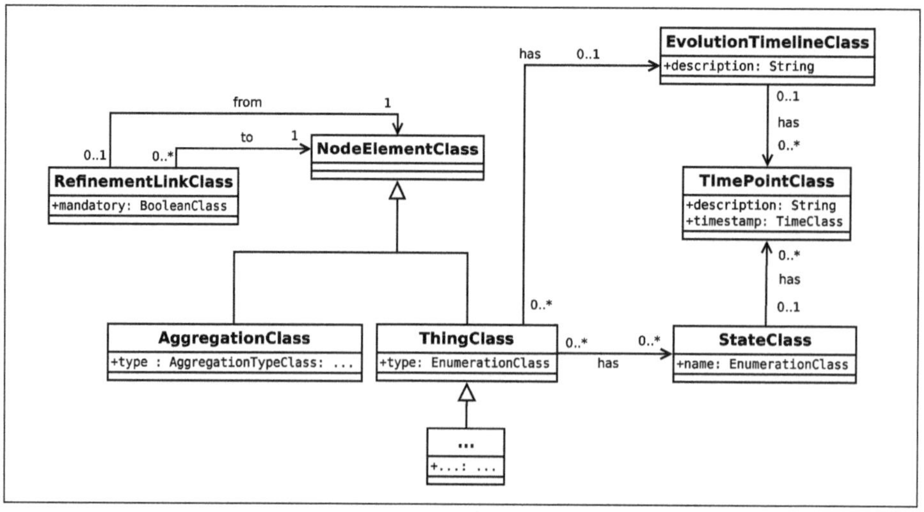


An UML Class diagram for the BIM's abstraction mechanism.

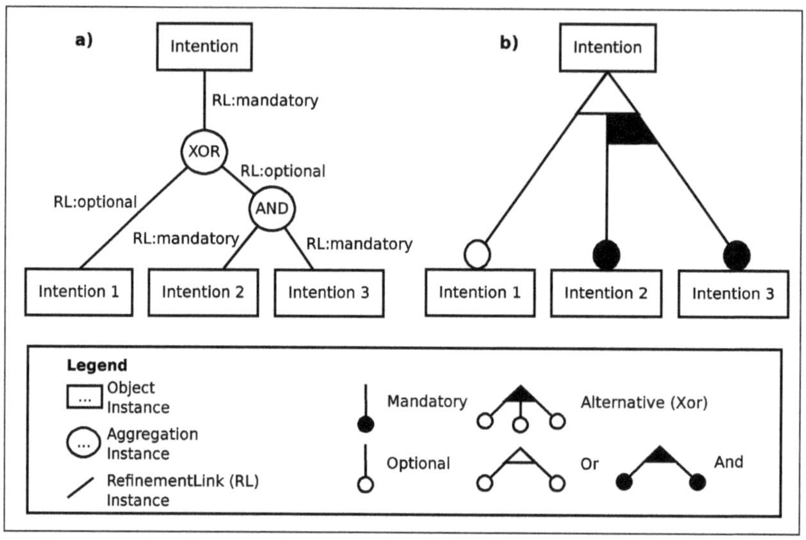


An example of aggregation using (b) the feature model visual notation and (a) the underlying UML Class Diagram.

## Strategic Analysis through Mappings

We illustrate how the richness and flexibility of BIM can be used to represent widespread strategic planning models. Moreover, since the final aim of BIM is to support analysis activities for answering questions such as "What will happen next?" or "Where exactly is the problem?", we describe how BIM can be projected onto different analysis models.

In particular, the following target models are considered:

- A goal reasoning model based on a formal goal model,
- The SWOT analysis model,
- The Strategic Map model,
- The Balanced SCorecards (BSCs) (and Key Performance Indicators ) model.

## Goal (Intention) Reasoning: A Formal (Axiomatic) Model

In the BIM, Intention analysis and reasoning are given a prominent role to help stakeholders in the definition of their intentions and relationships among them, such as conflicts and negative or positive contributions.

The Intention primitive type can be used to define the hierarchy of the Vision, Goals, and Objectives of an organization in which nodes can be connected by influence links.

Here, we want to provide an underneath algorithm which enables the reasoning on the Intentions belonging to such a hierarchy.

At this aim, we project the BIM toward the goal reasoning model. Notice that, the model is used in the context of the Tropos methodology which adopts the i *modeling framework for analyzing requirements (Early Requirements and Late Requirements ).

In particular, the formal model goals is used by the software engineer to cope with qualitative relationships and inconsistencies among goals during the early requirements phase.

The formal model description resides in the definition of the notions of goal graphs and the axiomatic representation of goal relations. The goal graphs is defined trough a set of goal nodes $G_i$ and of relations $(G_1, \ldots, G_n) \overset{r}{\mapsto} G \mapsto$ over them, including the (n+1)- any relations and, or and the binary relations +S, -S, +D, -D, ++S, - -S, +,-++, - -. For a in depth description we remand to while here we briefly recall the intuitive meaning of such relationships.

For and and or we have that:

- $(G_1, \ldots, G_n) \overset{and}{\mapsto} G$ means that G is satisfied (resp. denied) if all $G_1, \ldots, G_n$ are satisfied (resp. if at least one $G_i$ is denied);
- $(G_1, \ldots, G_n) \overset{or}{\mapsto} G$ means that G is denied (resp. satisfied) if all $G_1, \ldots, G_n$ are denied (resp. if at least one $G_i$ is satisfied);

For the other binary relationships, an example is provided by: $G_2 \overset{+S}{\mapsto} G_1$(resp. $G_2 \overset{++S}{\mapsto} G_1$) means that if $G_2$ is satisfied, then there is some (resp. a full) evidence that G1 is satisfied, but if G2 is denied, then nothing is said about the denial of $G_1$.

To generalize the previous $G_2 \overset{+S}{\mapsto} G_1$ relationship, we said that, the "S" (resp. "D") symbol denotes the fact that the satisfiability (resp. deniability) value of the source goal, e.g., $G_2$, is propagated; the "+" (resp. "-") symbol denotes the fact that the propagation is positive (resp. negative), in the sense that satisfiability propagates to satisfiability (resp. deniability) and deniability propagates to deniability (resp. satisfiability).

Finally, the relations +, -, ++, - - are defined such that $G_2 \overset{r}{\mapsto} G_1$ is a shorthand for the combination of the two corresponding relationships $G_2 \overset{r_s}{\mapsto} G_1$ and $G_2 \overset{r_D}{\mapsto} G_1$ e.g., $G_2 \overset{+}{\mapsto} G_1$ is a shorthand for the combination of $G_2 \overset{+S}{\mapsto} G_1$ and $G_2 \overset{+D}{\mapsto} G_1$. The first kind of relationships are called symmetric and the latter two asymmetric.

Now, a set of four distinct predicates over goals are introduced to be used with ground axioms in order to reasoning on the goal model. They are: F S(G), F D(G) and P S(G), P D(G); which mean, respectively, that there is (at least) full evidence that goal G is satisfied and that G is denied, and that there is at least partial evidence that G is satisfied and that G is denied. An example of relation axiom is: $G_2 \overset{+S}{\mapsto} G_1 : PS(G_2) \rightarrow PS(G_1)$.

Given a goal graph and an initial values assignment to some goals, the underlying algorithm exploits the ground axioms for forward and backward reasoning tasks. In particular, for the forward reasoning the assigned goals are called input goals (typically the leaf goals) while for the backward reasoning the assigned goals are called target goals (typically root goals).

The aim of the forward reasoning is the propagation of initial values (i.e., the input goals) to all other goals of the graph; the user can look the final values of the goals of interest (i.e., the target goals).

Instead, the aim of the backward reasoning is the backward search of the possible input values (i.e., the input goals) leading to some desired final value (i.e., the target values), under desired constrains, e.g., avoiding conflicts among goals.

In general, the forward reasoning is used for evaluating the impact of the adoption of the different alternatives with respect to the root goals; while, the backward reasoning, is used to analyze goal models and find the set of goals at the minimum costs that if achieved can guarantee the achievement of the desired top goals and softgoals.

The algorithm of the formal goal model can be used within the BIM to allow such reasoning. In fact, the goal relationships are accounted for within BIM through the InfluenceClass metaclass illustrated in Figure.

Notice how the qualitativeStrength and the quantitativeStrengh allow, respectively, to record the qualitative (e.g., + or - -) or quantitative (e.g., 0.7 or -0.3) strength of an influence. The type attribute allows to specify whether the satisfiability or deniability is propagated, i.e., S or D. The StateClass, which is inherited from the ObjectClass, is used to record the four states associated to F S(G), F D(G), P S(G) and P D(G) predicates.

Finally, the ResourceClass, can help in the backward "search" when we desire to find the set of Intentions at the minimum cost that, if achieved, can guarantee the achievement of the desired top Intentions. Indeed, the ResourceClass can represent the monetary resource required for the achievement (through a Process) of an Intention which is used in the minimum cost analysis.

Figure shows an example of Intentions reasoning with respect to the example described in figure.

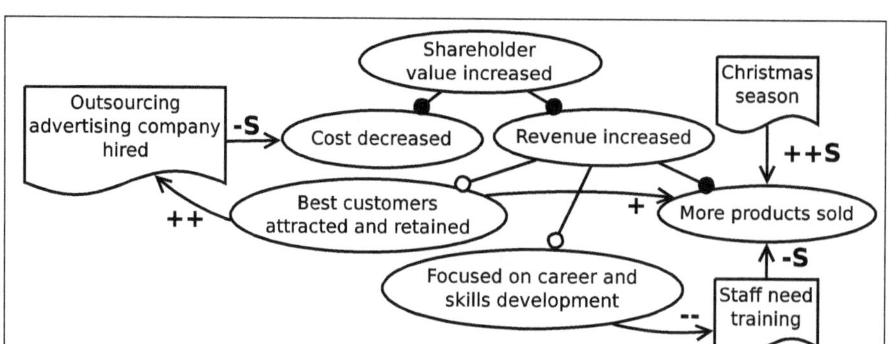


An example of Intentions reasoning with BIM.

Notice how the formal model is used for both Situations and Intentions. In the figure, the semantic of the influence relationships is the following:

- The satisfiability of "Outsourcing advertising company hired" Situation is propagated negatively (-S) to the "Cost decreased" Intention; this means that if the former holds the latter is partial denied; nothing is said about the denial of the "Outsourcing advertising company hired".
- The satisfiability (resp. Deniability) of "Best customers attracted and retained" Intention is propagated positively (++) to the "Outsourcing advertising company hired" Situation; this means that if the former is satisfied (resp. Denied) the latter holds (resp. Does not hold).
- The satisfiability (resp. Deniability) of "Best customers attracted and retained" Intention is propagated positively (+) to the "More products sold" Intention; this means that if the former is satisfied (resp. Denied) the latter is partial satisfied (resp. Denied).
- The satisfiability of "Staff need training" Situation is propagated negatively (- S) to the "More products sold" Intention; this means that if the former holds the latter is partial denied; nothing is said about the denial of the "Staff need training" Situation.
- The satisfiability of "Christmas season" Situation is propagated positively (++S) to the "More products sold" Intention; this means that if the former holds the latter is (at least partial) satisfied; nothing is said about the denial of the "Christmas season" Situation.

In order to show an example of forward reasoning on the model defined in figure, we input such a model in the same tool used in. The result is as shown in figure.

Table shows the results obtained by applying forward reasoning. The first three rows correspond to Situations, followed by three rows for the top Intentions and three rows for the bottom Intentions with respect to the Intentions hierarchy. In the table, three experiments are described through initial values (Init) and final values (Fin) for satisfiability (S) and deniability (D) of Situations/Intentions. In particular, these values can be: full (F); partial (P); an empty cell when the corresponding element is not involved in the reasoning; or, a question mark symbol (?) when a result cannot be calculated.

A brief description of the experiments is the following:

- Exp 1: The "Christmas season" Situation is satisfied (see the F value for the [S]-Init column) so is the "Best customers attracted and retained" Intention. As result, we have that the "Shareholder value increased" is partial denied due to the partial denying of the "Cost decreased" Intention.
- Exp 2: The "Christmas season", the "Staff need training", and "Focused on career and skills development" initial values are set to full satisfied (F). As result, we have a full "Revenue increased" satisfaction (see below for the semantic of the conflicts) but no information for the "Shareholder value increased" Intention (represented by the question mark). This result is due to the fact that the ground axioms, in this case $\left(G_1,\ ...,\ G_n\right) \overset{and}{\mapsto} G$, are not able to work with uncertainties. In fact, we have no information for the "Cost decreased" Intention.

- Exp 3: The “Christmas season”, the “Staff need training”, “Best customers attracted and retained” and “Focused on career and skills development” initial values are set to full satisfied (F). As result, we have that the “Shareholder value increased” is partial denied due to the partial denying of the “Cost decreased” Intention and a conflict (i.e., full satisfied and partial denied) on the “Revenue increased” Intention.

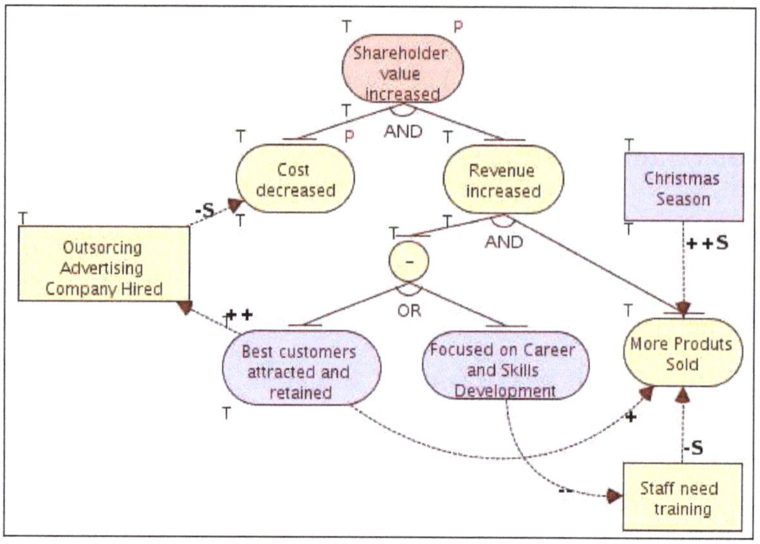

An example of Intention reasoning using the tool.

Therefore, in the three experiments we use different strategies to satisfy the top “Shareholder value increased” Intention which lead to different results.

A final observation regarding the influence from intentions towards Situations must be made. In fact, an Intention can lead to (++) or avoid/mitigate (- -) a Situation.

A clear example is shown in the analysis performed in Table where the “Outsourcing advertising company hired” can hold as the result of the satisfaction of the “Best customers attracted and retained” Intention; vice-versa, we have also that “Staff need training” Situation is avoided or mitigated by the satisfaction of “Focused on career and skills development”.

The latter is the semantic associated to the conflicting values (S=F and D=F) for the “Staff need training” Situation which is propagated towards the“More products sold” Intention. Notice also that, the formal model is not able to deal with with uncertainty when some Intentions have not an initial value since the ground axioms require a complete information for the reasoning algorithm.

Table: A formal forward reasoning example.

| Situation / Intention | Exp 1 | | | | Exp 2 | | | | Exp 3 | | | |
|---|---|---|---|---|---|---|---|---|---|---|---|---|
| | Init | | Fin | | Init | | Fin | | Init | | Fin | |
| | S | D | S | D | S | D | S | D | S | D | S | D |
| Outsourcing advertising company hired | | | F | | | | | | | | F | |
| Christmas season | F | | F | | F | | F | | F | | F | |
| Staff need training | | | | | F | | F | F | F | | F | F |
| Shareholder value increased | | | | P | | | | ? | | | | P |

| | | | | | | | | | | | | |
|---|---|---|---|---|---|---|---|---|---|---|---|---|
| Cost decreased | | | | P | | | | ? | | | | P |
| Revenue increased | | | F | | | | F | P | | | | P |
| Best customers attracted and retained | | | | | | | | | F | | F | |
| Focused on career and skills development | | | | | F | | F | | F | | F | |
| More products sold | | | F | | | | F | P | | | F | |

Finally, a similar analysis for the backward reasoning can be performed using similar experiments as shown in both considering or not a cost criteria. As a summary, we can said that the Intention reasoning model enables to:

- Perform forward reasoning, in order to evaluate different strategies for the satisfaction of top Intentions elements;
- Perform backward reasoning (considering also cost constrains), in order to evaluate the optimal input values leading to some desired final value;
- Perform analysis on Intention inconsistencies and conflicts in the Intention hierarchy.

## The SWOT Analysis with the BIM

The SWOT analysis is a strategic planning method which is used to evaluate the Strengths, the Weaknesses, the Opportunities, and Threats which are involved in a business environment. The purpose of the analysis is to specify the goals of the organization, business venture or project and identifying those internal and external factors that are favorable and unfavorable to achieve these goals.

Since a scan of the internal and external environment covers an fundamental role in the strategic planning process, the SWOT analysis can be considered as the first stage of such a process in which an organization is helped to focus on key issues.

Therefore, a SWOT analysis starts with the definition of a desired state of the world in terms of a set of strategic goals. Than, the identification of SWOTs with respect to the these strategic goals is performed. The result is an essential information which helps the decision makers in understanding the attainability of the selected strategic goals given such SWOTs. If the goals are not attainable different objectives must be selected and the process repeated.

In detail, the description of SWOT factors is:

- Strengths are resources and capabilities of an organization which can be used as a basis for developing a competitive advantage since they are are helpful to achieve the strategic goals;
- Weaknesses are absence of (certain) strengths as resources and capabilities which may be viewed as a weakness since they are are harmful to achieve strategic goals;
- Opportunities are external conditions which can be helpful to achieve the strategic goals since represent favorable circumstances for profit and growth;
- Threats are external conditions, usually due to changes in the external environment, which can be harmful to the strategic goals.

The results of a SWOT analysis are often presented in the form of a matrix.

Notice how, some factors may be viewed as strengths/opportunities or weaknesses/threats depending upon their impact on the organization's goals, e.g, the opportunity or threat "changing of customer tastes".

Another way to use SWOT is for the matching and converting activities. The matching is used to find competitive advantages by "matching" the strengths to opportunities, while converting is the act of guide strategies in order to convert weaknesses or threats into strengths or opportunities. Usually, if the threats or weaknesses cannot be converted an organization should try to minimize or avoid them.

In particular, an organization can use a SWOT analysis to define:

- S-O strategies, which pursue opportunities that fit good to the organization's strengths.
- W-O strategies, which overcome or avoid weaknesses to pursue opportunities.
- S-T strategies, which identify ways to use organization's strengths to reduce its vulnerability to external threats.
- W-T strategies, which establish a defensive plan to avoid that organization's weaknesses accentuate external threats.

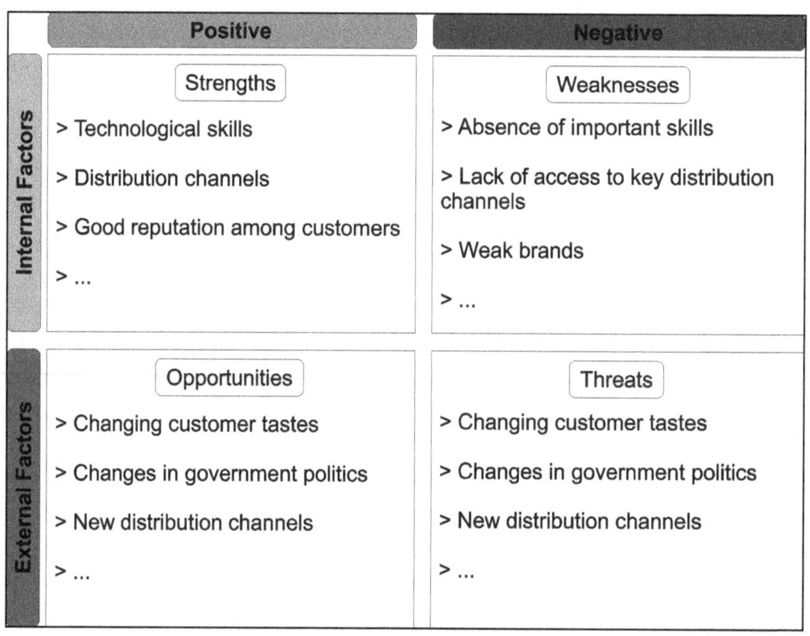


An example of SWOT matrix.

The BIM provides a formal way to perform the SWOT analysis since: i) allows to link the SWOT factors directly to the strategic goals they impact upon; ii) allows a formal reasoning on the set of strategic goals, SWOT factors and influences relationships among them.

The latter can be very useful for the definition of S-O, W-O, S-T, W-T strategies since make feasible the exploration of the different alternatives relying on the forward reasoning and backward reasoning approaches.

We use Situation to represent those internal and external factors which can contribute positively or negatively to the achievement of Intention, i.e., strategic goals.

Notice that, when a schema is defined, some Intention can be introduced to mitigate or avoid some Situations and some (harmful) Situations can arise due to the presence, in the schema, of specific Intentions.

Moreover, it must be said that, in the BIM, we characterized as strength, weakness, opportunity or threat the "influence" that exist from a Situation to an Intention. This allows to represent those cases in which the same Situation can represent, for example, a strength with respect to an Intention while representing a weakness with respect to another.

Table shows how to map the SWOT influences to the formal model presented in figure illustrates an example.

In the figure, the "More products sold" is defined to exploit the "Christmas season" external opportunity. This opportunity is matched by the"Efficient and effective distribution channels" internal strength that allows to deal with the high demand during Christmas.

Table: SWOT and formal model mapping.

| SWOT Influence | Formal Model Influence |
|---|---|
| Strength | +S, ++S |
| Weakness | -S, –S |
| Opportunity | +S, ++S |
| Threat | -S, - -S |

A SWOT analysis example with BIM.

Moreover, in order to avoid and mitigate weaknesses and threats, two strategic goals are also defined in the schema, namely "Focused on career and skills development" and "New set of products researched" strategic goals.

The former attempts: i) to mitigate the lack of Staff's skills in order to be prepared for the Christmas; and ii) to reduce the organization vulnerability to the external threat helping the Staff to turn the customer's taste toward the Organization's products.

The latter, the "New set of products researched", is defined and pursued as a defensive plan to match the new customer's taste.

## Define Strategic Map, Balanced Scorecard and Key Performance Indicators with BIM

Important instruments for strategic planning are Strategic Maps (SMs) and Balanced SCorecards (BSCs). The former are visual representation of the strategy of an organization which shows organization plans used to achieve missions and visions. In particular, a Strategic map illustrates the cause-and-effect relationships between different strategic goals and the associated measures, the key performance indicators (KPIs).

These measures are included in the latter, the BSC, which represents a "balanced" range of metrics against which to measure the Organization's performance. The meaning of "balance" is provided by the fact that the broader view of leading indicators of performance includes also non-financial metrics, such as "learning and growth of employees", "customer satisfaction", etc.

The combination of SMs and BSCs follows the principle of "you cannot measure what you cannot describe". In fact, SMs aim to describe the direction of an organization while BSCs aim to define a comprehensive set of performance measures that provides the framework for a strategic measurement and a management system.

Both the SMs and BSCs describe and measure organizational performance across four balanced perspectives: financial, customers, internal business processes, and learning and growth. In general, these perspectives, allow to see the organization and the business environment from different viewpoints and not only from the financial aspects.

The four perspectives have been found to be robust across a wide variety of companies and industries but should be considered a template. Indeed, no mathematical theorem exists to proof that four perspectives are both necessary and sufficient.

Within each of the four perspectives, the organization must define the following elements:

1. Strategic goals: Strategies which must be achieved in that perspective;
2. Measures: The progresses toward that particular strategic goals;
3. Targets: The target value sought for each measure;
4. Initiatives: What should be done to facilitate the achievement of the target;
5. Cause-effect relationships: Influences among strategic goals (or measures).

Figure illustrates an example of such elements in which only Targets are missing. A typical target can be, for example, a value of $10,000 for the Revenue measure for satisfying the "Revenue increased" strategic goal.

A common approach to evaluate the performance of an organization and how successful it is in achieving short and long-term goals, is the use of KPIs. KPIs are quantifiable measurements which reflect the performance of an organization towards its goals. Therefore, BSCs can express measures and targets through a set of KPIs.

BIM integrates in a single conceptual framework the primitive concepts that characterize SMs, BSCs and KPIs, as well as requirements models in Software Engineering. Through projection mappings on a global BIM model, it is possible to obtain partial models that can be analyzed through SM, BSC, KPI and formal goal reasoning techniques.

Using the fragment in Figure and the IndicatorClass described in figure, we are able to represent both SMs and BSCs (i.e., a set of KPIs). In particular, Intentions and Indicators represent strategic goals, their measures and associated targets. Processes with the type attribute set to Initiative describe initiatives used to reach targets. Instances of the Influence metaclass address causeeffect relationships (both in quantitative and qualitative ways). Finally, the perspective attribute helps to characterize elements along the four different perspectives.

An example of such mapping is shown in figure, corresponding to the model of figure.

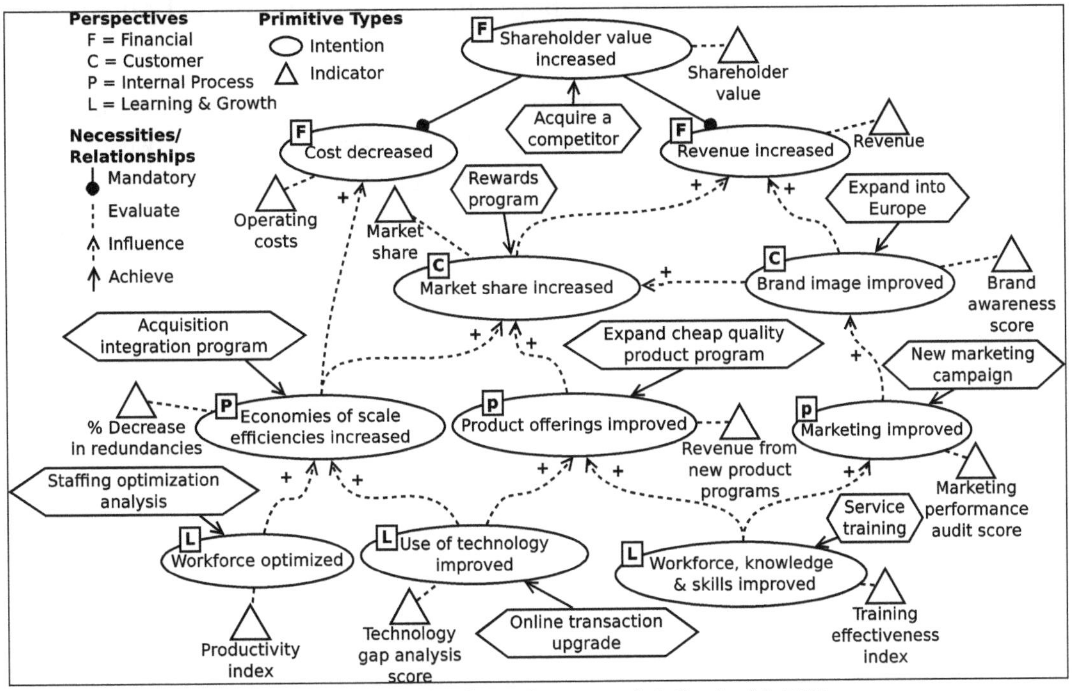


Strategic Map and Balanced Scorecard defined with BIM.

Notice how, the BIM model can represent a possible underneath formal schema for the SM and BSC described in figure. Therefore, SM and BSC should be used for illustration purpose, since familiar to executives, middle managers, etc., while BIM should be used to formalize such abstracted human-language to a machine-readable language on which queries, in depth analysis, etc., can be performed.

In conclusion we can affirm that, as SMs and BSCs do, the BIM is: i) a way of providing a macro view of an organization's strategy using the Intention primitive type to describe strategic and tactical goals; and ii), a way of constructing metrics to evaluate performance against these strategies using the Indicator primitive type. However, at the contrary of SMs and BSCs, the BIM allows more in depth analysis on the schema obtained after the designing activity.

## Probabilistic Graphical Model for Intention Reasoning

We described a solution based on formal logic model to provide a reasoning mechanism on Intentions. However, we also highlighted that such kind of model is able to provide only partial results in condition of uncertainty. For example, we would recall the experiment two in table in which a question mark symbol (?) was introduced for the "Cost decreased" and "Shareholder value increased" Intentions.

The issue of treat with uncertainty is an inescapable aspect of most real-world applications; indeed, it is quite common to have not a complete information during an analysis activity.

Probabilistic graphical models are approaches model-based which allow interpretable models to be constructed and then manipulated by reasoning algorithms. These models can be defined by an analyst or can be learned automatically from data in order to facilitate their construction when a manual design is difficult or even impossible. Different Probabilistic graphical models have been defined in the scientific community, such as Bayesian networks, undirected Markov networks, Influence Diagrams, etc.

One of our goals within BIM, is to adapt such models in order to manage uncertainty to perform causal reasoning and decision making under such circumstances. In particular, we are concentrating on Bayesian networks and in providing a first step toward the use of Influence Diagrams.

# 8

# Business Intelligence Tools and Software

Business intelligence consists of various applications such as spreadsheets, online analytical processing, digital dashboards, business activity monitoring, etc. It makes use of several software to aid these applications such as BIRT project, JasperReports, TACTIC and Orange. These diverse applications and software of business intelligence have been thoroughly discussed in this chapter.

## Business Intelligence Tools

### Spreadsheets

A spreadsheet or worksheet is a file made of rows and columns that help sort data, arrange data easily, and calculate numerical data. What makes a spreadsheet software program unique is its ability to calculate values using mathematical formulas and the data in cells. A good example of how a spreadsheet may be utilized is creating an overview of your bank's balance.

Below is a basic example of what a Microsoft Excel spreadsheet looks like, as well as all the important features of a spreadsheet highlighted.

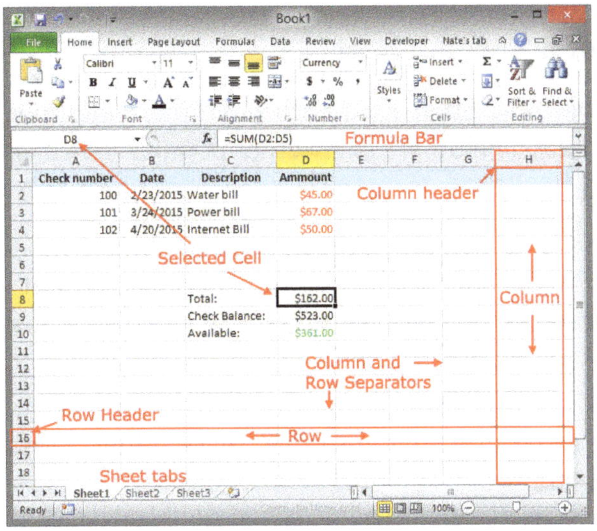

In the above example, this spreadsheet is listing three different checks, the date, their description, and the value of each check. These values are then added together to get the total of $162.00 in cell D6. That value is subtracted from the check balance to give an available $361.00 in cell D8.

## Difference between a Workbook, Worksheet and Spreadsheet

Because the terms spreadsheet, workbook, and worksheet are so similar, there can be a lot of confusion when trying to understand their differences. When you open Microsoft Excel (a spreadsheet program), you're opening a workbook. A workbook can contain one or more different worksheets that can be accessed through the tabs at the bottom of the worksheet your currently viewing. What's often most confusing is that a worksheet is synonymous with a spreadsheet. In other words, a spreadsheet and worksheet mean the same thing. However, most people only refer to the program as a spreadsheet program and the files it creates as spreadsheet files or worksheets.

## Examples of Spreadsheet Programs

Today, Microsoft Excel is the most popular and widely used spreadsheet program, but there are also many alternatives. Below is a list of spreadsheet programs that can be used to create a spreadsheet.

- Google Sheets - (online and free).
- iWork Numbers - Apple Office Suite.
- LibreOffice -> Calc (free).
- Lotus 1-2-3 (discontinued).
- Lotus Symphony - Spreadsheets.
- Microsoft Excel.
- OpenOffice -> Calc (free).
- VisiCalc (discontinued).

## Examples and uses of a Spreadsheet

Although spreadsheets are most often used with anything containing numbers, the uses of a spreadsheet are almost endless. Below are some other popular uses of spreadsheets.

### Finance

Spreadsheets are ideal for financial data, such as your checking account information, budgets, taxes, transactions, billing, invoices, receipts, forecasts, and any payment system.

### Forms

Form templates can be created to handle inventory, evaluations, performance reviews, quizzes, time sheets, patient information, and surveys.

### School and Grades

Teachers can use spreadsheets to track students, calculate grades, and identify relevant data, such as high and low scores, missing tests, and students who are struggling.

### Lists

Managing a list in a spreadsheet is a great example of data that does not contain numbers, but still can be used in a spreadsheet. Great examples of spreadsheet lists include telephone, to-do, and grocery lists.

### Sports

Spreadsheets can keep track of your favorite player stats or stats on the whole team. With the collected data, you can also find averages, high scores, and statistical data. Spreadsheets can even be used to create tournament brackets.

Spreadsheets are used in varied ways within business contexts. In general, spreadsheets store data sets, but they also provide a range of utilities to manage and process the data sets. This makes them particularly useful to businesses. Through preset and user-defined formulas, spreadsheets can perform mathematical, statistical, financial and organizational transformations on sets of data. Spreadsheets help to present data in organized ways and to inform future planning decisions. Businesses use spreadsheets in ways that are suited to their own services, but these uses tend to fall into a few general categories.

### Storing Data

The primary purpose of a spreadsheet is to store data in a structured way. Data values are entered into cells in a worksheet. These data values can be formatted using various categories of data types, including numerical and textual types. The cells in a worksheet can refer to other cells, using the location of a cell within the rows and columns in the sheet. Individual parts of a worksheet can be contained within tables, with a single worksheet potentially holding a range of information sets. Spreadsheet programs such as Excel provide templates for common business tasks, such as expenses recording.

### Analyzing Data

Once a spreadsheet has some data values in it, you can perform various analytical tasks on this data. This includes mathematical functions, such as adding or counting values. By entering a formula or choosing from one of many preset functions, you can analyze your data sets. This allows business users to sort data, filter it and process it. For financial data, you can calculate profits and losses. In a general sense, spreadsheet formulas and functions allow you to carry out performance measurements for many aspects of your business.

### Presentation

Spreadsheet applications such as Excel include tools for data visualization. You can take an existing data set within a spreadsheet and present it within a chart, with various types of graph and chart options to choose from. The resulting charts let business managers gain insight into the data by presenting it in graphical ways. These charts can also be used in corporate contexts, such as within presentations. You can manually control all aspects of a chart display, including chart type, labeling and colors. You can also print spreadsheet tables and charts for use within reports and other publications.

## Future Planning

Spreadsheets facilitate future planning in two ways. First, being able to analyze and visualize data gives you an insight into how well your business is currently performing, highlighting areas for growth or reconsideration. Second, you can use a spreadsheet to calculate the potential effects of changes to your business model. For example, if you use existing information together with a potential change, such as a sales fluctuation in a retail context, you can determine the impact of this change. Spreadsheets also use conditional formulas, in which you can carry out conditional tests on data values, filtering or manipulating the values as a result of these tests.

## Online Analytical Processing (OLAP)

Online analytical processing, or OLAP, is an approach to answer multi-dimensional analytical (MDA) queries swiftly in computing. OLAP is part of the broader category of business intelligence, which also encompasses relational databases, report writing and data mining. Typical applications of OLAP include business reporting for sales, marketing, management reporting, business process management (BPM), budgeting and forecasting, financial reporting and similar areas, with new applications emerging, such as agriculture.

The term *OLAP* was created as a slight modification of the traditional database term online transaction processing (OLTP).

OLAP tools enable users to analyze multidimensional data interactively from multiple perspectives. OLAP consists of three basic analytical operations: consolidation (roll-up), drill-down, and slicing and dicing. Consolidation involves the aggregation of data that can be accumulated and computed in one or more dimensions. For example, all sales offices are rolled up to the sales department or sales division to anticipate sales trends. By contrast, the drill-down is a technique that allows users to navigate through the details. For instance, users can view the sales by individual products that make up a region's sales. Slicing and dicing is a feature whereby users can take out (slicing) a specific set of data of the OLAP cube and view (dicing) the slices from different viewpoints. These viewpoints are sometimes called dimensions (such as looking at the same sales by salesperson, or by date, or by customer, or by product, or by region, etc.)

Databases configured for OLAP use a multidimensional data model, allowing for complex analytical and ad hoc queries with a rapid execution time. They borrow aspects of navigational databases, hierarchical databases and relational databases.

OLAP is typically contrasted to OLTP (online transaction processing), which is generally characterized by much less complex queries, in a larger volume, to process transactions rather than for the purpose of business intelligence or reporting. Whereas OLAP systems are mostly optimized for read, OLTP has to process all kinds of queries (read, insert, update and delete).

At the core of any OLAP system is an OLAP cube (also called a 'multidimensional cube' or a hypercube). It consists of numeric facts called *measures* that are categorized by *dimensions*. The measures are placed at the intersections of the hypercube, which is spanned by the dimensions as a vector space. The usual interface to manipulate an OLAP cube is a matrix interface, like Pivot tables in a spreadsheet program, which performs projection operations along the dimensions, such as aggregation or averaging.

The cube metadata is typically created from a star schema or snowflake schema or fact constellation of tables in a relational database. Measures are derived from the records in the fact table and dimensions are derived from the dimension tables.

Each *measure* can be thought of as having a set of *labels*, or meta-data associated with it. A *dimension* is what describes these *labels*; it provides information about the *measure*.

A simple example would be a cube that contains a store's sales as a *measure*, and Date/Time as a *dimension*. Each Sale has a Date/Time *label* that describes more about that sale.

For example:

```
 Sales Fact Table
+-------------+----------+
| sale_amount | time_id  |
+-------------+----------+          Time Dimension
|      2008.10|     1234 |----+   +---------+-------------------+
+-------------+----------+    |   | time_id | timestamp         |
                              |   +---------+-------------------+
                              +---->|  1234   | 20080902 12:35:43 |
                                  +---------+-------------------+
```

## Multidimensional Databases

Multidimensional structure is defined as "a variation of the relational model that uses multidimensional structures to organize data and express the relationships between data". The structure is broken into cubes and the cubes are able to store and access data within the confines of each cube. "Each cell within a multidimensional structure contains aggregated data related to elements along each of its dimensions". Even when data is manipulated it remains easy to access and continues to constitute a compact database format. The data still remains interrelated. Multidimensional structure is quite popular for analytical databases that use online analytical processing (OLAP) applications. Analytical databases use these databases because of their ability to deliver answers to complex business queries swiftly. Data can be viewed from different angles, which gives a broader perspective of a problem unlike other models.

## Aggregations

It has been claimed that for complex queries OLAP cubes can produce an answer in around 0.1% of the time required for the same query on OLTP relational data. The most important mechanism in OLAP which allows it to achieve such performance is the use of *aggregations*. Aggregations are built from the fact table by changing the granularity on specific dimensions and aggregating up data along these dimensions, using an aggregate function (or *aggregation function*). The number of possible aggregations is determined by every possible combination of dimension granularities.

The combination of all possible aggregations and the base data contains the answers to every query which can be answered from the data.

Because usually there are many aggregations that can be calculated, often only a predetermined number are fully calculated; the remainder are solved on demand. The problem of deciding which aggregations (views) to calculate is known as the view selection problem. View selection can be constrained by the total size of the selected set of aggregations, the time to update them from changes in the base data, or both. The objective of view selection is typically to minimize the average time to answer OLAP queries, although some studies also minimize the update time. View selection is NP-Complete. Many approaches to the problem have been explored, including greedy algorithms, randomized search, genetic algorithms and A* search algorithm.

Some aggregation functions can be computed for the entire OLAP cube by precomputing values for each cell, and then computing the aggregation for a roll-up of cells by aggregating these aggregates, applying a divide and conquer algorithm to the multidimensional problem to compute them efficiently. For example, the overall sum of a roll-up is just the sum of the sub-sums in each cell. Functions that can be decomposed in this way are called decomposable aggregation functions, and include `COUNT`, `MAX`, `MIN`, and `SUM`, which can be computed for each cell and then directly aggregated; these are known as self-decomposable aggregation functions. In other cases the aggregate function can be computed by computing auxiliary numbers for cells, aggregating these auxiliary numbers, and finally computing the overall number at the end; examples include AVERAGE (tracking sum and count, dividing at the end) and `RANGE` (tracking max and min, subtracting at the end). In other cases the aggregate function cannot be computed without analyzing the entire set at once, though in some cases approximations can be computed; examples include `DISTINCT COUNT`, `MEDIAN`, and `MODE`; for example, the median of a set is not the median of medians of subsets. These latter are difficult to implement efficiently in OLAP, as they require computing the aggregate function on the base data, either computing them online (slow) or precomputing them for possible rollouts (large space).

## Types

OLAP systems have been traditionally categorized using the following taxonomy:

## Multidimensional OLAP (MOLAP)

MOLAP (multi-dimensional online analytical processing) is the classic form of OLAP and is sometimes referred to as just OLAP. MOLAP stores this data in an optimized multi-dimensional array storage, rather than in a relational database.

Some MOLAP tools require the pre-computation and storage of derived data, such as consolidations – the operation known as processing. Such MOLAP tools generally utilize a pre-calculated data set referred to as a data cube. The data cube contains all the possible answers to a given range of questions. As a result, they have a very fast response to queries. On the other hand, updating can take a long time depending on the degree of pre-computation. Pre-computation can also lead to what is known as data explosion.

Other MOLAP tools, particularly those that implement the functional database model do not pre-compute derived data but make all calculations on demand other than those that were previously requested and stored in a cache.

## Advantages of MOLAP

- Fast query performance due to optimized storage, multidimensional indexing and caching.
- Smaller on-disk size of data compared to data stored in relational database due to compression techniques.
- Automated computation of higher level aggregates of the data.
- It is very compact for low dimension data sets.
- Array models provide natural indexing.
- Effective data extraction achieved through the pre-structuring of aggregated data.

## Disadvantages of MOLAP

- Within some MOLAP systems the processing step (data load) can be quite lengthy, especially on large data volumes. This is usually remedied by doing only incremental processing, i.e., processing only the data which have changed (usually new data) instead of reprocessing the entire data set.
- Some MOLAP methodologies introduce data redundancy.

## Products

Examples of commercial products that use MOLAP are Cognos Powerplay, Oracle Database OLAP Option, MicroStrategy, Microsoft Analysis Services, Essbase, TM1, Jedox, and icCube.

## Relational OLAP (ROLAP)

ROLAP works directly with relational databases and does not require pre-computation. The base data and the dimension tables are stored as relational tables and new tables are created to hold the aggregated information. It depends on a specialized schema design. This methodology relies on manipulating the data stored in the relational database to give the appearance of traditional OLAP's slicing and dicing functionality. In essence, each action of slicing and dicing is equivalent to adding a "WHERE" clause in the SQL statement. ROLAP tools do not use pre-calculated data cubes but instead pose the query to the standard relational database and its tables in order to bring back the data required to answer the question. ROLAP tools feature the ability to ask any question because the methodology is not limited to the contents of a cube. ROLAP also has the ability to drill down to the lowest level of detail in the database.

While ROLAP uses a relational database source, generally the database must be carefully designed for ROLAP use. A database which was designed for OLTP will not function well as a ROLAP database. Therefore, ROLAP still involves creating an additional copy of the data. However, since it is a database, a variety of technologies can be used to populate the database.

## Advantages of ROLAP

- ROLAP is considered to be more scalable in handling large data volumes, especially models with dimensions with very high cardinality (i.e., millions of members).
- With a variety of data loading tools available, and the ability to fine-tune the extract, transform, load (ETL) code to the particular data model, load times are generally much shorter than with the automated MOLAP loads.
- The data are stored in a standard relational database and can be accessed by any SQL reporting tool (the tool does not have to be an OLAP tool).
- ROLAP tools are better at handling non-aggregatable facts (e.g., textual descriptions). MOLAP tools tend to suffer from slow performance when querying these elements.
- By decoupling the data storage from the multi-dimensional model, it is possible to successfully model data that would not otherwise fit into a strict dimensional model.
- The ROLAP approach can leverage database authorization controls such as row-level security, whereby the query results are filtered depending on preset criteria applied, for example, to a given user or group of users (SQL WHERE clause).

## Disadvantages of ROLAP

- There is a consensus in the industry that ROLAP tools have slower performance than MOLAP tools.
- The loading of aggregate tables must be managed by custom ETL code. The ROLAP tools do not help with this task. This means additional development time and more code to support.
- When the step of creating aggregate tables is skipped, the query performance then suffers because the larger detailed tables must be queried. This can be partially remedied by adding additional aggregate tables, however it is still not practical to create aggregate tables for all combinations of dimensions/attributes.
- ROLAP relies on the general purpose database for querying and caching, and therefore several special techniques employed by MOLAP tools are not available (such as special hierarchical indexing). However, modern ROLAP tools take advantage of latest improvements in SQL language such as CUBE and ROLLUP operators, DB2 Cube Views, as well as other SQL OLAP extensions. These SQL improvements can mitigate the benefits of the MOLAP tools.
- Since ROLAP tools rely on SQL for all of the computations, they are not suitable when the model is heavy on calculations which don't translate well into SQL. Examples of such models include budgeting, allocations, financial reporting and other scenarios.

## Performance of ROLAP

In the OLAP industry ROLAP is usually perceived as being able to scale for large data volumes, but suffering from slower query performance as opposed to MOLAP. The OLAP Survey, the largest independent survey across all major OLAP products, being conducted for 6 years (2001 to 2006) have consistently found that companies using ROLAP report slower performance than those using MOLAP even when data volumes were taken into consideration.

However, as with any survey there are a number of subtle issues that must be taken into account when interpreting the results.

- The survey shows that ROLAP tools have 7 times more users than MOLAP tools within each company. Systems with more users will tend to suffer more performance problems at peak usage times.
- There is also a question about complexity of the model, measured both in number of dimensions and richness of calculations. The survey does not offer a good way to control for these variations in the data being analyzed.

## Downside of Flexibility

Some companies select ROLAP because they intend to re-use existing relational database tables—these tables will frequently not be optimally designed for OLAP use. The superior flexibility of ROLAP tools allows this less than optimal design to work, but performance suffers. MOLAP tools in contrast would force the data to be re-loaded into an optimal OLAP design.

## Hybrid OLAP (HOLAP)

The undesirable trade-off between additional ETL cost and slow query performance has ensured that most commercial OLAP tools now use a "Hybrid OLAP" (HOLAP) approach, which allows the model designer to decide which portion of the data will be stored in MOLAP and which portion in ROLAP.

There is no clear agreement across the industry as to what constitutes "Hybrid OLAP", except that a database will divide data between relational and specialized storage. For example, for some vendors, a HOLAP database will use relational tables to hold the larger quantities of detailed data, and use specialized storage for at least some aspects of the smaller quantities of more-aggregate or less-detailed data. HOLAP addresses the shortcomings of MOLAP and ROLAP by combining the capabilities of both approaches. HOLAP tools can utilize both pre-calculated cubes and relational data sources.

## Vertical Partitioning

In this mode HOLAP stores aggregations in MOLAP for fast query performance, and detailed data in ROLAP to optimize time of cube processing.

## Horizontal Partitioning

In this mode HOLAP stores some slice of data, usually the more recent one (i.e. sliced by Time dimension) in MOLAP for fast query performance, and older data in ROLAP. Moreover, we can store some dices in MOLAP and others in ROLAP, leveraging the fact that in a large cuboid, there will be dense and sparse subregions.

## Products

The first product to provide HOLAP storage was Holos, but the technology also became available in other commercial products such as Microsoft Analysis Services, Oracle Database OLAP Option, MicroStrategy and SAP AG BI Accelerator. The hybrid OLAP approach combines ROLAP and MOLAP technology, benefiting from the greater scalability of ROLAP and the faster computation of MOLAP. For example, a HOLAP server may store large volumes of detailed data in a relational database, while aggregations are kept in a separate MOLAP store. The Microsoft SQL Server 7.0 OLAP Services supports a hybrid OLAP server

## Comparison

Each type has certain benefits, although there is disagreement about the specifics of the benefits between providers.

- Some MOLAP implementations are prone to database explosion, a phenomenon causing vast amounts of storage space to be used by MOLAP databases when certain common conditions are met: high number of dimensions, pre-calculated results and sparse multidimensional data.
- MOLAP generally delivers better performance due to specialized indexing and storage optimizations. MOLAP also needs less storage space compared to ROLAP because the specialized storage typically includes compression techniques.
- ROLAP is generally more scalable. However, large volume pre-processing is difficult to implement efficiently so it is frequently skipped. ROLAP query performance can therefore suffer tremendously.
- Since ROLAP relies more on the database to perform calculations, it has more limitations in the specialized functions it can use.
- HOLAP attempts to mix the best of ROLAP and MOLAP. It can generally pre-process swiftly, scale well, and offer good function support.

## Other Types

The following acronyms are also sometimes used, although they are not as widespread as the ones above:

- WOLAP: Web-based OLAP.
- DOLAP: Desktop OLAP.
- RTOLAP: Real-Time OLAP.
- GOLAP: Graph OLAP.
- CaseOLAP: Context-aware Semantic OLAP, developed for biomedical applications. The CaseOLAP platform includes data preprocessing (e.g., downloading, extraction, and parsing text documents), indexing and searching with Elasticsearch, creating a functional document structure called Text-Cube, and quantifying user-defined phrase-category relationships using the core CaseOLAP algorithm.

## APIs and Query Languages

Unlike relational databases, which had SQL as the standard query language, and widespread APIs such as ODBC, JDBC and OLEDB, there was no such unification in the OLAP world for a long time. The first real standard API was OLE DB for OLAP specification from Microsoft which appeared in 1997 and introduced the MDX query language. Several OLAP vendors – both server and client – adopted it. In 2001 Microsoft and Hyperion announced the XML for Analysis specification, which was endorsed by most of the OLAP vendors. Since this also used MDX as a query language, MDX became the de facto standard. Since September-2011 LINQ can be used to query SSAS OLAP cubes from Microsoft .NET.

## Digital Dashboards

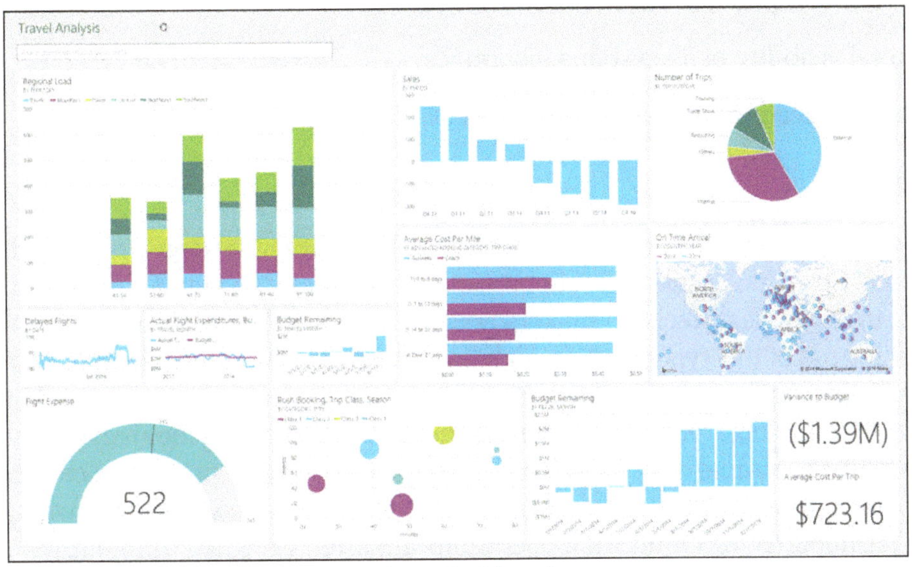


Business Dashboards.

A dashboard is a type of graphical user interface which often provides at-a-glance views of key performance indicators (KPIs) relevant to a particular objective or business process. In other usage, "dashboard" is another name for "progress report" or "report."

The "dashboard" is often displayed on a web page which is linked to a database that allows the report to be constantly updated. For example, a manufacturing dashboard may show numbers related to productivity such as number of parts manufactured, or number of failed quality inspections per hour. Similarly, a human resources dashboard may show numbers related to staff recruitment, retention and composition, for example number of open positions, or average days or cost per recruitment.

The term dashboard originates from the automobile dashboard where drivers monitor the major functions at a glance via the instrument cluster.

### Benefits

Digital dashboards allow managers to monitor the contribution of the various departments in their organization. To gauge exactly how well an organization is performing overall, digital dashboards allow you to capture and report specific data points from each department within the organization, thus providing a "snapshot" of performance.

Benefits of using digital dashboards include:

- Visual presentation of performance measures.
- Ability to identify and correct negative trends.
- Measure efficiencies/inefficiencies.
- Ability to generate detailed reports showing new trends.
- Ability to make more informed decisions based on collected business intelligence.
- Align strategies and organizational goals.
- Saves time compared to running multiple reports.
- Gain total visibility of all systems instantly.
- Quick identification of data outliers and correlations.

## Classification

Dashboards can be broken down according to role and are either strategic, analytical, operational, or informational. Strategic dashboards support managers at any level in an organization, and provide the quick overview that decision makers need to monitor the health and opportunities of the business. Dashboards of this type focus on high level measures of performance, and forecasts. Strategic dashboards benefit from static snapshots of data (daily, weekly, monthly, and quarterly) that are not constantly changing from one moment to the next. Dashboards for analytical purposes often include more context, comparisons, and history, along with subtler performance evaluators. Analytical dashboards typically support interactions with the data, such as drilling down into the underlying details. Dashboards for monitoring operations are often designed differently from those that support strategic decision making or data analysis and often require monitoring of activities and events that are constantly changing and might require attention and response at a moment's notice.

## Types of Dashboards

Digital dashboards may be laid out to track the flows inherent in the business processes that they monitor. Graphically, users may see the high-level processes and then drill down into low level data. This level of detail is often buried deep within the corporate enterprise and otherwise unavailable to the senior executives.

Three main types of digital dashboard dominate the market today: stand alone software applications, web-browser based applications, and desktop applications also known as desktop widgets. The last are driven by a widget engine.

Specialized dashboards may track all corporate functions. Examples include human resources, recruiting, sales, operations, security, information technology, project management, customer relationship management and many more departmental dashboards. For a smaller organization like a startup a compact startup scorecard dashboard tracks important activities across lot of domains ranging from social media to sales.

Digital dashboard projects involve business units as the driver and the information technology department as the enabler. The success of digital dashboard projects often depends on the metrics that were chosen for monitoring. Key performance indicators, balanced scorecards, and sales performance figures are some of the content appropriate on business dashboards.

## Dashboards and Scoreboards

Balanced Scoreboards and Dashboards have been linked together as if they were interchangeable. However, although both visually display critical information, the difference is in the format: Scoreboards can open the quality of an operation while dashboards provide calculated direction. A balanced scoreboard has what they called a "prescriptive" format. It should always contain these components (Active Strategy).

- Perspectives: Group.
- Objectives: Verb-noun phrases pulled from a strategy plan.
- Measures: Also called Metric or Key Performance Indicators (KPIs).
- Spotlight Indicators: Red, yellow, or green symbols that provide an at-a-glance view of a measure's performance.

Each of these sections ensures that a Balanced Scorecard is essentially connected to the businesses critical strategic needs.

The design of a dashboard is more loosely defined. Dashboards are usually a series of graphics, charts, gauges and other visual indicators that can be monitored and interpreted. Even when there is a strategic link, on a dashboard, it may not be noticed as such since objectives are not normally present on dashboards. However, dashboards can be customized to link their graphs and charts to strategic objectives.

## Design

Digital dashboard technology is available "out-of-the-box" from many software providers. Some companies however continue to do in-house development and maintenance of dashboard applications. For example, GE Aviation has developed a proprietary software/portal called "Digital Cockpit" to monitor the trends in aircraft spare parts business.

Good dashboard design practices take into account and address the following:

- The medium it is designed for (desktop, laptop, mobile, tablet).
- Use of visuals over tabular presentation of data.
    - Bar charts: To visualize one or more series of data.
    - Line charts: To track changes in a number of dependent data sets over a period of time.
    - Sparklines: To show the trend in a single data set.
    - Use of legends anytime more than one color or shape is present on a graph.
    - Spatial arrangement: Place your most important view on the top left (if the language is written left to right) then arrange the following views in a Z pattern with the most important information following the top-to-bottom, left-to-right pattern.

  - Color palettes to be colorblind friendly.

A good information design will clearly communicate key information to users and makes supporting information easily accessible.

## Assessing the Quality of Dashboards

There are a few key elements to a good dashboard:.

- Simple, communicates easily.
- Minimum distractions, it could cause confusion.
- Supports organized business with meaning and useful data.
- Applies human visual perception to visual presentation of information.
- It can be accessed easily by its intended audience.

## Business Activity Monitoring

Business activity monitoring (BAM) is software that aids in monitoring of business activities, key performance indicators, business/operational exceptions and business risks, as those activities are implemented in computer systems.

The term was originally coined by analysts at Gartner, Inc. and refers to the aggregation, analysis, and presentation of real-time information about activities inside organizations and involving customers and partners. A business activity can either be a business process that is orchestrated by business process management (BPM) software, or a business process that is a series of activities spanning multiple systems and applications. BAM is an enterprise solution primarily intended to provide a real-time summary of business activities to operations managers and upper management.

## Goals and Benefits

The goals of business activity monitoring is to provide real time information about the status and results of various operations, processes, and transactions. The main benefits of BAM are to enable an enterprise to make better informed business decisions, quickly address problem areas, and re-position organizations to take full advantage of emerging opportunities.

## Key Features

One of the most visible features of BAM solutions is the presentation of information on dashboards containing the key performance indicators (KPIs) used to provide assurance and visibility of activity and performance. This information is used by technical and business operations to provide visibility, measurement, and assurance of key business activities. It is also exploited by event correlation to detect and warn of impending problems.

Although BAM systems usually use a computer dashboard display to present data, BAM is distinct from the dashboards used by business intelligence (BI) insofar as events are processed in real-time or near real-time and pushed to the dashboard in BAM systems, whereas BI dashboards refresh at predetermined intervals by polling or querying databases. Depending on the refresh interval selected, BAM and BI dashboards can be similar or vary considerably.

Some BAM solutions additionally provide trouble notification functions, which allows them to interact automatically with the issue tracking system. For example, whole groups of people can be sent e-mails, voice or text messages, according to the nature of the problem. Automated problem solving, where feasible, can correct and restart failed processes.

## Deployment Effort

In nearly all BAM deployments extensive tailoring to specific enterprises is required. Many BAM solutions seek to reduce extensive customization and may offer templates that are written to solve common problems in specific sectors, for example banking, manufacturing, and stockbroking. Due to the high degree of system integration required for initial deployment, many enterprises use experts that specialize in BAM to implement solutions.

BAM is now considered a critical component of Operational Intelligence (OI) solutions to deliver visibility into business operations. Multiple sources of data can be combined from different organizational silos to provide a common operating picture that uses current information. Wherever real-time insight has the greatest value, OI solutions can be applied to deliver the needed information.

## Processing Events

All BAM solutions process events. While most of the first BAM solutions were closely linked to BPM solutions and therefore processed events emitted as the process was being orchestrated, this had the disadvantage of requiring enterprises to invest in BPM before being able to acquire and use BAM. The newer generation of BAM solutions are based on complex event processing (CEP) technology, and can process high volumes of underlying technical events to derive higher level business events, therefore reducing the dependency on BPM, and providing BAM to a wider audience of customers.

Examples:

A bank might be interested in minimizing the amount of money it borrows overnight from a central bank. Interbank transfers must be communicated and arranged through automation by a set time each business day. The failure of any vital communication could cost the bank large sums in interest charged by the central bank. A BAM solution would be programmed to become aware of each message and await confirmation. Failure to receive confirmation within a reasonable amount of time would be grounds for the BAM solution to raise an alarm that would set in motion manual intervention to investigate the cause of the delay and to push the problem toward resolution before it becomes costly.

Another example involves a mobile telecommunications company interested in detecting a situation whereby new customers are not set up promptly and correctly on their network and within the various CRM and billing solutions. Low-level technical events such as messages passing from one application to another over a middleware system, or transactions detected within a database logfile, are processed by a CEP engine. All events relating to an individual customer are correlated in order to detect an anomalous situation whereby an individual customer has not been promptly or correctly provisioned, or set up. An alert can be generated to notify technical operations or to notify business operations, and the failed provisioning step may be restarted automatically.

## Local Information Systems

A Local information system (LIS) is a form of information system built with business intelligence tools, designed primarily to support geographic reporting. They overlap with some capabilities of geographic information systems (GIS), although their primary function is the reporting of statistical data rather than the analysis of geospatial data. LIS also tend to offer some common knowledge management functionality for storage and retrieval of unstructured data such as documents. They deliver functionality to load, store, analyse and present statistical data that has a strong geographic reference. In most cases the data is structured as indicators and is linked to discrete geographic areas, for example population figures for US counties or numbers claiming unemployment benefit across wards in England. The ability to present this data using data visualization tools like charts and maps is also a core feature of these systems.

The term "LIS" has emerged since 2004, primarily in the UK public sector. To date it is not widely used elsewhere although other terms like Community Information Systems apply to solutions, primarily in North America, that have a great deal of overlap. Another widely used and largely synonymous term is Data Observatory. Data Observatory is a more widely used term internationally particularly within the area of public health where sites which often include this type of statistical reporting application are often termed a health observatory.

The primary application for LIS is to provide a place-focused evidence base that is easily accessible to a wide range of users including data experts, managers, policy makers, front-line staff and citizens. They provide a wide range of statistics and reports allowing users to review the current evidence base and build a picture of localities and neighbourhoods for their area of interest. LIS are commonly used by partnerships where they need to come together to provide joined-up services for a common area. The ability to have a common evidence base and a platform to share sensitive and non-sensitive data is critical in this situation. LIS enables partners to publish a wide range of indicators in the form of defined outputs which combine locally and nationally available data into more meaningful intelligence aimed at specific user groups

In the UK, like many other countries, there has been a rapid growth in the availability of small area statistics. National Neighbourhood Statistics projects across the UK, set up as a result of the PAT 18 report, have opened up access to a wide range of government small area based statistics. This has been accompanied by a gradual shift across the public sector, a shift that remains very much on-going, towards the recognition that policy and decisions should be influenced to a greater degree by evidence. There also continues to be a growing acceptance that some services can be more effectively delivered by targeting resources at specific areas of need – the idea of high demand 'hotspots'. This relies on having reliable and detailed data about the needs of customers, in this case citizens, and where they live, work and take leisure time.

In England in particular this has led to a rapid increase in the number of Local Information Systems particularly within local Authorities and Local Strategic Partnerships. This development has been actively supported by the Department of Communities and Local Government (CLG) under their 'Neighbourhood Renewal' agenda. A national research project was funded to identify examples and disseminate best practice – this reported publicly in 2004 and led to a more formal report being published in 2006. CLG's role as a catalyst in this area is further re-enforced through its provision of Neighbourhood Renewal Funds (NRF) - this funding was used by a number of authorities to pump-prime their initial LIS developments.

An initiative is currently on-going through the CLG Information Management Programme to co-ordinate all LIS activity across local government and partnerships. This has led to regular national LIS meetings and a dedicated LIS forum. To date it is estimated that approximately 50 per cent of top tier authorities in England now have some form of LIS. In some cases these have been built as bespoke solutions, in other cases they are based on off-the-shelf products. Elsewhere within the UK this figure is lower although an initiative has been launched in Scotland in 2009 resulting in a Scottish LIS Toolkit to complement the English version.

## Data

The range of data managed within a LIS can be wide and classified in many different ways. Most common is some form of domain specific classification where indicators are grouped into top level categories like 'Demography', 'Health and Welfare', 'Crime and Community Safety', 'Education and Children's Services', 'Environment' and 'Economy'. There may also be cross-cutting themes such as 'Performance' and 'Social Disadvantage'. In the UK key government data sources include ONS Neighbourhood Statistics, CLG, Dept for Work and Pensions, NOMIS, Audit Commission and several areas of NHS information services. However the real value of LIS is their ability to combine national data with local data available from a wide range of internal business systems including those of partners. This local data is often not provided to central government and, even when it is, it tends to be in a form that limits its value.

## Data Cleansing

Data cleansing or data cleaning is the process of detecting and correcting (or removing) corrupt or inaccurate records from a record set, table, or database and refers to identifying incomplete, incorrect, inaccurate or irrelevant parts of the data and then replacing, modifying, or deleting the dirty or coarse data. Data cleansing may be performed interactively with data wrangling tools, or as batch processing through scripting.

After cleansing, a data set should be consistent with other similar data sets in the system. The inconsistencies detected or removed may have been originally caused by user entry errors, by corruption in transmission or storage, or by different data dictionary definitions of similar entities in different stores. Data cleaning differs from data validation in that validation almost invariably means data is rejected from the system at entry and is performed at the time of entry, rather than on batches of data.

The actual process of data cleansing may involve removing typographical errors or validating and correcting values against a known list of entities. The validation may be strict (such as rejecting any address that does not have a valid postal code) or fuzzy (such as correcting records that partially match existing, known records). Some data cleansing solutions will clean data by cross checking with a validated data set. A common data cleansing practice is data enhancement, where data is made more complete by adding related information. For example, appending addresses with any phone numbers related to that address. Data cleansing may also involve harmonization (or normalization) of data, which is the process of bringing together data of "varying file formats, naming conventions, and columns", and transforming it into one cohesive data set; a simple example is the expansion of abbreviations ("st, rd, etc." to "street, road, etcetera").

## Motivation

Administratively, incorrect or inconsistent data can lead to false conclusions and misdirected investments on both public and private scales. For instance, the government may want to analyze population census figures to decide which regions require further spending and investment on infrastructure and services. In this case, it will be important to have access to reliable data to avoid erroneous fiscal decisions. In the business world, incorrect data can be costly. Many companies use customer information databases that record data like contact information, addresses, and preferences. For instance, if the addresses are inconsistent, the company will suffer the cost of resending mail or even losing customers. The profession of forensic accounting and fraud investigating uses data cleansing in preparing its data and is typically done before data is sent to a data warehouse for further investigation. There are packages available so you can cleanse/wash address data while you enter it into your system. This is normally done via an application programming interface (API).

## Data Quality

High-quality data needs to pass a set of quality criteria. Those include:

- Validity: The degree to which the measures conform to defined business rules or constraints. When modern database technology is used to design data-capture systems, validity is fairly easy to ensure: invalid data arises mainly in legacy contexts (where constraints were not implemented in software) or where inappropriate data-capture technology was used (e.g., spreadsheets, where it is very hard to limit what a user chooses to enter into a cell, if cell validation is not used). Data constraints fall into the following categories:
    - Data-Type Constraints: E.g., values in a particular column must be of a particular datatype, e.g., Boolean, numeric (integer or real), date, etc.
    - Range Constraints: Typically, numbers or dates should fall within a certain range. That is, they have minimum and/or maximum permissible values.
    - Mandatory Constraints: Certain columns cannot be empty.
    - Unique Constraints: A field, or a combination of fields, must be unique across a dataset. For example, no two persons can have the same social security number.
    - Set-Membership constraints: The values for a column come from a set of discrete values or codes. For example, a person's gender may be Female, Male or Unknown (not recorded).
    - Foreign-key constraints: This is the more general case of set membership. The set of values in a column is defined in a column of another table that contains unique values. For example, in a US taxpayer database, the "state" column is required to belong to one of the US's defined states or territories: the set of permissible states/territories is recorded in a separate States table. The term foreign key is borrowed from relational database terminology.
    - Regular expression patterns: Occasionally, text fields will have to be validated this way. For example, phone numbers may be required to have the pattern (999) 999-9999.

  - Cross-field validation: Certain conditions that utilize multiple fields must hold. For example, in laboratory medicine, the sum of the components of the differential white blood cell count must be equal to 100 (since they are all percentages). In a hospital database, a patient's date of discharge from hospital cannot be earlier than the date of admission.

- Accuracy: The degree of conformity of a measure to a standard or a true value - Accuracy is very hard to achieve through data-cleansing in the general case, because it requires accessing an external source of data that contains the true value: such "gold standard" data is often unavailable. Accuracy has been achieved in some cleansing contexts, notably customer contact data, by using external databases that match up zip codes to geographical locations (city and state), and also help verify that street addresses within these zip codes actually exist.

- Completeness: The degree to which all required measures are known. Incompleteness is almost impossible to fix with data cleansing methodology: one cannot infer facts that were not captured when the data in question was initially recorded. (In some contexts, e.g., interview data, it may be possible to fix incompleteness by going back to the original source of data, i,e., re-interviewing the subject, but even this does not guarantee success because of problems of recall - e.g., in an interview to gather data on food consumption, no one is likely to remember exactly what one ate six months ago. In the case of systems that insist certain columns should not be empty, one may work around the problem by designating a value that indicates "unknown" or "missing", but supplying of default values does not imply that the data has been made complete.

- Consistency: The degree to which a set of measures are equivalent in across systems. Inconsistency occurs when two data items in the data set contradict each other: e.g., a customer is recorded in two different systems as having two different current addresses, and only one of them can be correct. Fixing inconsistency is not always possible: it requires a variety of strategies - e.g., deciding which data were recorded more recently, which data source is likely to be most reliable (the latter knowledge may be specific to a given organization), or simply trying to find the truth by testing both data items (e.g., calling up the customer).

- Uniformity: The degree to which a set data measures are specified using the same units of measure in all systems. In datasets pooled from different locales, weight may be recorded either in pounds or kilos, and must be converted to a single measure using an arithmetic transformation.

The term integrity encompasses accuracy, consistency and some aspects of validation but is rarely used by itself in data-cleansing contexts because it is insufficiently specific. (For example, "referential integrity" is a term used to refer to the enforcement of foreign-key constraints above.)

## Process

- Data auditing: The data is audited with the use of statistical and database methods to detect anomalies and contradictions: this eventually gives an indication of the characteristics of the anomalies and their locations. Several commercial software packages will let you specify constraints of various kinds (using a grammar that conforms to that of a standard programming language, e.g., JavaScript or Visual Basic) and then generate code that checks the data for violation of these constraints. This process is referred to below in the bullets "workflow specification" and "workflow execution." For users who lack access to high-end cleansing software, Microcomputer database packages such as Microsoft Access or File Maker Pro will also let you perform such checks, on a constraint-by-constraint basis, interactively with little or no programming required in many cases.

- Workflow specification: The detection and removal of anomalies is performed by a sequence of operations on the data known as the workflow. It is specified after the process of auditing the data and is crucial in achieving the end product of high-quality data. In order to achieve a proper workflow, the causes of the anomalies and errors in the data have to be closely considered.
- Workflow execution: In this stage, the workflow is executed after its specification is complete and its correctness is verified. The implementation of the workflow should be efficient, even on large sets of data, which inevitably poses a trade-off because the execution of a data-cleansing operation can be computationally expensive.
- Post-processing and controlling: After executing the cleansing workflow, the results are inspected to verify correctness. Data that could not be corrected during execution of the workflow is manually corrected, if possible. The result is a new cycle in the data-cleansing process where the data is audited again to allow the specification of an additional workflow to further cleanse the data by automatic processing.

Good quality source data has to do with "Data Quality Culture" and must be initiated at the top of the organization. It is not just a matter of implementing strong validation checks on input screens, because almost no matter how strong these checks are, they can often still be circumvented by the users. There is a nine-step guide for organizations that wish to improve data quality:

- Declare a high level commitment to a data quality culture.
- Drive process reengineering at the executive level.
- Spend money to improve the data entry environment.
- Spend money to improve application integration.
- Spend money to change how processes work.
- Promote end-to-end team awareness.
- Promote interdepartmental cooperation.
- Publicly celebrate data quality excellence.
- Continuously measure and improve data quality.

Others include:

- Parsing: For the detection of syntax errors. A parser decides whether a string of data is acceptable within the allowed data specification. This is similar to the way a parser works with grammars and languages.

- Data transformation: Data transformation allows the mapping of the data from its given format into the format expected by the appropriate application. This includes value conversions or translation functions, as well as normalizing numeric values to conform to minimum and maximum values.
- Duplicate elimination: Duplicate detection requires an algorithm for determining whether data contains duplicate representations of the same entity. Usually, data is sorted by a key that would bring duplicate entries closer together for faster identification.
- Statistical methods: By analyzing the data using the values of mean, standard deviation, range, or clustering algorithms, it is possible for an expert to find values that are unexpected and thus erroneous. Although the correction of such data is difficult since the true value is not known, it can be resolved by setting the values to an average or other statistical value. Statistical methods can also be used to handle missing values which can be replaced by one or more plausible values, which are usually obtained by extensive data augmentation algorithms.

### System

The essential job of this system is to find a suitable balance between fixing dirty data and maintaining the data as close as possible to the original data from the source production system. This is a challenge for the Extract, transform, load architect. The system should offer an architecture that can cleanse data, record quality events and measure/control quality of data in the data warehouse. A good start is to perform a thorough data profiling analysis that will help define to the required complexity of the data cleansing system and also give an idea of the current data quality in the source systems.

### Tools

There are lots of data cleansing tools like Trifacta, OpenRefine, Paxata, Alteryx, Data Ladder, WinPure and others. It's also common to use libraries like Pandas (software) for Python (programming language), or Dplyr for R (programming language).

One example of a data cleansing for distributed systems under Apache Spark is called Optimus, an OpenSource framework for laptop or cluster allowing pre-processing, cleansing, and exploratory data analysis. It includes several data wrangling tools.

### Quality Screens

Part of the data cleansing system is a set of diagnostic filters known as quality screens. They each implement a test in the data flow that, if it fails records an error in the Error Event Schema. Quality screens are divided into three categories:

- Column screens: Testing the individual column, e.g. for unexpected values like NULL values; non-numeric values that should be numeric; out of range values; etc.
- Structure screens: These are used to test for the integrity of different relationships between columns (typically foreign/primary keys) in the same or different tables. They are also used for testing that a group of columns is valid according to some structural definition to which it should adhere.

- Business rule screens: The most complex of the three tests. They test to see if data, maybe across multiple tables, follow specific business rules. An example could be, that if a customer is marked as a certain type of customer, the business rules that define this kind of customer should be adhered to.

When a quality screen records an error, it can either stop the dataflow process, send the faulty data somewhere else than the target system or tag the data. The latter option is considered the best solution because the first option requires, that someone has to manually deal with the issue each time it occurs and the second implies that data are missing from the target system (integrity) and it is often unclear what should happen to these data.

### Criticism of Existing Tools and Processes

Most data cleansing tools have limitations in usability:

- Project costs: Costs typically in the hundreds of thousands of dollars.
- Time: Mastering large-scale data-cleansing software is time-consuming.
- Security: Cross-validation requires sharing information, giving an application access across systems, including sensitive legacy systems.

### Error Event Schema

The Error Event schema holds records of all error events thrown by the quality screens. It consists of an Error Event Fact table with foreign keys to three dimension tables that represent date (when), batch job (where) and screen (who produced error). It also holds information about exactly when the error occurred and the severity of the error. In addition there is an Error Event Detail Fact table with a foreign key to the main table that contains detailed information about in which table, record and field the error occurred and the error condition.

## Business Intelligence Software

BI solutions come in various forms. Some act as standalone applications while others are part of an enterprise suite. Some are targeted at large enterprises, still others are primarily for small businesses. To give you an idea how they are packaged, here are some examples of business intelligence software that are popular on the market:

- Sisense: A leading BI software known for robust features and advanced technologies like its InChip engine and single-stack architecture.
- GoodData: Features a growth-centric advanced analytics ideal for finding new revenue streams or understanding customer behavioral trends
- Looker: A data discovery app with intuitive data exploration tools that let users build and share reports on the fly. It's a solid GoodData alternative.

- Tableau: A highly visual BI platform with extensive access across devices from PC to iPad, this software leverages its Tableau Service for smooth data flow across platforms.
- Domo: Features a wide range of self-service BI tools with extensive data connectors and social collaboration features which make it a worthwhile Looker alternative.
- Klipfolio: This simple yet very powerful business data platform that allows businesses to turn their company data accessible and visible to their people, with all information updated constantly for real-time accuracy.
- Engtics: A behavior tracking, engagement, and analytics suite that helps you view and assess your users and how they relate to the performance of your products, websites, applications, and more.
- Artivatic: An end to end plug-in-play business intelligence with neuroscience focused automated decision making advanced AI/ML platform.
- GroupThinq: A cloud-based project management and business intelligence software designed primarily for consulting firms and professionals, helping them manage their processes and grow their business.
- Qubida: An end-to-end business intelligence and big data integration platform that enables businesses and enterprises to prepare, analyze, and visualize data without having to rely on multiple data platforms and systems.

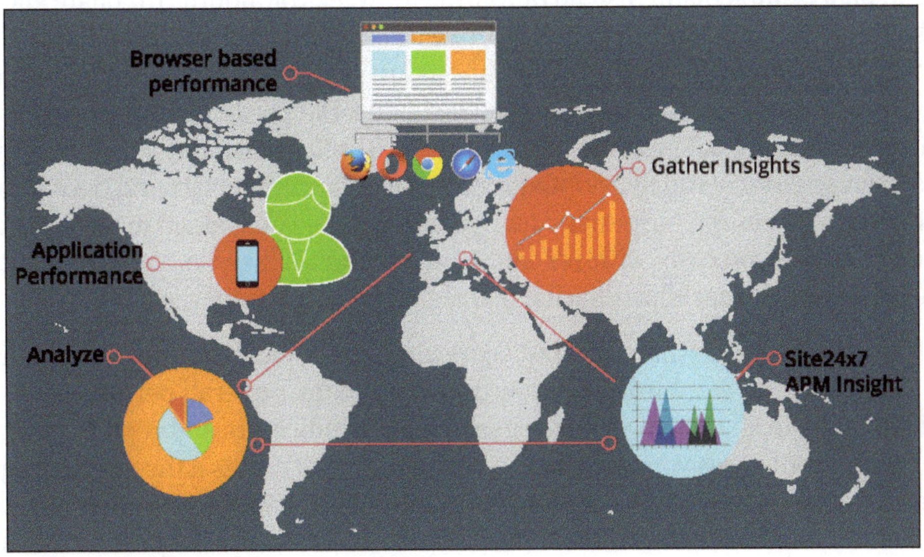


## Using Business Intelligence Software

Now that you know the answer to what is business intelligence software it's also important to understand why you should use one.

IDC predicted that big data and business analytics will grow to $187 billion global market in 2019, an impressive 50% jump from 2015. Clearly, more companies today understand the myriad benefits of BI solutions across the organization and overall business competitiveness. Here are the main benefits of a business intelligence software:

1. Gain insight for growth: This is the main definition of BI. You can optimize business intelligence for sales opportunities, lead generation, market analysis, customer segmentation, etc. Combining relational database and multidimensional data models with real-time data and cross-departmental collaboration, you can manipulate huge volumes of data and surface insights in almost unlimited ways.Among others, you can identify growth areas, assess supply and demand, measure product viability and determine your market position. Moreover, data is sourced in real-time and analyzed through collaboration, further enhancing your market knowledge. For instance, customer-facing staff like support and sales can share feedback updates with top-level management, giving the latter an accurate picture of current market behavior.

2. Address urgent issues: Crises can be immediately addressed if you have the right information. BI solutions feature ad hoc reporting that let you input data and generate insights in minutes, if not seconds. You can take a more informed action before a crisis further escalates.Through a wizard interface, these solutions let you locate and extract critical data off volumes of datasets and generate reports on the fly. This alone saves you time from mindlessly browsing through databases. Does a social media rant affecting your whole market or is it limited to a segment? Which branch has inventory surplus you can reallocate to a needy branch in the next hour? How much a sudden current event set to impact on your project? These questions need answers now and a BI solution makes that happen.

3. Ground data is immediate: Instead of waiting for weeks or months to collate and process raw market data from frontline departments like sales, marketing and support, you can now access real-time ground movement. BI solutions are equipped with powerful multidimensional analytics that can be simultaneously used by teams. Data is dynamic and moves with market events as they happen. Moreover, because many BI solutions today are intuitive for non-tech users, data analysis is widely adopted across the organization. Ground data sourced by your frontline employees can be immediately cleansed, sorted and added to the central repository, empowering the company with the latest information. Likewise, most BI solutions feature collaboration tools that allow sharing of insights and best practices.

4. Get the big picture: Dashboards and scorecards are typical features in BI solutions. They give senior executives a bird's eye view of the company's overall performance. Metrics can be customized to align with your key performance indicators and reports generated in real time. With dashboards you can plot the business health across a threshold range. Automatic alerts can be triggered if you reach a minimum or maximum tolerance within the range. Meanwhile, scorecards can be set to deliver periodic snapshots of your company's progress vis-a-vis its goals. Metrics and milestones are customized to align with your objectives and overall strategy.

5. "See" the future: The more advanced BI solutions feature predictive analytics and forecasting that enable you to anticipate future outcomes. These tools leverage historical, recurring and current patterns to churn out calculated forecasts. The ability to anticipate events lends to your company agility and flexibility, critical factors in highly disruptive industries like tech, retail and entertainment.

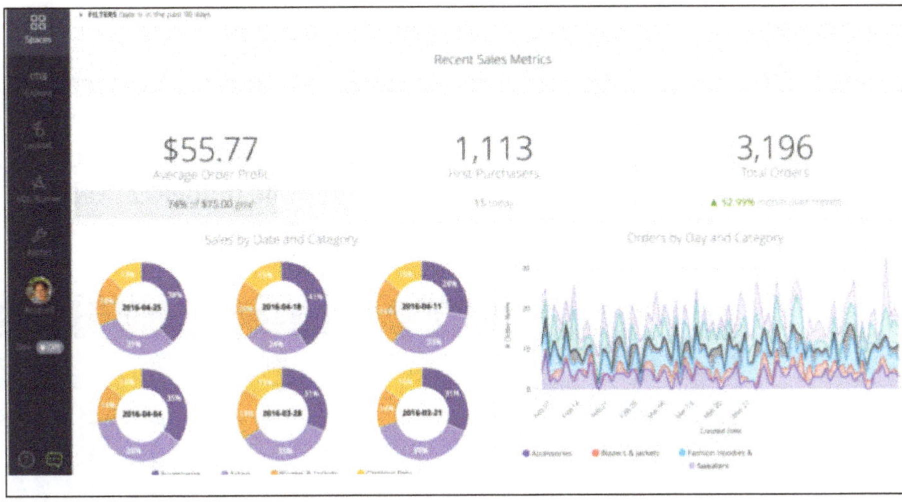


Looker is a data discovery app that let users build and share reports on the fly.

## Types of Business Intelligence Software

### Data Management

A BI can primarily function to clean your existing data. Raw data is messy and disparate. It needs to be prepared for processing such as for analytics or reporting. A data management BI software uses a standardized approach for indexing and archiving. This tool ensures you get clean, accurate raw data to process and that you are conducting an apple-to-apple comparison.

Likewise, this BI software type follows ETL processes (extract, transform and load) to gather data from various sources and load them into a target platform, such as, spreadsheets, data containers and data warehouses. Most top BI software solutions include data management as a major feature.

Example: Sisense, GoodData

### Data Discovery

When users say BI software today, they're likely referring to its data discovery function. This is where real intelligence is unearthed, when data silos are mined and consolidated for patterns and insights.

Most BI solutions are data mining tools capable of integrating with different business systems and datasets. These include spreadsheets, mailing lists, reports, website content, etc. BI software funnels their data into a centralized platform, where processing takes place and the output literally, the "business intelligence" asset.

Most data discovery BI solutions feature an online analytical processing, which is often considered as its own classification. But OLAP is really just the "processing" part of the broader data discovery spectrum. It needs other data discovery tools, such as, relational database, predictive analytics, semantic analytics and report writing to churn out intelligent assets. Together, these tools parse data, carve huge datasets into digestible bits and present them in meaningful reports.

Example: Looker, Tableau, Domo

## Reporting Platform

Some BI solutions focus on how data is presented intuitively that they become popular among non-technical users like senior executives and managers. These solutions offer visualizations that simplify complex data, dashboards that highlight KPIs, report writers for customize outputs and scorecards that display overall business health with a measurable numerical value.

Example: Sisense

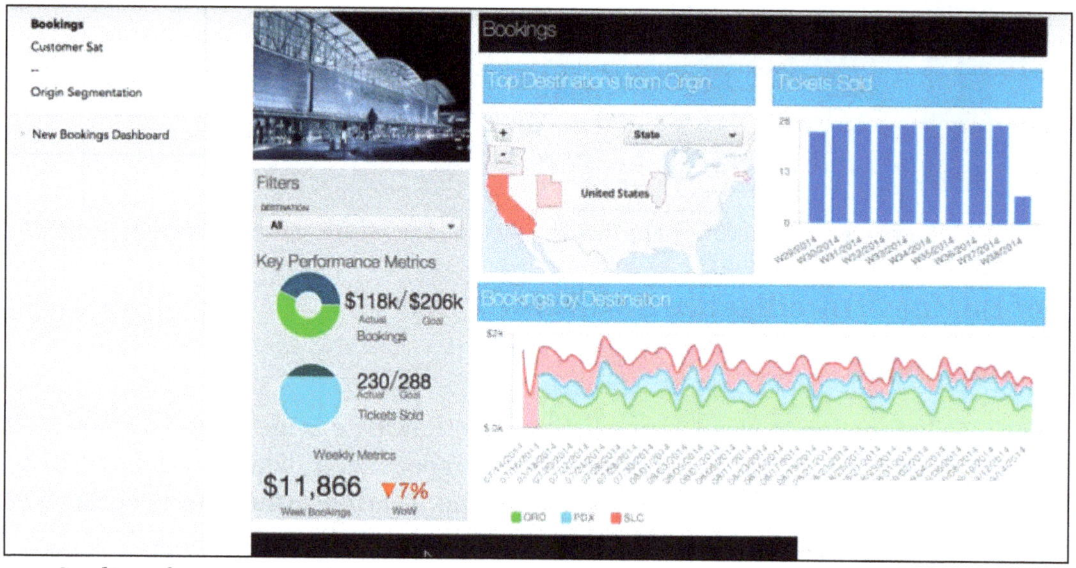


GoodData features a growth-centric advanced analytics ideal for finding new revenue streams.

## Workings of a Business Intelligence Software

Business intelligence solutions come with myriad features, but in general they let you accomplish all or some of these processes:

- Compare, match different outcomes via A/B or multivariate testing.
- Forecast outcomes through predictive modeling.
- Surface insights off patterns or relationships.
- Present cause-effect scenarios.

When comparing, try matching the main features of a business intelligence software, which should include all or at least some the following:

- Online analytical processing (OLAP) or business analytics: OLAP runs the gamut of data preparation, processing and delivering outcomes for reporting. At the core of BI solutions are OLAP tools that enable you to analyze multidimensional data in real-time or simultaneously with other analytics processing.

  For example, a user aggregates the company's sales data by location, while another one uses the same data source and mashes it with real-time online purchases. The same dataset is used interactively by two users with different purposes.

A great BI software should allow you to perform the three OLAP operations: consolidate or roll up disparate sources; drill down to details; and slice and dice. Generally, the more ways you can isolate data from a dataset (called OLAP cube) and view it, the more flexible you can interpret data. When reviewing BI solutions, you'll come across terms like data mashups, data unification and complex business queries, which are OLAP functionalities.

- Reporting and querying: Reporting and querying is another key feature of BI software–how complex data is sorted and generated. Integration is key here to tap into external sources. Likewise, mobile access for query and reports lets you leverage the flexibility afforded by cloud computing and real-time data.

  Generally, business intelligence reporting falls into two types: customized and ad hoc. Customized reports let you sort data subsets, arrange the order of data points, and use specific metrics that matter to you. On the other hand, ad hoc reports are quick data outputs generated by the solution during an urgent situation to help you, among others, make on-the-spot decisions.

  In both instances, reports can be presented as quick lookups or in drill-down details and can be shared across the organization.

  Meanwhile, advanced BI solutions today feature intuitive querying that enables users to surface complex data even without SQL writing or coding skills. OLAP automatically prepares the datasets for every new query. This ability, in fact, allows companies to adopt BI tools organizational wide, beyond the traditional realm of the IT department.

- Digital or visual dashboards: Data visualization is the end-stage of reporting and, in fact, one of the most identifiable elements of BI solutions. Executives and non-technical users often regard BI through this lens, enabling them to generate charts, graphs and dashboard widgets. Advanced visualizations include geospatial reports, heat maps and funnels.

  In many ways, visual dashboards are the sum of the BI solution's capabilities. Behind the chart or graph are the OLAP, reporting-querying, integration, customization and other features at work.

  Although BI solutions have varied visual dashboards by color, location, clusters and any other metrics, they usually feature sharing and commenting capabilities.

- Integration: Integration is also a key factor in answering–what does a business intelligence software do? BI solutions rely on different data sources to churn out meaningful and deep insights, so integration is key. In fact, many vendors tie up BI tools with other business applications, such as, CRM, salesforce automation and shopping cart software.

  Integration can be native (with vendor's own apps), pre-built (arrangement with third-party apps) or via API (with your own apps). Many top BI software solutions integrate with key business applications like CRM, sales, accounting, content management, and project management.

## Potential Issues with Business Intelligence Software

Despite its clear benefits BI solutions are not without issues. Here are the common problems associated with BI software:

- Inaccurate data leads to wrong forecasting: Too much dependence on BI software can lead to clunky data gathering. Sales may feed the system with guesswork just to comply with management's requirement. As a result, BI software churns out misleading or inaccurate reports.
- Unused or under-utilized complex and expensive BI tools: Some BI solutions have comprehensive set features in an attempt to cover the whole range of business analytics. But not all companies need to cover the whole nine yards, leading to some of these sophisticated tools unused or underutilized. Partly, the BI solution becomes a liability as its cost isn't optimized.
- Steep learning curve: Because it involves complex analytics and uses data sources managed by different teams, BI software has a higher-than-average learning curve among SaaS solutions. It has a lot of moving hardware and software parts like multiple-stack architecture and predictive analytics. Likewise, it leverages frontier technologies like multidimensional analytics, big data and OLAP. These technologies are fast evolving that both vendors and users have to play catch-up.
- Difficulty in rollout among large enterprise: In a survey of 2,500 users, one in ten enterprise Bl system rollouts take a year or more to implement. However, small businesses only take one to three months, according to the survey.
- Some of the reasons cited for the slow pace among large enterprises are incompatibility with legacy systems, varied user requirements and corporate politics. The study suggested that incremental rollouts marked by success stages can make BI software adoption faster and smoother.

## BIRT Project

The Business Intelligence and Reporting Tools (BIRT) Project is an open source software project that provides reporting and business intelligence capabilities for rich client and web applications, especially those based on Java and Java EE. BIRT is a top-level software project within the Eclipse Foundation, an independent not-for-profit consortium of software industry vendors and an open source community.

The project's stated goals are to address a wide range of reporting needs within a typical application, ranging from operational or enterprise reporting to multi-dimensional online analytical processing (OLAP). Initially, the project has focused on and delivered capabilities that allow application developers to easily design and integrate reports into applications.

The project is supported by an active community of users at BIRT Developer Center and developers at the Eclipse.org BIRT Project page.

BIRT has two main components: a visual report designer within the Eclipse IDE for creating BIRT Reports, and a runtime component for generating reports that can be deployed to any Java environment. The BIRT project also includes a charting engine that is both fully integrated into the report designer and can be used standalone to integrate charts into an application.

BIRT Report designs are persisted as XML and can access a number of different data sources including JDO datastores, JFire Scripting Objects, POJOs, SQL databases, Web Services and XML.

The BIRT project was first proposed and sponsored by Actuate Corporation when Actuate joined the Eclipse Foundation as a Strategic Developer on August 24, 2004. The project was subsequently approved and became a top-level project within the Eclipse community on October 6, 2004 The project contributor community includes IBM, and Innovent Solutions.

In 2007 IBM's Tivoli Division adopted BIRT as the infrastructure for its Tivoli Common Reporting (TCR) product. TCR produces historical reports on Tivoli-managed IT resources and processes.

The initial project code base was designed and developed by Actuate beginning in early 2004 and donated to the Eclipse Foundation when the project was approved.

## JasperReports

JasperReports is an open source Java reporting tool that can write to a variety of targets, such as: screen, a printer, into PDF, HTML, Microsoft Excel, RTF, ODT, comma-separated values (CSV) or XML files.

It can be used in Java-enabled applications, including Java EE or web applications, to generate dynamic content. It reads its instructions from an XML or .jasper file.

## Features

JasperReports is an open source reporting library that can be embedded into any Java application. Features include:

- Scriptlets may accompany the report definition, which the report definition can invoke at any point to perform additional processing. The scriptlet is built using Java, and has many hooks that can be invoked before or after stages of the report generation, such as Report, Page, Column or Group.
- Sub-reports.

For users with more sophisticated report management requirements, reports designed for JasperReports can be easily imported into the *JasperServer* - the interactive report server.

## Jaspersoft

Teodor Danciu began work on JasperReports in June 2001, the sf.net project was registered in September 2001 and JasperReports 0.1.5 was released on November 3, 2001.

Jaspersoft was originally called Panscopic, and was founded by Al Campa, CEO, and Raj Bhargava, VP of Products in 2001. Panscopic raised $23M from Doll Capital, Discovery Ventures, Morgenthaler Ventures, and Partech. In 2004 Panscopic teamed up with Teodor Danciu, acquired the intellectual property of JasperReports, and changed the name of the company to Jaspersoft. Brian Gentile became CEO in 2007.

Jaspersoft provides commercial software around the JasperReports product, and negotiate contracts with software developers that wish to embed the JasperReports engine into a closed source product.

Jaspersoft's main related product is JasperReports Server, a Java EE web application that provides advanced report server capabilities such as report scheduling and permissions. It is available under an open source license for use in conjunction with open source infrastructure such as MySQL and JBoss, or a commercial license for enterprise deployments involving commercial databases and application servers.

Jaspersoft is a gold partner with MySQL, and JasperReports was included in the PostgreSQL distribution Bizgres version 0.7.

On April 28, 2014, TIBCO announced it had acquired Jaspersoft for approximately $185 million.

## JRXML

JasperReports reports are defined in an XML file format, called JRXML, which can be hand-coded, generated, or designed using a tool. The file format is defined by a Document Type Definition (DTD) or XML schema for newer versions, providing limited interoperability. JRXML files have the filename extension *.jrxml.*

A *.jasper* file is a compiled version of a *.jrxml* file. iReport does the compilation on the fly, but the compilation can also get achieved at runtime using the JasperCompileManager class.

## IDE Integration

Several Java IDEs, such as NetBeans, Eclipse and IBM Websphere Studio Application Developer provide instructions for users wishing to integrate JasperReports into a project.

## Palo

Palo is a memory resident multidimensional (online analytical processing (OLAP) or multidimensional online analytical processing (MOLAP)) database server and typically used as a business intelligence tool for controlling and budgeting purposes with spreadsheet software acting as the user interface. Beyond the multidimensional data concept, Palo enables multiple users to share one centralised data storage (single version of the truth).

This type of database is suitable to handle complex data models for business management and statistics. Apart from multidimensional queries, data can also be written back and consolidated in real-time. To give rapid access to all data, Palo stores them in the memory during run time. The server is available as open-source and proprietary software.

Jedox was founded by Kristian Raue in 2002 and developed by Jedox AG, a company based in Freiburg, Germany. The firm currently employs approximately 100 people. Kristian Raue's departure from Jedox was announced in June 2014.

## Features

Palo for Excel is an open source plug-in for Microsoft Excel. There is also an open source plug-in for OpenOffice.org named PalOOCa (discontinued), with Java and web client also available from the JPalo project. Palo can also be integrated into other systems via its client libraries for Java, PHP, C/C++, or .NET Framework. It is fairly easy to communicate with Palo OLAP Server, since it uses representational state transfer (REST).

Starting in October 2008, Palo supports XML for Analysis and MultiDimensional eXpressions (MDX) APIs for connectivity, and OLE DB for OLAP interface which allows standard Excel pivot tables to serve as a client tool. Starting September 2011, Palo supports SDX dialect of LINQ.

Palo also provides a web-based spreadsheet interface called Palo Web.

## Architecture

Palo Suite is a tightly integrated framework consisting of: Palo MOLAP Server, Palo ETL Server, Palo Web (Palo Spreadsheet - Connection, User, ETL, File and Report Manager), Palo for Excel, Palo Supervision Server and the Palo Client Libraries.

The Data in Palo database is stored as a cube in the Palo MOLAP server. The Palo Excel Add-In component is used as a service to communicate between the Excel and the Palo MOLAP Server.

## Licensing

Jedox announced only commercial licensing is available since 5.1 version (2015).

## Pentaho

Pentaho is business intelligence (BI) software that provides data integration, OLAP services, reporting, information dashboards, data mining and extract, transform, load (ETL) capabilities. It is headquartered in Orlando, Florida. Pentaho was acquired by Hitachi Data Systems in 2015. On September 19, 2017, Pentaho became part of Hitachi Vantara, a new company that unifies the operations of Pentaho, Hitachi Data Systems and Hitachi Insight Group.

Pentaho offers an enterprise and community edition of the software. The enterprise software is obtained through an annual subscription and contains extra features and support not found in the community edition. Pentaho's core offering is frequently enhanced by add-on products, usually in the form of plug-ins, from the company and the broader community of users.

## Licensing

Pentaho follows an open core business model. It provides two different editions of Pentaho Business Analytics: a community edition and an enterprise edition. The enterprise edition needs to be purchased on a subscription model. The subscription model includes support, services, and product enhancements via annual subscription. The enterprise edition is available under a commercial license. Enterprise license goes with 3 levels of Pentaho Enterprise Support: Enterprise, Premium and Standard. The community edition is a free open source product licensed under the GNU General Public License version 2.0 (GPLv2), GNU Lesser General Public License version 2.0 (LGPLv2), and Mozilla Public License 1.1 (MPL 1.1).

## Tactic

TACTIC is a web-based, open source smart process application and digital asset management system supported by Southpaw Technology in Toronto, ON. Designed to optimize busy production environments with high volumes of content traffic, TACTIC applies business or workflow logic to combined database and file system management. Using elements of digital asset management, production asset management and workflow management, TACTIC tracks the creation and development of digital assets through production pipelines. TACTIC is available under both commercial and open-source licenses, and also as a hosted cloud service through Amazon Web Services Marketplace.

## Key Features

### Web Framework

TACTIC is a web-based platform or framework for delivering enterprise data- driven HTML5 applications. It uses a hierarchical drawing engine to deliver self-contained HTML5 widgets to a browser. Each widget is an encapsulated bundle of HTML, JavaScript, CSS (cascading style sheets) and server-side Python code. Widgets can contain other widgets, and can be dynamically loaded through AJAX. TACTIC also includes tools that allow it to deliver branded customized widgets or themes.

By coupling standard web technologies with TACTIC's asset management and ability to handle complex data models, TACTIC can be used to deliver enterprise applications to any device with a browser. TACTIC also uses standard web technologies such as HTML5, CSS and AJAX to make the customization process easy and accessible. An embedded expression language provides simplified access to complex data models without having to build up large SQL statements.

Reviewers write that TACTIC's key strengths are its strong workflow capabilities and its suitability for managing large volumes of production assets, especially big files. Features of TACTIC include a flexible data model, a visual workflow designer, powerful API connectivity and an adaptable plug-in architecture.

### Workflow Management

TACTIC organizes workflows through pipelines, production command chains that grant users the ability to define discrete processes within a workflow. In each process, files can be checked in and versioned, tasks created, notes added and triggers responding to events in the process executed. Users can also configure their workflows to assign arbitrary metadata, send notifications and update the status of projects. TACTIC's trigger system allows custom business logic to be attached to any event in the system, including every data change and file check-in.

### File System Management

TACTIC deploys several technologies to manage its file systems: strict file naming conventions, check-in/out or gatekeeper/librarian function, and versioning. First TACTIC breaks up all the business entities into assets. In the TACTIC world, a user works on assets, or more specifically on some part of the process in the workflow that produces assets. Assets are organized into "types of searchable assets", or "sTypes" in TACTIC terminology. This configuration provides a space or sandbox for a user to do his or her work. The sandbox is generally a freeform area designated by TACTIC where a user can create and manage his or her files.

When the work evolves to a stage where it requires an external review or is ready to be pushed on to the next process, the user checks in his or her files. This check-in process hands files off to TACTIC, which acts as a gatekeeper to the repository where all the files are kept. TACTIC also acts as a librarian, sorting the files it receives into the appropriate location in the repository. If specified by the system, file names will also be renamed accordingly to make their locations more identifiable (a function cognate to card cataloguing). TACTIC's automated file management system ensures that files are uniformly named and appear in predictable and reliable locations, effectively eliminating human error in the repository.

## Data Management

TACTIC's data management strategy is rooted in its flexible data model, which makes no assumptions about structure or file type. Instead, the TACTIC framework adapts to any type of file, including audio, video, graphic and enterprise content. Data models can either be built in TACTIC or TACTIC can be mapped onto a pre-existing data model. This capability allows TACTIC to provide an updated web interface for legacy systems with critical data.

Instead of relying on classifications based on file type, TACTIC manages data by defining an overall "schema" for each project. Each schema contains sTypes ("types of searchable assets"), with each type representing a different category or classification of entities. This structure is largely arbitrary but can follow good database table design. TACTIC can also access multiple databases simultaneously, regardless of platform. TACTIC projects can view databases from multiple disparate locations, including Oracle, MySQL, SQLite, PostgreSQL and Microsoft SQLServer, and unify the user experience.

TACTIC's built-in expression language simplifies the process of extracting data from the database, making the overall system much easier to navigate. It provides an interface that removes the complexity of reiterating relationships on every query inherent in SQL. TACTIC's expression language is particularly useful in scenarios with complex enterprise data models where deep relationships between tables must be navigated in order to retrieve and operate on the data.

## Support Platforms and Environments

TACTIC is written almost entirely in Python programming language and will run on most platforms where Python is available. This includes Windows, OS X and the various Unix flavours and distributions (RHEL, CentOS, Ubuntu, etc.). TACTIC is one of the largest projects written in Python, clocking in at 198949 lines of code.

"TACTIC Team" is a self-contained stand-alone version of TACTIC that runs on SQLite and embeds the Python language and required modules, as well as Cherrypy for web service. It is distributed with an installer and is executable for both Windows and OS X.

## Orange

Orange is an open-source data visualization, machine learning and data mining toolkit. It features a visual programming front-end for explorative data analysis and interactive data visualization.

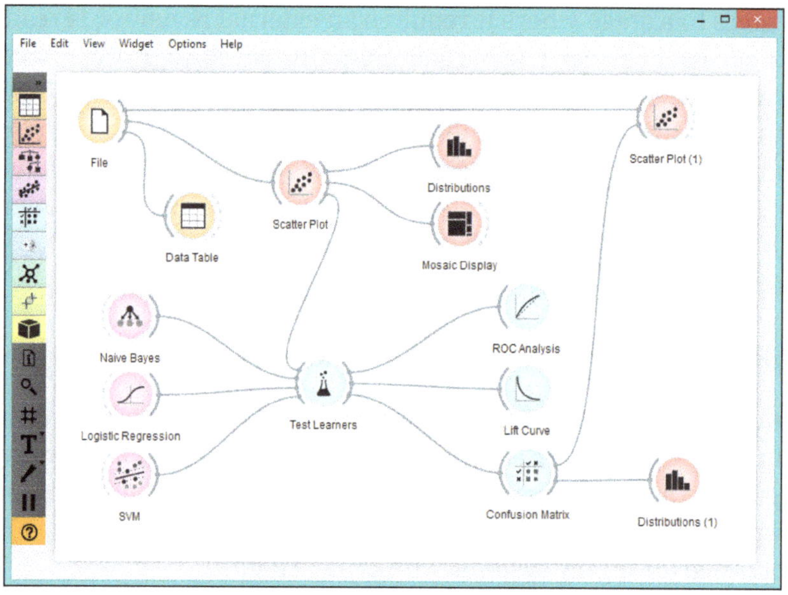


A typical workflow in Orange 3.

Orange is a component-based visual programming software package for data visualization, machine learning, data mining, and data analysis.

Orange components are called widgets and they range from simple data visualization, subset selection, and preprocessing, to empirical evaluation of learning algorithms and predictive modeling. Visual programming is implemented through an interface in which workflows are created by linking predefined or user-designed widgets, while advanced users can use Orange as a Python library for data manipulation and widget alteration.

## Software

Orange is an open-source software package released under GPL. Versions up to 3.0 include core components in C++ with wrappers in Python are available on GitHub. From version 3.0 onwards, Orange uses common Python open-source libraries for scientific computing, such as numpy, scipy and scikit-learn, while its graphical user interface operates within the cross-platform Qt framework.

The default installation includes a number of machine learning, preprocessing and data visualization algorithms in 6 widget sets (data, visualize, classify, regression, evaluate and unsupervised). Additional functionalities are available as add-ons (bioinformatics, data fusion and text-mining).

Orange is supported on macOS, Windows and Linux and can also be installed from the Python Package Index repository (*pip install Orange3*).

As of May 2018 the stable version is 3.13 and runs with Python 3, while the legacy version 2.7 that runs with Python 2.7 is still available.

## Features

Orange consists of a canvas interface onto which the user places widgets and creates a data analysis workflow. Widgets offer basic functionalities such as reading the data, showing a data table, selecting features, training predictors, comparing learning algorithms, visualizing data elements, etc. The user can interactively explore visualizations or feed the selected subset into other widgets.

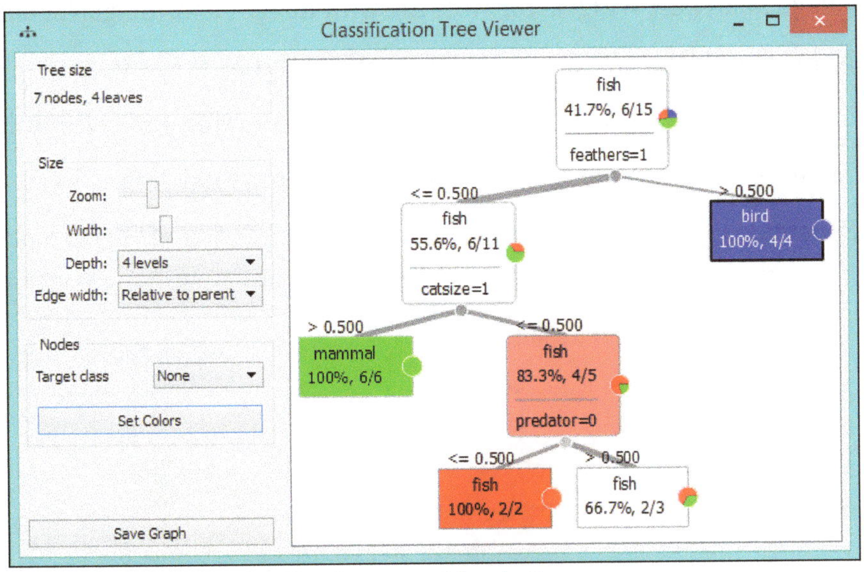


Classification Tree widget in Orange 3.0

- Canvas: Graphical front-end for data analysis.
- Widgets.
- Data: Widgets for data input, data filtering, sampling, imputation, feature manipulation and feature selection.
- Visualize: Widgets for common visualization (box plot, histograms, scatter plot) and multivariate visualization (mosaic display, sieve diagram).
- Classify: A set of supervised machine learning algorithms for classification.
- Regression: A set of supervised machine learning algorithms for regression.
- Evaluate: Cross-validation, sampling-based procedures, reliability estimation and scoring of prediction methods.
- Unsupervised: Unsupervised learning algorithms for clustering (k-means, hierarchical clustering) and data projection techniques (multidimensional scaling, principal component analysis, correspondence analysis).
  - Add-ons:
    - Associate: Widgets for mining frequent itemsets and association rule learning.
    - Bioinformatics: Widgets for gene set analysis, enrichment, and access to pathway libraries.
    - Data fusion: Widgets for fusing different data sets, collective matrix factorization, and exploration of latent factors.

- Educational: Widgets for teaching machine learning concepts, such as k-means clustering, polynomial regression, stochastic gradient descent, etc.
- Geo: Widgets for working with geospatial data.
- Image analytics: Widgets for working with images and ImageNet embeddings.
- Network: Widgets for graph and network analysis.
- Text mining: Widgets for natural language processing and text mining.
- Time series: Widgets for time series analysis and modeling.
- Spectroscopy: Widgets for analyzing and visualization of (hyper)spectral datasets.

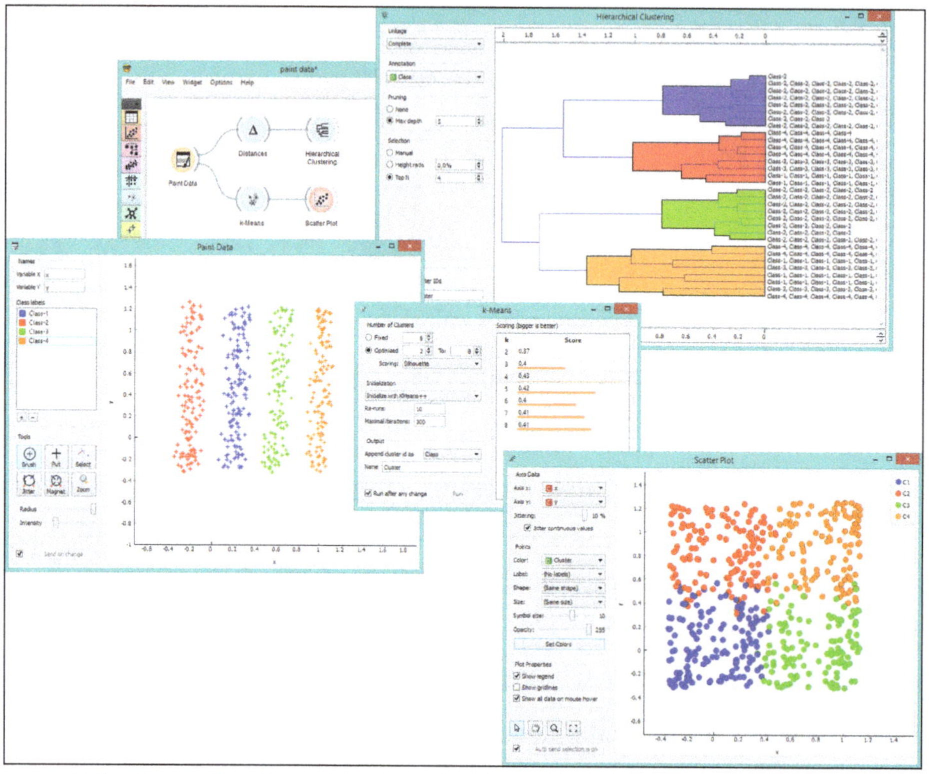


Paint Data widget in combination with hierarchical clustering and k-Means.

## Objectives

The program provides a platform for experiment selection, recommendation systems, and predictive modeling and is used in biomedicine, bioinformatics, genomic research, and teaching. In science, it is used as a platform for testing new machine learning algorithms and for implementing new techniques in genetics and bioinformatics. In education, it was used for teaching machine learning and data mining methods to students of biology, biomedicine, and informatics.

## Extensions

Various projects build on Orange either by extending the core components with add-ons or using only the Orange Canvas to exploit the implemented visual programming features and GUI.

- OASYS the ORange SYnchrotron Suite.
- scOrange for single cell biostatistics.
- Quasar for data analysis in natural sciences.

## Business Intelligence Markup Language (BIML)

The Business Intelligence Markup Language (Biml) is an XML dialect that specifies many aspects of a business intelligence solution, including relational models, data transformation packages, multi-dimensional models (OLAP), and permissions.

When Biml files are compiled, BI assets are generated for a target system. However, unlike other BI solutions, Biml can target multiple BI platforms with little to no code changes. Currently, Biml can be emitted for any version of SQL Server (2005, 2008, 2008 R2, and 2012), creating SQL Server Integration Services (SSIS) packages, SQL Server Analysis Services (SSAS) cubes and SQL Server DDL. This "write once, target many platforms" philosophy provides robustness in all of your Biml solutions.

Since basic Biml is just XML, you can easily use the broad ecosystem of tools for XML-based languages. Unlike DTSX and other SQL Server files, Biml is human readable and writable. This makes it easy to edit Biml files by hand, compare and merge changes across Biml files, automatically template code, and leverage team development tools.

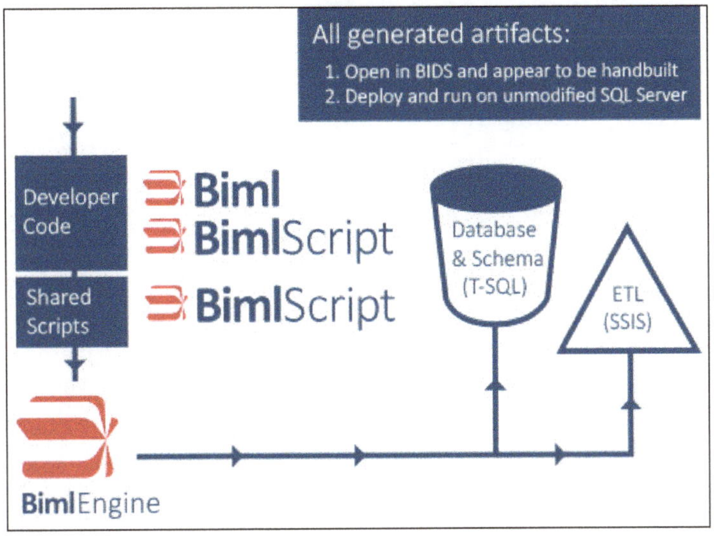


## BimlScript

BimlScript is an extension to the Biml language where C# or VB.NET code nuggets are embedded directly within Biml. BimlScript's relation to Biml is analogous to ASP.NET's relation to HTML. By incorporating BimlScript, it's possible to turn tedious, repetitive work into reusable scripts. Furthermore, BimlScript's power extends to automating package generation and building reusable patterns for common BI tasks. BimlScript particularly shines when metadata from various sources (relational database structure, relational data, flat files, annotations, and more) is used to automatically generate Biml code for your solution.

## References


- What-is-Medical-Tourism, health: news-medical.net, Retrieved 23 May, 2019
- Woodman, Josef (2015-02-17). Patients Beyond Borders: Everybody's Guide to Affordable, World-Class Medical Travel. ISBN 978-0990315407
- Hughes EG, Dejean D (June 2010). "Cross-border fertility services in North America: a survey of Canadian and American providers". Fertility and Sterility. 94 (1): e16–9. doi:10.1016/j.fertnstert.2009.12.008. PMID 20149916
- Dental-Tourism-Global-Competition-in-Health-Care- 226018768: researchgate.net, Retrieved 04 August, 2019

# Permissions

All chapters in this book are published with permission under the Creative Commons Attribution Share Alike License or equivalent. Every chapter published in this book has been scrutinized by our experts. Their significance has been extensively debated. The topics covered herein carry significant information for a comprehensive understanding. They may even be implemented as practical applications or may be referred to as a beginning point for further studies.

We would like to thank the editorial team for lending their expertise to make the book truly unique. They have played a crucial role in the development of this book. Without their invaluable contributions this book wouldn't have been possible. They have made vital efforts to compile up to date information on the varied aspects of this subject to make this book a valuable addition to the collection of many professionals and students.

This book was conceptualized with the vision of imparting up-to-date and integrated information in this field. To ensure the same, a matchless editorial board was set up. Every individual on the board went through rigorous rounds of assessment to prove their worth. After which they invested a large part of their time researching and compiling the most relevant data for our readers.

The editorial board has been involved in producing this book since its inception. They have spent rigorous hours researching and exploring the diverse topics which have resulted in the successful publishing of this book. They have passed on their knowledge of decades through this book. To expedite this challenging task, the publisher supported the team at every step. A small team of assistant editors was also appointed to further simplify the editing procedure and attain best results for the readers.

Apart from the editorial board, the designing team has also invested a significant amount of their time in understanding the subject and creating the most relevant covers. They scrutinized every image to scout for the most suitable representation of the subject and create an appropriate cover for the book.

The publishing team has been an ardent support to the editorial, designing and production team. Their endless efforts to recruit the best for this project, has resulted in the accomplishment of this book. They are a veteran in the field of academics and their pool of knowledge is as vast as their experience in printing. Their expertise and guidance has proved useful at every step. Their uncompromising quality standards have made this book an exceptional effort. Their encouragement from time to time has been an inspiration for everyone.

The publisher and the editorial board hope that this book will prove to be a valuable piece of knowledge for students, practitioners and scholars across the globe.

# Index

CPSIA information can be obtained
at www.ICGtesting.com
Printed in the USA
LVHW060859030122
707669LV00002B/260

9 781682 859766